HOW IOWA COOKS

A collection of
recipes from
people of
Iowa

PELICAN PUBLISHING COMPANY
GRETNA 1992

First printing, March 1964
Second printing, July 1964
Third printing, June 1965
Fourth printing, September 1969
Fifth printing, February 1973
Sixth printing, September 1977
First Pelican edition, January 1983
Eighth printing, September 1985
Ninth printing, April 1992

Library of Congress Cataloging in Publication Data
Main entry under title:

How Iowa cooks.

Includes index.
1. Cookery, American--Iowa. I. Tipton Woman's Club.
TX715.H839 1982   641.5   82-9070
ISBN 0-88289-321-1   AACR2

Cover design by Libbie Sparks

Manufactured in the United States of America

Published by Pelican Publishing Company, Inc.
1101 Monroe Street, Gretna, Louisiana 70053

FOREWORD

The cornucopia is a symbol of abundance. The cornucopia on tne cover of "How Iowa Cooks" is a symbol of Iowa's abundance of food, for our state is recognized as a leader in production. Included in this book are all-time favorites as well as gay new ideas and recipes— all part of Iowa's heritage of food.

Recipes gleaned from many other states and countries, from our immigrant ancestors, our vacation travels, our foreign students and our own inventiveness are all represented. There is a miscellany of traditional foods set out in a special section, and this tradition continues to be threaded through the various sections, pointing out specialties of many homes.

Not only does our state grow a variety of foods, but we have many industries based on food processing and these staples appear frequently in the cookbook.

If you should come to Tipton, located in the center of this "market basket" of plenty, you might observe the feeding of harvest workers, morning coffee groups, church suppers, family reunions, luncheons for organizations and picnics, all exemplifying the recipes we've shared with you here.

Iowa, Beautiful Land, with fields of corn, pastures of dairy cattle and stocky beeves, acres of rolling hills covered with grain, stretches from the Mississippi to the Missouri. It is intended that the scope of cookery represented in this book be as broad and diverse as the needs and interests of Iowa.

There's something to appeal to everybody in this appetizing array of recipes found in "How Iowa Cooks."

—Ruth Clark

PREFACE

The Tipton Woman's Club, sponsor of two successful Tastee Teas, where foods were tested and recipes sold, knew of no cookbook that featured favorite recipes of Iowans from every section of the State.

The members set a goal for themselves to prepare and have published such a book.

Recipes were solicited and gathered from wives of state and national officials, wives of mayors and county fair secretaries, radio and TV personalities, women who are prominent in professions and organizations, and women with no claim to fame. One thing they had in common: all were Iowa homemakers with recipes to share.

In the early spring of 1964, "How Iowa Cooks" was introduced at another Tastee Tea. The first printing of 2,500 copies was sold in less than six weeks!

The more than six hundred recipes will be easily understandable to the new cook and will still challenge the experienced. There are party foods and plain foods, family sized recipes and recipes to serve large groups, all checked and double checked for accuracy. Only a few call for ingredients from specialty shops.

Corn, Iowa's most talked about crop from our fertile lands, rated a special section.

Iowans are hearty meat eaters. Thick, juicy steaks, broiled indoors or out, succulent beef and pork roasts, baked hams, fried chickens and lamb are common fare. Since directions for preparing these are available from many sources, our meat section features mostly combination type meat dishes.

Many tourists crossing Iowa on Interstate highway 80 plan to stop at West Branch, the home of former President Herbert Hoover and the site of his Presidential Library. One of the eating places there regularly features recipes from "How Iowa Cooks." Now, in this supplement it shares with you some of its specialties.

We might have included a chapter on the preservation of our garden products, but because this was not intended to be a textbook based on authoritative and scientific testing, we recommend, instead, that you contact the Extension Service in your own state for the best up to date information on this type of cookery.

There has been united effort by all the members of the Tipton Women's Club in this project. Without the help of those who gathered the recipes, the typists, the proof readers and those who made the final selections, it would have been impossible. Each lady who had a part in preparing this book hopes you will enjoy using "How Iowa Cooks."

—Darlene Donohue

Table of Contents

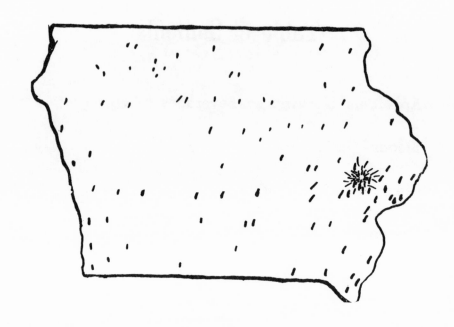

Good cooks abound in every corner of Iowa. A dot marks each community represented by recipes in "How Iowa Cooks."

The cluster of dots in the eastern part of the map represents the Tipton area.

Appetizers
Sandwiches
Beverages

If you need a bit of magic,
Try these and you'll agree
A meal turns out a party
As easy as —— one, two, three.

Crabmeat Dip

1 garlic clove
⅓ cup cream
1 8-ounce package cream cheese
1 cup flaked crabmeat

2 teaspoons lemon juice
1½ teaspoons Worcester-
    shire sauce
Dash of salt
Dash of pepper

Rub bowl with the garlic clove. Gradually add the cream to the cream cheese in the bowl, blending until smooth. Add the remaining ingredients, and mix well.

Mrs. Walter Schnelle, Tipton

Cucumber Dip

1 pint commercial sour cream
1 envelope dried onion soup

1 medium cucumber
    (diced fine)

Add cream for right consistency.

Mrs. E. J. Wilson, Tipton

Deviled Ham Dip

1 5-ounce jar pimento cheese
1 2¼-ounce can deviled ham
½ cup mayonnaise
2 tablespoons minced parsley

1 tablespoon minced onion
4 drops tabasco sauce
Dash monosodium glutamate

Mix in order given and serve with potato chips or crackers.

Mrs. J. L. Fraseur, Tipton

Sweet-Sour Dip

1 cup (8 ounces) currant jelly
⅓ cup yellow prepared mustard

Melt jelly in double boiler and add mustard. Heat meat in the mixture. Keep hot in a chafing dish and serve with toothpicks.

This makes enough dip for 1 pound of wieners cut in fourths, cubed luncheon meat or vienna sausages.

Mrs. J. F. Casterline, Tipton

Cheese Balls

½ pound processed cheese   ¼ pound sharp cheddar cheese

Cut into small cubes and add:

1 4-ounce glass blue cheese. Let stand until it reaches room temperature. Cream well with electric mixer.

Add to the above and mix well:

½ cup mayonnaise
1 tablespoon chopped sweet
  pickle

2 teaspoons Worcestershire
  sauce
1 teaspoon onion, chopped
  fine

Place in small bowl; cover and let stand in refrigerator at least 6 hours. Remove from bowl, shape into balls the size of grapefruit. Roll in mixture of:

½ cup chopped pecans   ½ cup chopped parsley.

Recipe makes 2 balls. Will keep in refrigerator for 2 weeks. By adding small amount of cream and bringing to room temperature, this may also be used as a dip rather than a spread.

Martha Gaul, Tipton

Krispy Cocktail Mix

1 box rice chex
1 box wheat chex
1 box kix
1 box cheerios
1 box pretzel sticks

1 pound Spanish peanuts
1 pound cashew nuts
¼ pound butter
¾ cup salad oil
½ teaspoon each of salt, garlic
  salt, and celery salt

Melt butter and mix with salad oil. Pour over remainder of ingredients which have been mixed together. Bake 2 hours in 200 degree oven, stirring every 20 minutes. Cool and store in plastic bags.

Mrs. W. E. Hutchison, Tipton

3

Versatile Punch

1 6-oz. can frozen lemonade plus liquid according to directions on can
1 package lime jello, dissolved in 2 cups hot water
1 No. 5 can pineapple juice   1 quart ginger ale
1 pint lime sherbet

Mix first three ingredients. Just before serving add ginger ale and sherbet. If ice is added, it should be substituted for part of water in recipe. This amount makes about 5 quarts and will serve between 40 and 50 punch cups.

The recipe may be varied to fit any color scheme or flavor desired. For strawberry, use strawberry jello and add vanilla ice cream or a white sherbet in place of the lime. Other flavors may be substituted in a similar way. Ice cream or sherbet may be omitted if a clear punch is desired.

Mrs. Max Crawford, Tipton

Bride's Punch

3 packages raspberry jello   4 cups boiling water
          1½ cups sugar (combine and dissolve)

4 cups cold water   ½ cup lime juice
2¼ cups orange juice   1¼ cups lemon juice
1 quart ginger ale   2 10-ounce packages frozen
                                   raspberries

Mix all ingredients, adding ginger ale and partially thawed raspberries last. Serves 40 people.

Kathryn Gruenwald, Tipton

Wedding Punch

1 tall can pineapple juice   2 6-ounce cans lemonade
1 6-ounce can orange juice   (1 may be the pink)
1 bottle cranberry cocktail juice

Prepare the juices as suggested on the cans and mix all. Chill. Just before serving, add 1 quart ginger ale and a few ice cubes. Serves 30.

Mrs. Ruth L. Liddy, Keosauqua
Wife of Iowa's Secretary of Agriculture

4

Tasty Quench

Simmer washed rhubarb stalks, cut in 4-6 inch lengths, until soft, in water to cover. Run through sieve.

1 quart liquid (sieved rhubarb)
1 can (6-ounce) frozen orange juice
2 cups sugar
1 package Koolade to give color to drink

3½ quarts water
4 ounces real lemon, or 1 can frozen lemonade

Stir well, add ice cubes and serve. May add fruit slices for variety, or substitute pineapple juice for either of the fruit juices. A good recipe for lunch on the farm. The men relish it when making hay; it quenches their thirst without being too sweet—also healthful.

Mrs. Harold Eiler, Tipton

Orange Punch

1 6-ounce can frozen orange juice
1 6-ounce can frozen lemonade
1 6-ounce can frozen pineapple juice

1 quart ginger ale
1½ quarts water

Mix all together and serve over crushed ice. This makes 15 large glasses of drink.

Mrs. Walter Kopsa, Tipton

Teen Snow Punch

1½ cups mashed bananas
½ cup lemon juice
1 cup sugar

1 cup light cream
4 7-ounce bottles carbonated water

1 pint lemon or lime sherbet

You may sprinkle top with coconut before serving, if desired. This only adds to the appearance, not to the taste.

Mrs. Lester Davis, Tipton

5

Cranberry Punch

1 6-ounce can frozen orange
  juice
½ cup boiling water
2 7-ounce bottles ginger ale
2 7-ounce bottles seven-up

¼ cup sugar
1 pint cranberry-juice
  cocktail

Add sugar to water to dissolve. Add fruit juice. Chill well.
Just before serving add ginger ale and seven-up.

Mrs. Bill Woods, Spencer

Garnet Punch

¼ cup instant tea
2 cups cranberry juice

2 cups apple juice
1 quart lemon-lime soda

Place the tea in a punch bowl, add cranberry and apple juice,
stir until tea is dissolved. Refrigerate. Just before serving add
lemon-lime soda.

Mrs. Hans Freese, Tipton

1 gallon punch — 35 servings in punch cups

1 gallon punch — 20 servings in glasses

Noodle Nibblers

Mix: 1 3-ounce package softened cream cheese with 1 can
deviled ham. Season to taste. Roll mixture into 24 small
balls. Pop 'em into your refrigerator. Just before you
serve, roll the balls in one cup broken chow mein noodles.
(a real treat)

Mrs. W. E. Hutchison, Tipton

6

Hot Cranberry Punch

1 quart cranberry juice
1 pint pineapple juice
⅓ cup brown sugar
½ cup water

½ teaspoon cloves
¼ teaspoon allspice
¼ teaspoon cinnamon
⅛ teaspoon nutmeg

⅓ teaspoon salt

Mix all together; heat. Serve hot. Dot with butter.

Mrs. Keith Fields, Tipton

Hot Spiced Tea

1 teaspoon whole cloves
3 quarts water
Juice of 3 oranges

1 inch stick cinnamon
2½ tablespoons black tea
1½ lemons

1 cup sugar

Tie spices loosely in a bag and bring to a boil in water. Add tea, tied loosely in a bag; steep 5 minutes; remove bags. Heat fruit juices and sugar; add to tea. Serves 20 — 24.

Mrs. M. E. Conrad, Winthrop

Hot Spiced Tea

5 quarts water
1 teaspoon whole cloves
1 stick cinnamon

2 cups sugar
1 can frozen orange juice, small
1 can frozen lemon juice, small

10 tea bags, orange pekoe

Bring water and spices to full boil. Remove from heat. Immediately add tea, let stand 4 minutes. Stir and strain. Add sugar and fruit juices, stirring until sugar is dissolved. Serve hot. Serves 30-35.

To reheat for serving, place over low heat. Do not boil.

Mrs. W. E. Hutchison, Tipton

If ice tea clouds, add a small amount of boiling water to clear it up.

Hot Tomato Juice

6 cups tomato juice
1 can condensed consomme
1 teaspoon horseradish
1 teaspoon Worcestershire
    sauce

1 teaspoon grated onion or
    onion salt
Dash of pepper

In sauce pan, combine juice, consomme, onion, horseradish, Worcestershire sauce and pepper. Stud slices of one lemon with whole cloves and add to the juice. Heat just to boiling point, serve at once. Use lemon slices as floaters in each cup. Makes 8 servings.

Mrs. B. C. Bunker, Tipton

Hot Chicken Sandwiches

1 cup cubed (yellow) cheese
2 tablespoons olives, chopped
3 hard cooked eggs, chopped
1 cup cubed chicken
2 tablespoons chopped onion
2 tablespoons chopped pickle
½ cup salad dressing

Mix above and put in 8 large buns. Wrap in foil. Bake in 250 degree oven 30 minutes or 350 degree 10 to 15 minutes. These may be frozen and heated as needed.

Mrs. Raymond Spencer, Tipton

Bar B Q Hamburgers

2 pounds hamburger
1 onion
1 green pepper (optional)
1½ cups catsup
4 tablespoons prepared mustard
3 to 4 tablespoons sugar
4 tablespoons vinegar
Water to make moist

Simmer until thoroughly cooked. Addition of ¼ cup quick oatmeal will keep hamburger moist and help hold it together.

Alice L. Moore, Tipton

Hamburger On Bun

1½ pounds hamburger
1 large onion
1 can chili beans
¾ teaspoon salt

Dash of pepper
1 can stewed tomatoes
   (with green peppers and
   onion combined)

Brown hamburger and onion. Add salt, pepper, beans, and tomatoes. Turn down to simmer. Stir occasionally; it thickens as it is slowly cooked (about 1 hour).

Mrs. James L. Steen, Tipton

Hamburger Filling

1 pound ground beef
1 diced onion
3 tablespoons catsup

1 tablespoon prepared mustard
Salt and pepper to taste
1 can cream of chicken soup

Brown the meat and onion. Put on low heat and add remaining ingredients. Simmer until mixture becomes thick enough to spread.

Blanche Owen, Tipton

Toasted Crab Meat Buns

1 dozen wiener buns
1 can crab meat (flaked)
1 pound processed cheese

¼ pound melted butter
Worcestershire sauce and
horseradish to taste

Melt butter and cheese. Add crab meat, sauce and horseradish. Spread on split buns. Toast under broiler until done.

Mrs. Bill Woods, Spencer

9

Bun-Steads

¼ pound American cheese (1 cup cubed)
2 tablespoons chopped green pepper
2 tablespoons chopped stuffed olives
3 hard cooked eggs, chopped
½ cup salad dressing

1 7-ounce can tuna, flaked
2 tablespoons chopped onion
2 tablespoons chopped sweet pickle

Combine. Split 6 coney buns and fill. Wrap in foil and place in oven at 250 degrees for 30 minutes. Serve hot.

Fern Raney, Tipton

Hot Tuna Sandwich

8 slices bread, remove crusts
2 tablespoons green pepper, chopped
2 tablespoons celery, chopped
1 cup tuna

½ cup grated cheese
3 eggs, beaten
1¼ cups milk
Salt and pepper to taste

Put 4 slices of bread in pan and spread with above mixture. Put 4 slices of bread on top. Bake 40 minutes at 350 degrees.

Fern Raney, Tipton

Corned Beef Bunwiches

1 12-ounce can corned beef, shredded
1 cup shredded American cheese
½ cup stuffed green olives

½ cup catsup
¼ cup minced onion
2 tablespoons Worcestershire sauce

Mix all ingredients and put in hot dog buns. Wrap in foil. Bake 375 degrees for 15 minutes. This is enough filling for 8 to 10 buns.

Mrs. Keith Fields, Tipton

10

Tuna Burgers

1 can cream of mushroom soup
1 can (7-ounce) tuna, drained
1 tablespoon minced onion
1 tablespoon minced green
   pepper

Combine and spoon into 4 or 5 hamburger buns which have been opened and brushed with butter. Broil until bubbly.

Mrs. John Kyl, Bloomfield
Wife of U. S. Representative, 4th Iowa District

Gooley Buns

1 pound large bologna
¼ cup prepared mustard
1 tablespoon minced onion
¾ pound sharp American
   cheese
2 tablespoons chopped
   sweet pickles
⅓ cup salad dressing

Grind bologna and cheese. Add remaining ingredients and mix well. Cut coney buns in half; spread with butter and then filling. Wrap each bun in foil. Heat in slow oven for 25 minutes at 325 degrees. Makes 12.

Fern Raney, Tipton

Broiled Bean and Cheese Sandwiches

1 can (1 pound 5 ounces)
   pork & beans
¼ cup pickle relish
½ teaspoon prepared
   mustard
⅛ teaspoon salt

Arrange 6 slices sandwich bread on foil lined cookie sheet. Spread bread slices with bean mixture. Place 6 slices sharp cheese over sandwiches. Top with 6 slices diced bacon. Broil, watching carefully, until bacon is done and cheese melted.

Mrs. Dwayne Drager, Tipton

Dogs In The Blanket (Kids' favorite)

Use basic roll recipe. Roll out as for cinnamon rolls. Cut into pieces large enough to roll a wiener in. Pinch ends and rolled edges so wiener is completely covered. Place in greased pan and let bread rise until it is light. Bake in 400 degree oven 15 to 20 minutes or until golden brown. Grease tops. Cut off end and add catsup, mustard, etc. Wieners should be room temperature so as not to slow up yeast action.

Mrs. Don Willcutt, Tipton

Left over sandwiches may be buttered and grilled for a second time treat.

Breads

Biscuits and muffins
Or homemade bread
Makes a house smell like heaven,
Puts a crown on your head!

Refrigerated Tea Muffin Mix

1 cup shortening
1½ cups sugar
2 eggs, beaten
2 cups milk
1½ cups raisins

4 cups sifted flour
2 teaspoons cinnamon
4 teaspoons baking powder
1 teaspoon salt

Cream shortening and sugar. Add rest of ingredients and mix lightly. Makes ½ gallon. Store in refrigerator up to 7 weeks. As needed, bake in greased muffin pans 25-30 minutes at 400 degrees.

Topping: Mix finely chopped nuts and brown sugar. Store in tightly closed jar. Sprinkle over top of muffins just before baking.

These may be frozen (unbaked) in muffin cups and then baked for about 45 minutes.

Mrs. Barbara Ann Grassley, New Hartford
Wife of Iowa State Representative

Spicy Apple Muffins

2 cups flour
¼ cup sugar
½ teaspoon salt
4 teaspoons baking powder
1 cup finely cut raw apple that has been sweetened with ¼ cup sugar

½ teaspoon cinnamon
1 egg, beaten
¼ cup melted shortening
1 cup milk

Combine sifted dry ingredients with liquid, adding sweetened apples last. Bake 20-25 minutes in 425 degree oven.

Mrs. John Miller, Tipton

Orange Muffins

Add grated orange peel to your favorite plain muffin dough and poke a sugar cube soaked in orange juice into the top of each muffin.

Mrs. B. C. Bunker, Tipton

14

Giant Muffin Mix

Better mix this in a dish pan! It's a large recipe!

Pour 2 cups boiling water over 4 cups all-bran cereal and 2 cups shredded wheat cereal. Let cool.

Cream together 3 cups sugar and 1 heaping cup shortening. Add 4 eggs. Beat well and stir in 1 quart buttermilk.

Sift together 5 cups flour, 5 tablespoons baking powder and 1 teaspoon salt.

Stir cooled cereal mixture into batter. Fold in dry ingredients until just barely moistened. Don't overmix!

Spoon into paper liners in muffin pans and bake in 425 degree oven for 20-25 minutes.

"I like to sprinkle a dab of cinnamon and sugar over the batter before baking. This batter will keep (completely mixed) in an air-tight container in your refrigerator at least 3 weeks. So bake as many as you like whenever you're just ready to eat them."

Jan Voss, Cedar Rapids
WMT-TV's Home Fare

Bran Bud or Flake Muffins

Pour 1 cup boiling water over 3 cups Bran Buds or Flakes; add 2 cups buttermilk and let cool. Cream together 1½ cups sugar and ½ cup margarine. Beat in 2 eggs and then add to bran mixture.

Sift 2½ cups flour, 2½ teaspoons soda, ⅔ teaspoon salt and fold into the above mixture.

Fill greased muffin pans ⅔ full.

Bake 25 minutes at 350 degrees. This will keep 2 weeks in the refrigerator.

Ruth Stewart, Washington

Mix equal parts of honey and butter — blend well — to use on muffins, biscuits, waffles or toast.

Coffee Cake Deluxe

Here is a favorite for a morning coffee. You can mix it up the night before and put in the oven in time to pop it out hot for company!

2 cups flour   ½ teaspoon salt
1 teaspoon cinnamon   3 teaspoons baking powder

Sift together into mixing bowl and add:

1 cup white sugar   ½ cup brown sugar

Cut in ⅔ cup butter or margarine. Add 2 beaten eggs and 1 cup buttermilk. Stir only until blended. Pour into 9" x 12" cake pan. Cover with topping before baking.

Topping: ½ cup brown sugar, ½ cup nuts, ½ teaspoon cinnamon, ½ teaspoon nutmeg.

Bake at 350 degrees for 30 minutes.

Marguerite Ashlock
WMT-TV's Home Fare

Southern Gal Biscuits

2 cups sifted flour   2 tablespoons sugar
4 teaspoons baking powder   ½ cup shortening
½ teaspoon cream of tartar   1 egg, unbeaten
½ teaspoon salt   ⅔ cup milk

Sift flour, baking powder, salt, sugar and cream of tartar into bowl. Add shortening and blend together until of cornmeal-like consistency. Pour milk into flour mixture slowly. Add egg. Stir to stiff dough. Knead 5 times. Roll to ½" thickness and cut with 1½" cutter. Bake at 450 degrees from 10-15 minutes.

Marion Jones, Tipton

Those who find adventure in making bread are probably the artists.

Delicious tea rusks are made by dipping buns (cut in half) in sweet milk, then toasting in a moderate oven until golden brown.

16

Sour Cream Coffee Cake

Cream ¼ pound butter and 1 cup sugar. Add 2 eggs and 1 cup sour cream.

Sift together 2 cups sifted flour, 1 teaspoon soda, 1 teaspoon salt and 1 teaspoon baking powder. Add to creamed mixture, plus 1 teaspoon vanilla.

Topping: ½ cup white sugar, ½ cup brown sugar, 1 teaspoon cinnamon, ground nuts.

Spread ½ batter in pan, then topping, then remainder of batter. Bake 35-40 minutes at 350 degrees.

Percie Van Alstine, Gilmore City
Iowa State Representative

Quick Coffee Cake

1 cup sugar
½ cup shortening
2 cups flour
1 cup milk

2 teaspoons baking powder
1 egg
½ teaspoon salt
½ teaspoon vanilla

Topping: Mix together 2 tablespoons flour, ½ cup sugar, 2 tablespoons butter, 1 teaspoon cinnamon.

Cream sugar and shortening. Add egg, flour, baking powder and milk. Beat well with electric mixer. Pour into oblong pan and sprinkle with topping mixture. Bake 20 minutes in 350 degree oven.

Beverly Stager, Iowa City

Coffee Cake

1 cup cold coffee or water
1 cup butter or margarine
1 cup raisins

1½ cups sugar
2 cups flour
2 eggs

1 teaspoon each of cloves, cinnamon, nutmeg and soda.

Cream sugar and shortening. Add beaten eggs, coffee or water. Mix soda, spices and raisins with the flour and add to the above mix.

Bake in either loaf or shallow pan 25-35 minutes at 375 degrees.

Mrs. George Wehde, Sr., Tipton

17

Apricot Horns

"I don't know whether to call this a cookie or a roll — but it is simply delicious."

1 pound butter or margarine   4 cups sifted flour (about)
1 pound creamed cottage cheese

Blend ingredients together with hands to form a dough. Add more flour if cheese is watery. Shape into 1-inch balls and refrigerate overnight. (Dough may be kept under refrigeration for one month).

Filling: 1 pound dried apricots and 2 cups sugar. Cook apricots until tender; drain and puree. Add sugar while still hot. Cool.

Coating: 1½ cups ground almonds, 1¼ cups sugar, 2 egg whites, slightly beaten. Mix sugar and nuts. Roll each dough ball into a 3-inch round. (Make only 10 horns at a time so dough will remain cold.) Place a teaspoon of apricot filling in center. Roll up in the shape of a horn. Dip into egg white and then roll in nut mixture. Place on greased cookie sheet and bake at 375 degrees for 12 minutes or until lightly browned. Sprinkle with confectioner's sugar. Makes 11 dozen horns.

Mrs. Evan Hultman, Waterloo
Wife of Iowa Attorney General

Southern Lemon Coffee Cake

½ cup butter   2 cups flour
1½ cups sugar   1 teaspoon baking powder
2 whole eggs   ¾ cup milk
        Rind and juice of 1 lemon

Cream butter and sugar, add one egg at a time and beat. Sift flour and baking powder, add to above alternately with milk.

Pour batter into 9x13-inch greased pan. Do not scrape bowl, but add enough flour to make crumbs and sprinkle on batter. Then mix ¼ cup butter, ½ cup sugar, 1 teaspoon cinnamon and pecan nuts. Put this over top and bake in 350 degree oven for 40 minutes. (Serve warm)

Bertha Sheets, Tipton

Pineapple Date Nut Bread

1 can (8½ ounces) crushed pineapple, undrained
1 package (8 ounces) coarsely chopped, pitted dates
¼ cup butter or margarine   ½ teaspoon salt
2¼ cups sifted flour   1 egg
2 teaspoons baking powder   ¼ cup sugar
½ teaspoon baking soda   1 cup finely chopped nuts

Add water to the crushed pineapple to measure 1½ cups.
Bring just to boiling, pour over chopped dates and butter in a medium sized bowl, stirring to melt the butter. Let cool to room temperature.

Sift flour with baking powder, soda and salt onto a shee' of waxed paper. Set aside.

In a large bowl, beat the egg and sugar until well combined.

Stir in the date mixture. Add flour mixture. Beat until smooth. Add nuts and mix well.

Turn batter into a well greased 9x5x3-inch loaf pan and bake at 350 degrees for 55-60 minutes or until cake tester, inserted in center, comes out clean. Cool in pan on wire rack 10 minutes. Run spatula around the sides of pan to loosen. Turn out on wire rack and let cool completely. If possible, wrap and let stand over night before using. Cut in thin slices with a sharp knife. Makes 1 loaf.

Mrs. Elizabeth Horrigan, Tipton

Banana Bread

¼ cup shortening   1½ cups flour
½ cup sugar   ½ teaspoon salt
1 beaten egg   2 teaspoons baking powder
1 cup bran   ½ teaspoon soda
2 tablespoons water   1 teaspoon vanilla
1½ cups mashed banana   ½ cup nuts

Mix ingredients. Bake in waxed paper lined loaf pan for 1 hour at 350 degrees.

Mrs. Kenneth Fulk, Des Moines
Wife of Secretary of Iowa State Fair

Traditional Christmas Date Nut Loaf

2 pounds dates, cut long way once
2 pounds English walnuts, left as whole as possible
Add: 1 cup cake flour sifted with 2 level teaspoons baking powder
1 cup sugar and a pinch of salt
4 beaten egg yolks

Fold in 4 beaten egg whites, 1 teaspoon vanilla

Pour batter into 2 greased and waxed paper lined bread pans. Set these pans in a pan of water and bake at 325 degrees at least 1¾ hours. Should be baked at least 2 weeks before using. Store in air-tight container.

> Bertha Reichert Penningroth, Cedar Rapids
> Wife of the District Judge

Grapenut Bread

2 cups buttermilk, (2 cups milk with 2 tablespoons vinegar added may be substituted). If vinegar and milk mixture is used, let stand for ½ hour.

Add 1 heaping cup of Grapenuts and let stand for ½ hour. Add 2 eggs and 1 tablespoon melted shortening.

Sift and add dry ingredients: 4 cups flour, 1 teaspoon soda, ½ teaspoon salt, 1½ cups white sugar, 2 teaspoons baking powder. Bake in well greased loaf pan for 1 hour at 325 degrees.

> Mrs. Roland Hambright, Bennett

Raisin Nut Bread

2 cups seedless raisins cooked in 2 cups boiling water. Drain off liquid (should be 1 cup) and add to it: 1 teaspoon salt, 2 teaspoons soda.

Mix together: 2 cups sugar, ½ cup butter or margarine, 2 eggs. Add liquid and mix well. Add 4 cups flour, ½ cup nuts, 1 teaspoon vanilla and raisins.

Pour into 3 7x3¼ inch greased pans, filling each ⅔ full. Bake for 1 hour at 300 degrees or until done. A larger loaf should be baked longer.

> Mrs. John Offringa, Tipton

Lemon Bread

1½ cups flour
½ teaspoon salt
2 teaspoons baking powder
2 tablespoons butter

1 cup white sugar
2 eggs
½ cup milk
1 lemon rind, grated

Combine ingredients. Pour into greased bread pan and let rise 20 minutes. Bake 45-50 minutes at 350 degrees. Remove from oven and turn out. Brush with juice of 1 lemon and ½ cup sugar, mixed. (Orange may be substituted).

Mrs. Lester Shick, Davenport

Nut Bread

1 cup sugar
2 cups graham flour
2 tablespoons shortening
4 teaspoons baking powder
1 cup white raisins

2 cups white flour
2 cups milk
2 eggs
2 cups black walnuts
1 teaspoon salt

Combine flour, baking powder, salt, nuts and raisins.

Beat eggs, sugar and shortening together. Add milk, then dry ingredients.

Pour into two 8x4x3-inch loaf pans and let stand 20 minutes.

Bake in 350 degree oven until bread is lightly browned and shrinks from sides of pans (about 1 hour).

Eleanor Buss, Pottawattamie County

Raisin Nut Wheat Bread

2 cups flour
3 teaspoons baking powder
1 teaspoon salt
½ teaspoon nutmeg
1 cup sugar
¾ cup wheat germ

½ cup raisins
½ cup chopped nuts
1 cup milk
⅓ cup melted butter or
    margarine

Combine ingredients. Turn into greased 9x5x3-inch loaf pan, bake in 350 degree oven for 55 minutes.

Edna White, Tipton

21

Olive Nut Bread

2½ cups cake flour
¾ teaspoon salt
½ cup chopped nuts
1 egg, well beaten

4 teaspoons baking powder
⅓ cup sugar
1 cup chopped stuffed olives
1 cup milk

Sift dry ingredients together. Add nuts and olives. Combine egg and milk. Add to dry ingredients and mix only enough to moisten flour.

Turn into a greased 9x5x3-inch loaf pan. Bake in a 350 degree oven for 45 minutes

Margaret Kuhn, Tipton

Butter and Egg Bran Bread

Dissolve 2 cakes of yeast in 1 cup lukewarm water.

Pour 1 cup boiling water over 1 cup all-bran and 1½ teaspoons salt. Add ¾ cup sugar and ⅓ cup soft shortening (butter or margarine). Cool to lukewarm.

Add yeast mixture and 2 well beaten eggs. Add 3 cups flour and beat well. Add 3½ cups more flour. Turn out on a board.

Knead until light and elastic.

Place in greased bowl. Cover. Let rise until doubled. Make into 2 large or 3 small loaves and place in greased pans. Let rise until doubled. Bake at 350 degrees for 45 minutes for small loaves and 1 hour for large loaves. Remove from pans. Brush with oil or butter. Cool on racks.

This is a very different bran bread, light in color, sweeter than most breads, and delicious toasted.

Mrs. Rex Berry, Tipton

The grocery shelves are filled with a variety of mixes that make good products and save time — but there is real satisfaction and joy in using a good recipe, and creating a "masterpiece" of your own!

22

Whole Wheat Bread

1 cup scalded milk   4 teaspoons salt
¼ cup lard   ¼ cup honey
Mix and let cool to lukewarm —about 85 degrees.
1 cup water, 110 degrees to 115 degrees

2 packages dry yeast   2 tablespoons brown sugar

Let stand to dissolve yeast, 2 to 3 minutes. Add yeast mixture to milk mixture. Add 3 cups whole wheat flour and 3 to 4 cups white flour. Mix well. Knead 5 to 10 minutes. Put in bowl to rise until double in size.

Punch down and divide into two portions.

Let rest 5 to 10 minutes and then shape into two loaves. Let rise in pans one hour or until double in bulk. Bake at 375 degrees for 5 minutes and 350 degrees for 30 to 35 minutes.

Remove from pans and let cool thoroughly before wrapping.

Excellent.

Jane Petersen and Phyllis Sywassink
Muscatine County

Modern Manna Yeast Bread

½ cup scalded milk   3 tablespoons sugar
2 teaspoons salt   3 tablespoons shortening

Cool to lukewarm

1½ cups lukewarm water   1 package dry yeast

Combine these mixtures. Beat in 3 cups unsifted flour to develop gluten. Add 2½ cups flour for soft dough. Lightly flour hands and board. Knead 8 to 10 minutes. Place in greased bowl, cover, and let rise until double in bulk. Divide and shape into 2 loaves. Put into greased loaf pans.

Let rise until double. Bake at 400 degrees for 30 minutes.

Rosemary Reed and Gina Marek
Washington County

The family will think you're pretty special if they are greeted by the smell of freshly baked bread.

23

Cinnamon Spiral Bread

½ cup warm water
1 package dry yeast
2 cups lukewarm milk
¼ cup brown sugar

2 cups quick cooking oats
2 tablespoons soft shortening
1 tablespoon salt
1 cup raisins
5½ — 6 cups sifted flour

Dissolve yeast in water in mixing bowl. Stir in remaining ingredients, except half of flour. Mix with a spoon until smooth.

Add remaining flour and mix with the hands. Turn onto a lightly floured board and knead 5 to 10 minutes.

Place in a greased bowl and let rise in a warm place until doubled (1½—2 hours). Divide dough into 2 parts and roll each into a 15x8-inch rectangle.

Sprinkle with all except 2 tablespoons of a mixture of ½ cup sugar and 2 teaspoons cinnamon. Roll up like a jelly roll, sealing tightly at the ends.

Divide in half, place in 2 loaf pans and let rise until doubled.

Brush top with corn syrup and sprinkle with remaining cinnamon-sugar mixture. Bake 1 hour at 350 degrees.

Thelma Kallenberger, Tipton

Oatmeal Bread

2 packages yeast
½ cup lukewarm water
2 cups milk, scalded
⅓ cup shortening

¼ cup brown sugar
1½ teaspoons salt
4 to 4½ cups sifted flour
2 cups rolled oats, uncooked,
    quick or old fashioned

Soften yeast in lukewarm water (use warm water for dry yeast).

Pour scalded milk over shortening, sugar and salt. Stir until shortening melts. Cool to lukewarm. Stir in 1 cup flour. Add softened yeast and oats. Stir in enough more flour to make a soft dough.

Turn dough out on lightly floured board or canvas. Knead until smooth and satiny (about 10 minutes). Round into ball, place

24

in greased bowl, brush lightly with melted shortening. Cover and let rise in warm place until nearly doubled in size (about 1 hour).

Punch dough down. Cover and let rest 10 minutes. Divide dough in half, forming each part to make a loaf. Place in well greased loaf pan (1 pound size). Brush tops with melted shortening.

Cover, let rise until nearly doubled in size (about 45 minutes).

Bake in 375 degree oven about 50 minutes. Remove from pans.

Brush lightly with melted butter.

Mrs. Cora Phillips, Tipton

Onion Bread

1 package yeast
1 cup creamed cottage cheese
1 tablespoon minced onion
  (dehydrated flakes)
2 tablespoons dill seed
¼ teaspoon baking soda

¼ cup warm water plus
1 teaspoon sugar
2 tablespoons sugar
1 tablespoon butter
1 teaspoon salt
1 egg
2¼ to 2½ cups flour

Sprinkle dry yeast over warm water. Heat cottage cheese to lukewarm, combine in mixing bowl with sugar, onion, butter, dill, salt, soda, egg and yeast mixture.

Add flour to form stiff dough, beating well after each addition.

A little more flour may have to be added. Dough may be kneaded lightly if desired. Cover and let rise until double.

Stir dough down and turn into a well greased, 1½ quart or 8 inch casserole. Let rise until light and bake in moderate oven at 350 degrees about 40-50 minutes. Take from casserole and brush with butter.

Frieda Fields, Tipton

Acorns were good until bread was found.

25

Bread Sticks

1 package dry yeast, dissolved in ⅔ cup warm water
1 teaspoon salt   ¼ cup soft shortening
1 tablespoon sugar   1 cup flour

Stir well. Add another cup of flour, then knead. Let rise until double. Cut into 48 pieces. Roll each 8" in length. Grease baking sheet. Place ½" apart.

Beat 1 whole egg with 1 tablespoon water. Brush over bread sticks. Sprinkle with coarse salt and sesame seed or poppy seed. Bake in 400 degree oven for 20 minutes. Watch closely.

Dorothy Albaugh, Tipton

Cinnamon Loaf

Soften 2 packages dry yeast or 2 cakes compressed yeast in ½ cup warm water.

Mix in large bowl:
⅓ cup sugar   1 teaspoon salt
¼ cup butter   ⅔ cup boiling water

Cool to lukewarm

Blend in 1 unbeaten egg and the softened yeast. Add 1 cup raisins and 3½ cups flour to form a soft dough. Beat well after each addition. Cover and let rise in a warm place until light, about 1 to 1½ hours.

Combine ⅔ cup sugar, 2 teaspoons cinnamon. Set aside.

Brush 2 quart casserole with butter and sprinkle with 3 tablespoons sugar mixture.

Stir down dough. Spread ⅓ of dough in casserole with lightly greased fingers. Sprinkle with 3 tablespoons sugar mixture. Repeat with remaining dough and sugar mixture, leaving the top plain. Shape to form a round loaf. Cover and let stand 30 minutes.

Bake at 350 degrees 45-55 minutes, until golden brown. Brush with butter and sprinkle with remaining sugar mixture. Makes 1 round loaf.

Mrs. Larry Hostler, Tipton

26

Sweet Coffee Rolls

2 cups milk
2 sticks margarine
¼ cup sugar

2 packages dry yeast
3 eggs, beaten
6 cups flour

Scald milk and add margarine and sugar. When cooled, add eggs and the yeast which has been dissolved in 3 tablespoons warm water. Add 1 cup flour at a time, beating well with a wooden spoon. This beats air into the dough.

Refrigerate over night. The next day take out as large a portion of the dough as you may need. Roll out lengthwise and butter half of it. Fold over other half. Cut 1" cross wise strips and twist each one to form a round circle roll. Let rise about 1 hour, on greased pans.

Bake at 450 degrees for 10 minutes.

Frost with powdered sugar frosting with almond or vanilla flavoring while they are warm. This is a large recipe.

Hertha Steffenson and
Christina Sondergard, West Branch

Sour Cream Twists

1 package active dry yeast
¼ cup very warm water
4 cups sifted flour
1 cup margarine, melted
1 cup sour cream

2 eggs, slightly beaten
1 teaspoon salt
1 teaspoon vanilla
1 cup sugar
1 teaspoon cinnamon

Sprinkle yeast into very warm water; stir until dissolved. Combine flour, margarine, sour cream, eggs, salt and vanilla in a large bowl. Stir in dissolved yeast; beat until smooth. Cover with damp cloth. Refrigerate at least 2 hours or up to 2 days.

Combine sugar and cinnamon. Sprinkle on board. Roll dough into rectangle about 15" x 18"; turn so both sides are coated to prevent sticking. Fold over three times, as you would a letter.

Roll into rectangle ¼ inch thick, using up all the sugar. Cut into 1 x 4 inch strips. Twist and place on greased baking sheet.

Bake at once for 15 minutes at 375 degrees. Makes 4-5 dozen.

Mrs. Keiffer Garton, Tipton

Orange Rolls

1 cup milk
3 tablespoons butter
1 package dry yeast
½ teaspoon salt
3 eggs
½ cup sugar
4 cups flour

Scald the milk, add the butter and cool to lukewarm. Sprinkle on the dry yeast and salt. Let sit, then stir to dissolve. Beat eggs until light. Add the sugar and combine all together. Then stir in 1 cup flour and mix well. Cover and let rise for 2 hours. Add the remaning 3 cups flour. DO NOT KNEAD.

Have the following FILLING prepared ahead:
½ cup soft butter ½ cup sugar
Grated rind of 1 large orange

Divide the soft dough into 3 pieces for ease in handling. Roll each into a rectangle on floured board. Spread with the filling. Roll up jelly roll fashion and cut into 1 inch slices. Place on well greased pan. Let rise for 2 hours. Bake in 400 degree oven for 20 minutes.

Best served hot.

Mrs. Norman Ludwick, Evansdale

Butterhorn Rolls

Dissolve 2 packages quick yeast in 1 cup lukewarm water. Melt ⅔ cup shortening in 1 cup hot water. Cool.

Combine above and add 2 teaspoons salt, ½ cup sugar and 2 beaten eggs.

Add 3 cups flour and beat well with mixer. Finish stirring about 4 cups flour in with a spoon.

This will be a real soft dough. Set in refrigerator to thicken up for about 1 hour. Then roll out like pie dough, cut in wedges and roll up from large end. Place on greased pan, let rise until real light.

Brush with butter or margarine, then bake at 375 degrees for 15 minutes.

This recipe may also be used for cinnamon, pecan or plain rolls.

Mrs. Earl Thomas, Washington

28

Ice Box Rolls

Measure into bowl:
¼ to ½ cup sugar   2 tablespoons lard
                        1 tablespoon salt

Pour 1 cup boiling water over these and let stand until luke warm. Soak 1 package or cake of yeast in 1 cup lukewarm water. Add 1 tablespoon sugar and let stand 5 minutes. Combine the two mixtures. Add 2 eggs. Mix well. Add 7 cups sifted flour or enough to make a stiff dough.

Toss onto floured board. Let rest 5 minutes. Knead well. Put into greased bowl and let rise until double in bulk, about 2 hours. Knead lightly. Cover and store in refrigerator until ready to use or shape rolls immediately. Oil tops. Let rise until light, about 1 hour and bake 15 to 20 minutes at 375 degrees.

Use above as plain rolls, cinnamon rolls or any variation desired.

For butterscotch rolls, butter muffin tin, add 1 teaspoon melted butter, 1 teaspoon brown sugar, ¼ teaspoon corn syrup and whole or chopped nuts. Place a plain or cinnamon roll in each, allow to rise and bake as above.

Glaze for rolls—
1 egg yolk   2 tablespoons sugar
                3 tablespoons water or milk

Beat egg slightly, add sugar and liquid and mix well. Then brush over rolls before baking. Sprinkle with sugar if desired. This gives a nice color to a plain roll.

Mrs. Ray Gammell, Red Oak

Tied Cinnamon Rolls

Soften 2 cakes yeast in 1 cup lukewarm water.

Cream 1 cup shortening and ½ cup sugar. Over this pour 1 cup boiling water. Add 2 beaten eggs, 1 tablespoon salt and the yeast mixture. Add 6 cups flour. Form a dough, but do not let rise.

Roll out and cut into 1x5 inch strips. Dip in melted butter. Roll in mixture of cinnamon and sugar. Tie in a knot. Place on greased pan. Let rise 1 hour. Bake until brown at 350 degrees (about 15 to 20 minutes).

Mrs. Charles Towle, Davenport

Crusty Casserolls

⅔ cup milk
1 tablespoon sugar
½ teaspoon salt

6 tablespoons butter
⅓ cup warm, not hot, water
1 package dry granular yeast

2 cups sifted flour

Scald milk, stir in sugar, salt, and 1 tablespoon butter. Cool to lukewarm. Melt rest of butter. Sprinkle yeast into water which should be warmer than lukewarm. Stir to dissolve. Combine lukewarm milk mixture, dissolved yeast and flour. Beat until smooth and elastic, about 50 strokes.

Brush top lightly with some melted butter. Cover and let rise in warm place until double in bulk—about 25 minutes. Stir dough down and drop by large tablespoons into shallow casserole containing half of melted and cooled butter. Spoon remaining melted butter over top of rolls. Cover and let rise until double in bulk—about 25 minutes. Sprinkle with sesame seed. Bake at 400 degrees about 35 minutes. Serve warm from casserole. Makes 10-12 rolls.

Mrs. Harold Johnson, Washington

Cinnamon Puffs

2 packages granular yeast
½ cup warm (not hot) water
¾ cup lukewarm milk
¼ cup sugar

1 teaspoon salt
½ cup shortening
2 eggs
3¼ cups sifted flour

1 tablespoon vanilla

Coating mixture: 1 cup sugar and 4 teaspoons cinnamon

Combine yeast and water. Let stand 5 minutes. In large bowl combine milk, sugar, salt, shortening, eggs, yeast mixture, and half of flour. Beat 2 minutes with electric mixer (medium speed) or by hand until smooth. Add remaining flour and vanilla. Beat 2 more minutes with spoon.

Drop 1 tablespoon batter into greased, medium sized muffin cups. Place in warm place and let rise until double and they reach tops of muffin pans (30-40 minutes). Bake in 375 degree oven 18-20 minutes or until golden brown. Remove from pans and dip top and sides in melted butter (½ cup), then into cinnamon-sugar coating mixture. Best served warm. Makes 2½ dozen.

Mrs. Albert Conrad, Tipton

Poppy Seed Crescents

¼ cup butter
⅓ cup boiling water
1 package yeast
¼ cup warm water

2 tablespoons sugar
1 teaspoon salt
1 egg, beaten
3 cups flour

⅔ cup undiluted, evaporated milk

Combine butter and boiling water, stir until butter is melted. Cool to lukewarm. Add yeast to warm water, stir until dissolved. Add sugar, salt and yeast to butter mixture. Blend in egg and milk.

Stir in flour, mix until well blended. Place in a greased bowl. Cover and let rise in a warm place for 1 hour.

Divide dough in half. Roll halves into 12 inch circles. Spread each with ½ of poppy seed mixture. Cut each circle into 8 to 12 pie shaped sections. Roll into crescents. Place on lightly greased baking sheet. Let rise until nearly doubled. Brush with 1 egg yolk and 1 tablespoon water mixed together. Bake 10 minutes at 425 degrees. Yields 16 to 24.

POPPY SEED FILLING: 2 tablespoons sugar, ¼ teaspoon cinnamon, 2 tablespoons poppy seed, 2 tablespoons water, ½ teaspoon grated lemon rind. Combine and heat to boiling. Cool.

Mrs. Austin Ford, Tipton

Cheese Sticks

½ cup butter or margarine
1 cup shredded sharp cheddar
    cheese

1 cup sifted flour
1 teaspoon salt

Cream butter, add cheese and beat well. Sift together flour and salt, stir into creamed mixture and mix to a smooth dough.

Force through ¾ to 1 inch wide saw tooth, flat attachment of cooky press. Press out in 5-inch lengths on ungreased cooky sheet.

Bake in 350 degree oven about 12 minutes. Let cool on sheet for a few minutes, then remove carefully. Makes 2½ dozen.

Mrs. Don Safley, Tipton

31

Special Cinnamon Rolls

2 packages dry yeast
½ cup lukewarm water
1 tablespoon sugar
Pinch of ginger
2 cups warm water
½ cup sugar

½ cup melted shortening, cooled
2 teaspoons salt
3 beaten eggs
3 cups flour
2 cups raisins
5 cups flour, more or less

In a big bowl place yeast, ½ cup lukewarm water, sugar and ginger. When yeast is dissolved, stir in well 2 cups warm water, ½ cup sugar, salt, eggs and 3 cups flour. Add raisins, which have plumped over hot water, shortening and more flour. Knead until smooth, place in a greased bowl, cover with a cloth and let rise until double.

Roll out in rectangle (or make 2 rectangles for ease in handling). Spread surface with butter, 1 cup brown sugar, and 4 teaspoons cinnamon.

Roll up and cut. Place cut side down on a greased pan. Let rise until almost double. TOPPING: 1 cup cream whipped, 1 teaspoon cinnamon, ½ cup brown sugar, and chopped nuts. Combine ingredients and spread on raised rolls. Bake at 375 for 20 to 25 minutes.

Mrs. H. L. Witmer, Tipton

Boston Brown Bread

2 cups graham (whole
    wheat) flour
1 cup white flour
2 cups buttermilk

½ cup dark cooking molasses
1 teaspoon soda
1½ cups raisins
½ teaspoon salt

Add milk to flour gradually until well mixed. Add soda to the molasses and stir until it foams. Then add to first mixture. Add raisins and salt and stir until well mixed.

Bake 35-45 minutes in a 350 degree oven in two medium sized (3x7 inch) bread tins. (You can use tin cans for this too).

This is delicious and especially good, served, not warm, but the same day it is baked, with lots of butter or cream cheese.

Mrs. Richard Dircks, Clarence

Sticky Cinnamon Rolls

¾ cup milk
¼ cup sugar
1 teaspoon salt
¼ cup butter

½ cup warm water
1 package yeast
1 beaten egg
3½ cups flour

Scald the milk. Stir in salt, sugar and butter. Cool to lukewarm.

Dissolve yeast in warm water and stir until dissolved. Add the lukewarm milk mixture, egg and 2 cups flour. Beat until smooth.

Add rest of flour. Let rise until doubled in bulk.

Roll out and spread with butter, cinnamon and sugar. Roll as for jelly roll, slice, and place in a pan, cut side up. Let rise until doubled in bulk.

Heat ½ cup dark syrup and ¼ cup butter until butter is melted.

Just before placing rolls in oven, pour this mixture over them.

Bake at 400 degrees for 20 minutes.

Edith Hambright, Bennett

Have fun — Make rolls! Kneading is easy; shaping is fun — when you've learned how.

Cherry Kringle

1 package yeast dissolved
   in ¼ cup warm water
⅓ cup warm milk
¼ cup sugar

1 egg
¼ cup oil
½ teaspoon salt
2⅓ cups flour

Mix warm milk, sugar, egg, oil and salt well. Add soaked yeast mixture. Add flour, 1 cup at a time. Let rise. Divide dough into 2 parts. Pat ½ into a 16x12 inch pan. Cover with 1 can cherry pie filling. Cover with the other half of dough, patted thin. Let rise and sprinkle with sugar. Bake 20-25 minutes in a 375 degree oven.

Thin frosting may be used.

Mrs. A. H. Schluntz, Cedar Rapids

Versatile Coffee Cake

Sift together 4 cups flour, 1 teaspoon salt, 3 tablespoons sugar.

Cut in with a blender, as for making pie crust, 1 cup vegetable shortening.

Scald and cool to lukewarm 1 cup milk and then dissolve in it 1 package dry yeast.

Add 2 beaten eggs to the milk.

Stir all together with a spoon and cover and store in refrigerator until well chilled at least 2 hours or it may be kept a week and baked as needed. When cold, will handle easily. Makes 3 coffee cakes. Roll each section into an oblong shape.

Variation Fillings:

Spread with any fruit filling, such as the prepared pie fillings, or jam, or sliced apples sprinkled with sugar and cinnamon, or cut up gum drops, or cranberries, or just spread with butter and sprinkle with cinnamon and sugar and cut up nuts.

Roll up jelly roll style. Tuck one end inside the other, making a ring. Place on greased pans. Let rise until double. Because it is cold, this will take 2 hours.

Bake at 350 degrees for ½ hour, until brown. Glaze or frost as desired and decorate with cherries or nuts.

"This is my most requested recipe. It is very like Danish Pastry, but without the bother. It's handy to have in the refrigerator for quick and easy refreshments with coffee."

Vern Berry, Tipton

Olivette suggests:
When freezing rolls, if you want them iced, make an icing of powdered sugar and evaporated milk. It will not melt when rolls are reheated for serving.

Vern adds: or keep a jar of icing covered in your refrigerator. Brush onto heated rolls just before serving.

Dumplings

1 cup flour
¼ teaspoon salt

2 teaspoons baking powder
1 egg
⅓ cup milk (scant)

Sift flour, baking powder and salt into a bowl. Add egg, stirring well. Add milk. Drop from spoon into hot stew or gravy. Cook uncovered for 5 minutes, then cover and steam gently for 15 minutes. May be covered immediately and baked in a 350 degree oven for 15 minutes.

Stella Dinsmore, Tipton

Feather Pancakes

1 cup sifted flour
2 tablespoons baking powder (no error, 2 tablespoons is correct!)
2 tablespoons sugar

¾ to 1 cup milk
½ teaspoon salt
1 slightly beaten egg
2 tablespoons melted shortening or salad oil

Combine egg, milk and shortening. (Use less milk for thick, fluffy cakes.) Add sifted dry ingredients, beat smooth.

Ann Owen, Tipton

Delicate Fluffy Pancakes

3 egg yolks
1⅔ cups thick buttermilk or sour cream
1 teaspoon baking powder
3 tablespoons soft butter

3 egg whites (stiffly beaten)
1 teaspoon soda
1½ cups flour
1 tablespoon sugar

Beat 3 egg yolks and buttermilk together. Add sifted dry ingredients. Stir in soft butter. Gently fold in egg whites. Bake on hot griddle. Amount 16, 4-inch cakes.

Margaret Kuhn, Tipton

35

Raised Waffles

Very convenient to prepare the night before for a fast breakfast!

Put into a large mixing bowl: ½ cup lukewarm water and 1 package yeast. Let stand 5 minutes. Add:

2 cups lukewarm milk   ½ cup melted butter or
1 teaspoon salt   salad oil
1 teaspoon sugar

Beat in 2 cups flour.

Cover the bowl. Let stand overnight or at least eight hours—not in refrigerator. When time to cook the waffles, add: 2 eggs and a pinch of baking soda.

Beat well. The batter will be very thin. Cook on waffle iron. Makes 6 or more large waffles.

Mrs. Washburn W. Steele, Cherokee
Wife of State Representative

Mix pancake or waffle batter in a wide mouth pitcher — then pour directly on the griddle.

Scotch Cream Scones

2 cups flour   4 teaspoons baking powder
2 teaspoons sugar   ⅓ cup cream
⅛ teaspoon salt   4 tablespoons butter
2 eggs, well beaten

Mix and sift together flour, baking powder, sugar and salt. Rub in butter with the tips of the fingers. Add eggs and the cream.

Toss on floured board, pat and roll to ¾ inch thickness.

Cut in squares, brush with white of egg, sprinkle with sugar and bake in 450 degree oven about 12 minutes, or until delicately browned.

Margaret Kuhn, Tipton

Glazed Raised Doughnuts

1 package dry yeast
1 cup sugar
2 cups lukewarm water
⅓ cup shortening
6 to 7 cups flour

1 egg (beaten)
2 teaspoons salt
2 teaspoons almond or
    vanilla extract

Dissolve yeast and 1 tablespoon sugar in cup lukewarm water. Melt shortening in remaining cup of water and add 2 cups flour, then add the yeast mixture and beat until bubbles appear. Let rise ½ hour. Add egg, salt, remaining sugar and flavoring.

Mix well and add remaining flour, enough to make a soft dough. Knead well for about 7 minutes on floured board. Place in a well greased bowl ond set in a warm place (95°F) until double in bulk (about an hour). Roll to ⅓ inch thickness and cut with a large holed donut cutter. Set in warm place to let rise.

When very light, fry in deep hot fat (365 to 375 degrees). Drain on unglazed paper. When cool sprinkle with sugar or while still slightly warm, they can be glazed with the following mixture: 1 cup powdered sugar, ½ cup water.

Makes 3 dozen doughnuts. (I use the holes and scraps of dough for sweet rolls and bake and freeze for future use).

Mrs. Virgil Walter, Stanwood

Potato Doughnuts

2 eggs well beaten
1 cup sugar
2 tablespoons salad oil
1 cup mashed potatoes
1 cup sour milk

4½ cups flour
1 teaspoon salt
4 teaspoons baking powder
1 teaspoon soda
1 teaspoon nutmeg

Beat eggs and sugar until light; add salad oil, potatoes, and milk. Beat until smooth. Sift dry ingredients and add to egg mixture and chill. On lightly floured surface roll dough to ½ inch thickness. Cut with doughnut cutter and fry in deep fat 365°. Drain on absorbent paper and shake in paper sack containing granulated or confectioner's sugar. Makes 3 dozen.

Clara Conrad, Burlington

The liquid in bread may be either water or milk. Milk adds food value. Bread made with milk has a velvety crumb and creamy color. It keeps well and toasts well, too. Fresh milk, evaporated, or reconstituted dry milk may be used. Bread made with water has a crisper crust.

The best possible place to store bread is in your freezer. Properly cooled, bread placed in plastic bags or wrapped in air tight moisture proof material, will keep fresh for several weeks when stored in a freezer. For quick defrosting, if sliced, pop bread, as needed, into the toaster until thawed. To defrost many slices, arrange them on a cooky sheet and warm under a broiler, watching closely and turning as needed.

Notes

Cakes
Cookies
Candies

Cakes and cookies

On a plate – – –

Oft have sealed

Some young man's fate!

Chocolate Cake

1⅞ cups sugar
3 eggs
½ teaspoon salt
½ cup cocoa
½ cup boiling water

1 tablespoon butter
1 cup cream, sweet or sour
2 cups cake flour
1 teaspoon soda
1 teaspoon vanilla

Beat eggs, add sugar and salt and beat well. Dissolve cocoa in boiling water and add fat, allowing it to melt, then add to egg mixture. Sift flour and soda together, and add alternately with cream. Add vanilla. Bake in 350 degree oven in a 9"x13" pan or two 9"-layer pans.

Filling:

1 cup milk or cream
½ cup sugar

4 tablespoons flour
½ cup dates

½ cup nutmeats

Mix together dates, flour and sugar, add milk or cream, and cook until thick. Add nuts. Spread hot filling on slightly cooled cake.

Icing:

2 cups powdered sugar
4 tablespoons cocoa
1 tablespoon soft butter

1 teaspoon vanilla
⅛ teaspoon salt
Cream to moisten

This icing should not be too thin as it is spread on the filling while still hot.

Mrs. Ralph Gaul, Tipton

Hundred Dollar Cake

2 cups flour
1 cup sugar
1½ teaspoons baking powder
1½ teaspoons soda

4 tablespoons cocoa
1 cup water
1 cup salad dressing
2 teaspoons vanilla

Sift together dry ingredients and add water, salad dressing and vanilla. Bake in greased 8" square pan 30 to 35 minutes at 350 degrees.

Mrs. Fred Schwengel, Davenport
Wife of Congressman from Iowa

Chocolate Cake

1¾ cups sugar
½ cup butter or margarine
½ teaspoon salt
½ cup cocoa
1 teaspoon vanilla

1 cup cold water
2 cups sifted cake flour
1 teaspoon soda
2 tablespoons hot water
3 beaten egg whites

Red food coloring if desired

Cream sugar and butter. Add salt, cocoa and vanilla which have been mixed with 2 tablespoons of the cold water. Add the sifted cake flour alternately with the remaining cold water. Dissolve soda in the 2 tablespoons of hot water and add to batter. Add food coloring. Fold in beaten egg whites. Pour into greased and floured 9x13-inch pan.

Bake in 350 degree oven until cake leaves sides of pan. Cover cake while still warm with waxed paper to avoid crust.

Serve with sauce made from:

1 cup sugar
1 cup cream or milk

Dash of salt
4½ tablespoons flour

Cook in double boiler until clear and thick. Add nuts and vanilla.

Serve warm. Cocoa may be added for a dark filling.

Mary Ferguson, Tipton

College Cup Cakes

1 cup sugar
½ cup butter or margarine
½ cup milk
1 egg
½ scant cup cocoa

½ teaspoon soda
1 teaspoon baking powder
½ teaspoon salt
1½ cups sifted all
purpose flour

½ cup boiling water

Combine above ingredients in bowl and mix well with electric mixer for three minutes. Line muffin tins with paper baking cups and fill about two-thirds full. Bake 25 to 30 minutes in 350 degree oven. Makes 18 cup cakes. Ice with favorite icing.

Note: Does cake go stale at your house? Make your favorite recipe into cup cakes and freeze part of them.

Mrs. Howard Hamilton, Tipton

Date Chocolate Chip Cake

Mix and let stand:
1½ cups chopped dates
1 teaspoon soda
1½ cups boiling water

Mix well:
1¼ cups sugar
½ cup shortening
2 eggs

Add date mixture to sugar-shortening mixture. To this add 2 cups all purpose flour, ¾ teaspoon soda and ½ teaspoon salt. Mix well and pour into large pan. Over the top sprinkle ½ cup sugar, 1 package chocolate chips, 1 cup nutmeats, chopped. Bake at 325 degrees for 40 minutes. May add a topping of whipped cream.

This is a large cake and is good to serve for a lunch with coffee.

Mrs. J. Henry Lucken, LeMars
Wife of State Senator

Coconut Frosting for Chocolate Chip Cake Mix

Make cake of chocolate chip cake mix and put on this frosting when cake is almost cool:

1 6-oz. can evaporated milk
3 egg yolks, beaten
1 cup sugar

1 stick margarine
1 teaspoon vanilla

Cook slowly until thick. Remove from stove and add 1 can coconut and enough chocolate chips to make it as dark as you wish.

Mrs. Harry Gerber, Tipton

Praline Prune Cake

Mix one package of burnt sugar cake mix according to directions.

Add ½ cup chopped prunes. Bake according to directions.

Penuche Prune Frosting: 2 cups light brown sugar, ¼ teaspoon salt, ½ cup milk, ½ cup butter or margarine. Cook over low heat until butter melts then cook until mixture forms a soft ball in cold water, 236 degrees. Beat until lukewarm and add ½ cup chopped prunes.

Mrs. C. S. Miller, Tipton

White Nut Cake
(With Variations)

2 cups sugar
¾ cup butter
1 cup milk
3 cups cake flour

2 teaspoons baking powder
Whites of 6 eggs
1 cup walnuts
1 teaspoon vanilla

Cream butter, add sugar gradually and cream together well. Sift flour before measuring. Measure flour and add baking powder.

Sift together several times. Add flour mixture alternately with milk.

Add broken nuts and vanilla. Beat egg whites until they form peaks and fold into batter. Bake in 9x13-inch pan 35 to 45 minutes at 350°.

I use a white boiled frosting on this cake. It can be a seven-minute frosting. For variety I cover the cake with a pineapple filling made from crushed pineapple, thickened, and then cover with frosting.

This makes a rich dessert.

Mrs. Leroy Getting, Sanborn
Wife of State Senator

Lazy Daisy Cake

2 eggs
2 cups flour
2 teaspoons vanilla

2 cups sugar
1 cup milk
2 tablespoons butter

2 teaspoons baking powder

Heat milk and butter. Beat eggs and sugar. Add rest of ingredients. Mix until moistened. Add hot milk last. Bake in a 13"x8" ungreased pan for 30 minutes at 350 degrees.

Topping: 1⅓ cups brown sugar, ⅔ cup butter and 2 tablespoons cream. Heat and stir until thick (5 to 7 minutes). Stir in 1 cup coconut. Spread on warm cake. Place in broiler for 1 to 2 minutes or until thoroughly browned.

Linda Dugger, Tipton

Wrap pennies in foil and place between layers of a child's birthday cake so each guest will find a surprise in his serving.

43

Toasted Pecan Cake

1 cup pecans, chopped
½ cup plus 2 tablespoons butter
¼ teaspoon salt
2 unbeaten eggs
1½ cups flour
1 teaspoon baking powder
1 cup sugar
½ cup milk
1 teaspoon vanilla

Method: Toast pecans in 2 tablespoons butter in 350 degree oven —20 minutes. Stir frequently.

Sift flour with baking powder and salt.

Cream butter; gradually add sugar. Blend in eggs. Beat well after each egg is added. Add dry ingredients alternately with milk. Blend well. Add vanilla and ⅔ cup pecans. Turn into 9x13-inch cake pan, well greased and floured on bottom. Bake at 350 degrees, 20 to 25 minutes. Cool. Frost with pecan frosting.

Butter Pecan Frosting

Cream 2 tablespoons butter

Add:
2 cups sifted powdered sugar
½ teaspoon vanilla
2 to 3 tablespoons cream

Method: Cream until spreading consistency. Stir in remaining pecans and spread on cooled cake.

Norma Horn, Tipton

Lace Cake

2 eggs
1 cup sugar
1 teaspoon vanilla
1 cup flour
1 teaspoon baking powder
¼ teaspoon salt
½ cup milk
1 tablespoon butter

Beat eggs until thick; add sugar gradually. Add vanilla. Sift flour, baking powder and salt and add to first mixture. Heat milk and butter to boiling point and mix with batter. Bake in 9"x13" pan at 350 degrees.

Topping: 3 tablespoons butter, 5 tablespoons brown sugar and 2 tablespoons sweet cream. Cook these ingredients until well blended. Sprinkle coconut over top of cake while still hot. pour hot syrup over coconut and return to oven for short time to brown.

Mrs. R. C. Mineck, Tipton

44

Oatmeal Cake

1½ cups boiling water
1 cup quick cooking oatmeal
1 cup brown sugar
1 cup white sugar
½ cup shortening

2 beaten eggs
1½ cups sifted flour
1 teaspoon soda
1 teaspoon cinnamon
½ teaspoon salt

Stir oatmeal into boiling water and let stand twenty minutes.

Cream shortening and sugar, then add eggs and beat. Add sifted dry ingredients. Beat in oatmeal mixture. Bake in 7½x12-inch pan at 325 degrees for 35 to 45 minutes. Remove from oven and spread with following topping:

½ cup butter or margarine
½ cup brown sugar
¼ cup cream

1 cup chopped pecans
1 cup coconut
1 teaspoon vanilla

Place cake and topping under broiler for about six minutes.

Mrs. Henry Mente, Tipton

Chocol-Oat Cake

Pour 1¼ cups boiling water over 1 cup quick oatmeal and ½ cup cocoa. Let stand 15 minutes.

Cream together ½ cup butter, 1 cup white sugar and 1 cup brown sugar. Add 2 eggs. Beat well.

Sift together 1⅓ cups flour, 1 teaspoon soda and 1 teaspoon salt.

Add the oatmeal and flour to creamed mixture and beat until smooth.

Bake in greased and floured 9"x13" pan for 40 minutes at 350 degrees. Remove from oven and cover with topping. Bake about 10 minutes more until topping is bubbly.

Topping: Mix together ⅔ cup brown sugar, 1 cup coconut, 1 cup nut meats, 6 tablespoons soft butter, 3 tablespoons cocoa and ¼ cup milk. Stir over low heat until well mixed.

Vern Berry, Tipton

Raw Apple Cake

1 cup sugar
½ cup butter
1 egg
1½ cups flour
½ cup nutmeats

1 teaspoon soda
1 teaspoon cinnamon
¼ teaspoon salt
½ cup cold coffee
2 cups diced raw apple

Sugar for topping

Cream sugar and butter. Add egg and beat. Sift flour, salt, soda and cinnamon and add alternately with coffee. Add nutmeats and diced raw apple. Bake in 7"x11"x2" pan in 350 degree oven approximately 40 minutes. Sprinkle sugar and nuts on top. Needs no frosting. Very good.

Norma Ramm, Durant

Banana Cake

½ cup shortening
1½ cups sugar
1 egg
¼ teaspoon salt
1 tablespoon vanilla

1 cup sour milk
2 cups flour
2 bananas, mashed
2½ teaspoons baking powder
½ teaspoon soda

½ cup chopped nuts

Cream shortening and sugar, add egg and beat well. Add mashed bananas. Sift dry ingredients together and add alternately with sour milk. Add vanilla and nuts. Bake in 8" or 9" layers in a 350 degree oven about 30 minutes.

Spread following filling between layers when cooled:

¼ cup butter or margarine
1 pound confectioner's sugar

½ cup mashed ripe bananas
1 teaspoon lemon juice

Spread a layer of whipped cream or dessert topping over top of cake. This makes a very good dessert and can be made the day before.

Mrs. Roy J. Smith, Spirit Lake
Wife of State Representative

Blackberry Cake

2 egg yolks	¾ teaspoon soda
1½ cups sugar	1 cup sour milk
½ cup shortening	¾ cup blackberry juice
1 teaspoon cinnamon	½ cup canned blackberries
¼ teaspoon cloves	3 teaspoons baking powder
½ teaspoon nutmeg	3 cups flour — enough to
¼ teaspoon allspice	make stiff batter

Cream shortening, of which half may be butter; add sugar and blend, then egg yolks. Mix dry ingredients and add alternately with liquids to first mixture. Fold in blackberries last. Bake in two 8x8-inch square pans for about an hour at 350 degrees. After cooling, ice with seven-minute frosting.

Mary Ingels, Manchester

Cherry Cake

1 cup sugar	1 teaspoon baking powder
½ cup shortening	1 teaspoon cinnamon
1 cup sour milk	½ teaspoon cloves
1 teaspoon soda	½ teaspoon nutmeg
2 cups flour	1 egg

Method: Cream sugar and shortening; add egg and mix well.

Add sifted dry ingredients alternately with sour milk.

Drain 1 cup sour cherries and put into cake mixture. Pour into a 9x13 inch pan and bake 45-50 minutes at 350°. Use cherry juice mixed with powdered sugar and butter for the frosting.

Enys Kautz, Tipton

Graham Cracker Cake

Cream ⅓ cup shortening, 1 cup sugar and 2 eggs. Mix 40 graham crackers (rolled fine), 2 teaspoons baking powder and 1 cup milk.

Add to shortening mixture. Then add 1 cup coconut and 1 cup nut meats (optional). Bake at 325 degrees for 30 minutes in an 8"x12" pan.

Topping: 1 small can crushed pineapple and 1 cup sugar. Boil 5 minutes. Pour on top of cake while hot.

Frances Hegarty, Tipton

Maraschino Cherry Cake

Grease and flour 2 round layer pans, 8" x 1½", or 1 square pan, 9" x 9" x 1¾".

Sift together into bowl:

2¼ cups cake flour
1⅓ cups sugar

3 teaspoons baking powder
¾ teaspoon salt

Add:

½ cup shortening
¼ cup juice from cherries
½ cup milk
12 maraschino cherries, cut in eighths

Mix with electric mixer for 2 minutes on medium speed. Add ½ cup unbeaten egg whites. Beat 2 minutes more. Fold in ½ cup chopped nuts. Pour batter into prepared pans. Bake at 350 degrees for 30 to 35 minutes for layers and 35 to 40 minutes for the square pan.

Mrs. Harold Hass, Tipton

Orange Cake

1 cup sugar
½ cup butter or margarine
1 egg
1 cup raisins (grind together with rind of 1 orange)

1 cup buttermilk or sour milk
1 teaspoon soda
⅛ teaspoon salt
2 cups flour

Cream butter and sugar. Add beaten egg, ground fruit, and alternate portions of sifted dry ingredients and liquid. Bake in 9" square pan in 350 degree oven for 45 minutes.

Frosting: Mix juice of 1 orange, 1 lemon, ½ cup sugar and ⅛ teaspoon salt. Pour over cake as soon as it is removed from the oven.

Mrs. Leigh R. Curran, Mason City
Wife of State Senator

Fruit Cake

2 pounds pitted (cut up) dates
4 packages candied red cherries (whole)
1 pound English walnuts (106 halves)
1 pound Brazil nuts (43 whole)
1 teaspoon baking powder

1½ cup sugar
1½ cup flour
½ teaspoon salt
4 large eggs

Put fruit, nuts, flour, baking powder, sugar, and salt in large bowl.

Mix well. Add beaten eggs. Mix.

Bake in oiled paper-lined 9"x13'" greased pan in 350 degree oven 1½ hours.

Mrs. Don Williams, Tipton

Fruit Salad Cake

1 package white cake mix
1 can fruit cocktail
2 eggs

Mix all together and bake in 9"x13" pan in 350 degree oven.

Frosting:
⅔ cup evaporated milk
1 stick margarine
⅔ cup sugar

Cook 5 minutes, take off heat and add 1 cup angel flake coconut. Pour over cake.

Mrs. Leonard Hayes, Tipton

Lemon Supreme Cake

Take a package of Lemon Supreme Cake Mix, add 4 eggs, 1 cup plus 2 tablespoons water, and 1 package lemon instant pudding. Beat all this together in your mixer and bake in 350 degree oven 35 to 40 minutes. Take out of oven, make holes in cake with a fork. (Make them quite large so that the mixture you pour over cake will go through).

Take one small can of frozen lemonade and 2½ cups powdered sugar. Mix this together and pour over cake. Put cake back in oven for 5 minutes.

This is a real tasty cake and if you wish you may put a little whipped cream on top when serving.

Mrs. Andy C. Hanson, Cedar Rapids

Gelatin Cake

Mix for 1 minute:
4 eggs
¾ cup cold water
1 package lemon gelatin

Add: 1 package lemon velvet cake mix. Beat 2 minutes. Add ¾ cup vegetable oil. Beat 1 minute. Pour into buttered 9"x13" pan and bake 40 minutes in 350 degree oven. When removed from oven prick with fork about 2 inches apart all over top of cake. Immediately cover with glaze of 2 cups powdered sugar and 5 tablespoons lemon juice which has been beaten together with mixer.

Spread over warm cake.

Mrs. Hans Henriksen, Clear Lake

Strawberry Dream Cake

1 package white cake mix
1 package strawberry gelatin
2 tablespoons flour
4 eggs
½ cup water
½ box (10 ounce) frozen sliced strawberries,
    thawed (Other half of box used in frosting)
¾ cup cooking oil

Mix together cake mix, gelatin, flour, eggs and water. Beat at medium mixer speed for 2 minutes. Add strawberries, including syrup, to batter. Beat 1 more minute. Add oil and beat 1 minute more. Divide batter evenly into two greased and floured 8" square pans or a 9"x13" oblong pan. Bake in moderate oven, 350 degrees, for 35 to 40 minutes. Cool on cake rack about 10 minutes, then remove from pan. When completely cool, fill and frost with strawberry frosting.

Strawberry Frosting: ½ cup butter or margarine, 1 pound powdered sugar, the other half box of strawberries, ½ teaspoon vanilla.

Beat butter or margarine until smooth. Add the sugar alternately with the strawberries, including syrup. Beat until smooth. Add vanilla. If frosting becomes too thick, thin with a little milk or cream.

Mrs. Joe Conway, Tipton

50

Carrot Cake

3 cups carrot, grated raw
4 eggs, unbeaten
2 cups sugar
1½ cups salad oil
2 teaspoons soda

½ teaspoon salt
2 cups flour
1 teaspoon cinnamon
1 teaspoon vanilla
1 cup chopped nuts

In electric mixer bowl, combine carrots, eggs, sugar and oil. Beat until ingredients are mixed. Add remaining ingredients and beat well. Pour into 2 oiled and floured 9 inch pans. Bake at 350 degrees for 40 to 45 minutes. Cool layers.

Put together with one 8 oz. package cream cheese, 1 pound powdered sugar. Soften cheese to room temperature, beat until fluffy and gradually beat in powdered sugar. Add small amount of cream or milk if needed.

Mrs. Lance Smith, Tipton

Date Cake

2 cups chopped dates
1 teaspoon soda

1 cup boiling water
1 cup nuts

Mix and let stand until you have the following ingredients ready:

1 cup sugar
1 egg
1⅓ cups flour

3 tablespoons butter
1 teaspoon vanilla
¼ teaspoon salt

Combine both mixtures and pour into greased 9"x13" pan. Use smaller pan if you wish the cake thicker. Bake at 350 degrees.

Serve with ice cream or whipped cream. This is also good with a sauce.

Mrs. Clifford Connelly, Washington

Cookery is not an art, but a master art.

51

Egg Yolk Layer Cake

11 egg yolks
2 cups sugar
½ teaspoon salt
2 teaspoons vanilla

6 tablespoons butter
1 cup scalded milk
2 cups sifted cake flour
2 teaspoons baking powder

Beat egg yolks until thick and lemon colored. Add sugar, salt and flavoring. Beat thoroughly. Melt butter in hot milk. Add to egg mixture, beating constantly. (If you are mixing cake by hand, be sure to keep stirring the batter while adding the milk. Likewise, keep the beaters revolving if you are using an electric mixer).

Sift together dry ingredients. Quickly add to egg mixture. Line bottoms of three 8x8x2-inch layer pans with oiled and floured waxed paper. Pour batter in pans and bake 25 or 30 minutes in a 350 degree oven.

Mrs. Elmer Petersen, Tipton

Poppy Seed Cake

1 cup whole poppy seed soaked in 1½ cups scalded milk over night.

Cream ½ cup butter and 1½ cups sugar. Add poppy seed mixture. Sift together 2 cups flour and 2 teaspoons baking powder.

Add to poppy seed, butter and sugar mixture.

Add 1 teaspoon vanilla and ½ teaspoon salt. Fold in 3 beaten egg whites and bake in two 9" layer pans in 350 degree oven.

Custard Filling:

Brown ½ cup sugar in heavy pan. Add 1 cup milk, 3 egg yolks and 1½ tablespoons cornstarch. Cook to a custard consistency.

Add ¼ cup nut meats. Frost as desired.

Mrs. R. C. Mineck, Tipton

Pumpkin Cake

Mix in a small bowl:

1 cup pumpkin   ¾ cup milk
            ½ teaspoon soda

Let above set while you mix and cream:

1¾ cup sugar   ⅔ cup shortening
                2 eggs

Add:

1½ cups flour   1 teaspoon salt
  2 teaspoons baking powder   1 teaspoon cinnamon
            1 teaspoon nutmeg

Add pumpkin mixture.

Nuts may be added to batter or sprinkled over top just before baking. Bake in 9"x13" pan for 30 to 35 minutes. Serve hot or cold with whipped cream or ice cream.

Mrs. Raymond E. Spencer, Tipton

Rhubarb Cake

1¼ cups sugar   1 teaspoon soda
½ cup vegetable shortening   1 teaspoon cinnamon
2 eggs   ¼ teaspoon cloves
½ cup milk   ¼ teaspoon salt
2 cups flour   ½ teaspoon allspice
            2 cups rhubarb, cut

Cream sugar, shortening and eggs. Sift flour, measure, and add soda, spices and salt to it. Mix well. Stir in rhubarb. Pour into 8"x12" pan and add following topping.

Topping: ⅓ cup brown sugar
                                ½ teaspoon cinnamon
                                ½ cup nuts

Sprinkle over top of batter. Bake at 350 degrees for 30 to 35 minutes.

Mrs. W. S. Bissell, Tipton

53

Easy Sponge Cake

Beat 4 egg whites just to stiff stage with ¼ teaspoon salt. Set aside.

With same beater in another bowl, beat the 4 egg yolks and 1¼ cups sugar. Add ½ cup cold water, 1¼ cups flour, and 3 teaspoons baking powder. Beat until smooth, adding flavoring to taste, preferably rind of lemon and 1 tablespoon juice. Fold in the beaten whites. Bake in a greased and floured 8"x12" pan at preheated 325 degree oven until it shrinks and springs up.

This is good with whipped cream and strawberries or plain with a caramel frosting or any fruit combination.

This recipe is from a cook in Old Manning Hotel at Keosauqua.

Mrs. L. B. Liddy, Keosauqua
Wife of Iowa Secretary of Agriculture

Burnt Sugar Sponge Cake

1 cup flour
1½ teaspoons baking powder
½ teaspoon salt
½ cup hot water

2 eggs
1 cup sugar
3 tablespoons burnt
sugar syrup

Beat eggs until very light, add sugar and beat again. Add salt and ½ cup hot water. Add flour, baking powder and the burnt sugar syrup. The more you beat this cake, the better. Bake in 9"x13" pan for 25 minutes in 350 degree oven.

Topping:

4 tablespoons melted butter
6 tablespoons brown sugar

½ cup coconut
3 tablespoons cream

Mix ingredients together and spread on baked cake. Place under broiler until bubbly and brown. Serve with or without whipped cream.

Mrs. Roy J. Smith, Spirit Lake
Wife of State Representative

Glorified Gingerbread

2 cups flour	1 cup sugar
½ cup lard	½ teaspoon cinnamon
	½ teaspoon ginger

Mix above together as for pie crust. Save ½ cup of mixture for top.

Add remainder to the following and beat:

1 egg	1 cup sour milk
2 tablespoons molasses	1 teaspoon soda
	¼ teaspoon salt

Pour into 9" square pan. Bake 30 minutes in 350 degree oven.

Mrs. Fred E. Wier, Letts
Wife of State Representative

Poor Man's Cake
(or depression cake)

2 cups brown sugar	1 teaspoon salt
2 cups hot water	1 teaspoon cloves
2 tablespoons shortening	1 teaspoon cinnamon
1 cup raisins	½ cup nutmeats

Boil above together 5 minutes. When cool add 2 cups flour, 1 teaspoon soda in 1 teaspoon water. Pour into greased 9"x13" pan and bake about 25 minutes in 350 degree oven. Tastes like a fruit cake.

Mrs. George Blazek, Cedar Rapids

Frostings

Chocolate Frosting

2 tablespoons margarine
2 tablespoons cocoa
1 teaspoon vanilla

¼ cup prepared coffee
⅛ teaspoon salt

Combine margarine, cocoa and coffee. Cook until margarine is melted, stirring constantly. Add salt, vanilla and enough powdered sugar for spreading consistency. The nice feature about this recipe is that it can be stretched by adding more coffee and/or more powdered sugar. This is a simple recipe for your youngsters who are just getting interested in cooking.

Darlene Donohue, Tipton

Chocolate Cream Frosting

1 cup brown sugar
½ cup water
Powdered sugar
1 teaspoon vanilla

2 squares chocolate
3 tablespoons butter
½ teaspoon salt

Mix brown sugar, chocolate, butter and water. Bring to boiling point and cook 3 minutes. Cool slightly. Add enough sifted powdered sugar to spread. Add vanilla. Spread between layers and on top of cake. This makes enough for a 2 layer cake. Nuts may be added.

Variations:

CARAMEL: Use the above recipe and omit chocolate.

BURNT SUGAR: Omit chocolate. Substitute white sugar for brown sugar and add burnt sugar syrup to suit taste.

DATE NUT FILLING: Omit the chocolate and add ½ package pitted dates, cut.

LEMON MELBA: Omit the chocolate. Substitute 1 cup white sugar for the brown. Add rind of 2 lemons, ¼ cup lemon juice and 1 egg. Cook until slightly thickened, cool slightly and add powdered sugar.

Olivette Werling, Tipton

56

French Cream Frosting

Cream ½ cup butter or margarine, gradually add 2½ cups sifted powdered sugar, creaming well. Add 1 egg, mix thoroughly. Blend in 3 squares melted unsweetened chocolate, cooled, and 1 teaspoon vanilla. Beat until spreading consistency. Thin with milk if necessary. Frosts two 8 or 9 inch layer cakes.

Mrs. Robert Hoffner, Clarence

Creamy Frosting

4 tablespoons shortening	2 egg whites
3 cups powdered sugar (sifted)	½ teaspoon vanilla

Cream sugar and shortening for 2 minutes. Beat egg whites until stiff, mix creamed ingredients into them. Add vanilla. Butter may be used but frosting will have a pale yellow color, while vegetable shortening will make it white.

Mrs. Robert Hoffner, Clarence

Topping for Angel Food Cake

1 package frozen raspberries or strawberries
16 marshmallows
1 pint cream (whipped)

Dice marshmallows and add to raspberries the day before. Add whipped cream just before serving.

Mrs. Charles Thomson, Stanwood

If you're tired of white or chocolate frosting, why not try a powdered sugar frosting where you use dark syrup for your liquid and add crunchy style peanut butter for flavoring? Children love this on white or spice cup cakes.

Andre's Chocolate Frosting

Heat until just melted — 3 tablespoons butter with ⅓ cup milk.

Sift together a mixture of 3½ cups powdered sugar, ½ cup cocoa and ⅛ teaspoon salt. Add about ½ of this mixture and beat until smooth. Stir in remaining dry mixture in two portions. Add 1½ teaspoons vanilla. If frosting is too thick, beat in ½ teaspoon of milk at a time.

Mrs. Robert Hoffner, Clarence

Miracle Icing

1½ cups sugar	2 unbeaten egg whites
⅓ cup water	¼ teaspoon cream of tartar
⅛ teaspoon salt	1 teaspoon vanilla

Mix sugar and water. Cook after boiling for 3 minutes. Place the unbeaten egg whites and cream of tartar into the small mixer bowl. Turn switch to fast and immediately add the hot syrup gradually. Continue to beat for 5 minutes. Add vanilla. Spread on cake. This is a soft frosting; does not become crusty over the top.

Olivette Werling, Tipton

Boiled White Frosting

½ cup sugar   ¼ cup water   1 egg white

Boil sugar and water to soft ball stage (238 degrees). Pour hot syrup slowly over stiffly beaten egg white, beating constantly. Add ½ teaspoon vanilla and 1 tablespoon heaped just as high as possible with powdered sugar. Continue beating until sugar is dissolved and frosting is smooth.

This small, basic recipe may be doubled, tripled or even quadrupled with good results. Because of the powdered sugar, this frosting is never sticky and never too hard.

Darlene Donohue, Tipton

Cookies

Butterscotch Chocolate Squares

Sift and set aside:

2¾ cup sifted flour   2½ teaspoons baking powder
                     ½ teaspoon salt
⅔ cup shortening   3 eggs
2¼ cups brown sugar (1 pound)   1 cup broken nut meats
               1 package chocolate bits

Melt the shortening and stir in brown sugar. Allow to cool slightly.

Beat in the eggs, one at a time, beating well after each addition.

Add flour mixture, nut meats, and chocolate bits. Blend well. Pour into greased pan 10½"x15½"x¾" or 2 smaller pans. Bake at 350 degrees for 25 to 30 minutes. When almost cool, cut into squares.

Mrs. Clifford Connelly, Washington

Chocolate Halfway Cookies

½ cup butter   1 teaspoon baking powder
½ cup white sugar   ½ teaspoon soda
½ brown sugar   1 package chocolate chips
4 egg yolks   1 teaspoon vanilla, or
1 teaspoon water   mint flavor
2 cups flour

Cream shortening and sugar, add egg yolks, water and flavoring.

Add sifted dry ingredients. Mix well. Spread on cookie sheet and sprinkle chips on top. Beat 4 egg whites with ½ cup sugar and put on top of chips. Sprinkle nuts on top if you like. Bake 25 minutes in 350 degree oven.

Rose Weih, Tipton

59

Raisin Drop Cookies

Cook 2 cups raisins and 1 cup water until raisins are tender. Remeasure water and add enough to make ⅔ cup.

1 cup butter or other shortening	½ teaspoon cinnamon
1½ cups sugar	½ teaspoon soda
2 eggs	3 cups flour (a little
½ teaspoon salt	more may be needed)
¾ cup nuts	

Cream fat and sugar; add eggs. Sift dry ingredients and add alternately with the ⅔ cup raisin water. Add raisins and nuts; mix well. Drop on greased cookie sheet. Bake 12 to 15 minutes at 350 degrees.

Mrs. Phil Sorensen, Mechanicsville

Boiled Candy Cookies

2 cups sugar	½ cup milk
3 tablespoons cocoa	1 stick margarine

Bring to full rolling boil. Remove from fire and add:

½ cup peanut butter	3 cups quick oats
½ cup nuts	1 teaspoon vanilla

Drop from teaspoon on waxed paper when they are cool enough to hold their shape.

Ann Owen, Tipton

Coconut Kisses

2 egg whites	1 cup sugar
½ teaspoon cream of tartar	1 teaspoon vanilla
⅛ teaspoon salt	1½ cups coconut

Beat first three ingredients, add sugar gradually and beat 10 minutes. Fold in remaining ingredients. Drop by spoonful onto greased cookie sheet.

Bake in 275 degree oven for 20 minutes, then reduce to 200 degrees and bake an additional 30 minutes. Makes 2½ dozen kisses.

Mrs. Arnold Miller, Clarence

Angel Cookies

Cream together: ½ cup butter   ½ cup brown sugar
                       ½ cup lard   ½ cup white sugar

Add: 1 egg; mix well.

Sift together and add: 2 cups flour   ½ teaspoon salt
                       1 teaspoon cream of tartar

Add: ½ cup nuts

Roll into balls size of a walnut or smaller. Dip the top half in cold water and then in sugar. Put in pan with sugared side up. Bake in 400 degree oven.

Mrs. Emil Licht, Lowden

Butterscotch Drop Cookies

1 cup white sugar	1 teaspoon salt
1 cup brown sugar	1 teaspoon soda
1 cup shortening	2 cups flour
2 eggs (beat in one at a time)	1 cup quick oats
1 teaspoon burnt sugar extract	1 package butterscotch chips
½ teaspoon vanilla	½ cup walnuts

Stir in order given. Drop on ungreased cookie sheet. Bake at 350 degrees 10-12 minutes.

Mrs. Bertel Berkeland, Fenton

Chip Kisses

1 egg white	¼ teaspoon salt
1 cup brown sugar	½ teaspoon lemon flavoring
1¼ cups crushed potato chips	

Beat egg white and gradually add sugar, salt, and lemon flavoring. Fold in potato chips. Drop from teaspoon on greased and floured cookie sheet. Bake at 350 degrees from 8-12 minutes.

Beulah Dodds, Tipton

61

French Apple Cookies

2 cups flour
3 teaspoons baking powder
½ teaspoon salt
1 teaspoon cinnamon
1 teaspoon cloves
½ teaspoon nutmeg

¾ cup shortening
1½ cups brown sugar
1 egg
½ cup milk
1 cup raisins
½ cup nuts

1 cup raw chopped apple

Mix in order given and drop by spoonfuls on cookie sheet. Bake at 375 degrees 12-15 minutes.

Mrs. William Kelting, Scott County

Banana Cookies

1½ cups shortening
1½ cups brown sugar
2 eggs

4 mashed ripe bananas
½ teaspoon salt
2 teaspoons soda

3½ to 4 cups flour—depending on size of bananas

Cream shortening and sugar, add eggs and mashed bananas.

Sift salt and soda with flour. Drop from tablespoon on greased cookie sheet. Bake in moderate oven about 10 minutes. Cool and frost. Yields 6½ dozen and is a soft cookie.

Icing for Banana Cookies

6 tablespoons brown sugar   4 tablespoons cream
4 tablespoons butter

Bring to a full rolling boil. Remove from heat and add powdered sugar to spreading consistency. Beat until smooth and add ½ teaspoon vanilla and frost cookies.

Mrs. Albert Norris, Graettinger

62

Pineapple Bars

½ cup butter   ¼ cup brown sugar
                      1¼ cups flour

Mix and pat in pan 9x9-inches. Bake 10 minutes at 350 degrees.

Remove from oven.

Mix together and spread on baked crust.

1 egg beaten   1 cup brown sugar
                      1 cup coconut

Spread on top of second layer:
1 small can sliced pineapple (much better than using crushed pineapple) cut in small pieces.

Bake 25 to 30 minutes in 350 degree oven. Cut in squares.

Mrs. Lee Cottingham, Russell

Gumdrop Cookies

1 cup brown sugar   1 cup gumdrops, cut finely
1 cup white sugar   2½ cups flour
1 cup butter or other   1 teaspoon soda
  shortening   1 teaspoon baking powder
2 eggs   ½ teaspoon salt
2 cups quick oatmeal   1 cup coconut

Cream fat and sugar; add eggs and mix well. Mix all dry ingredients together and add to the creamed mixture. Add gumdrops and coconut. Drop on greased baking sheet. Bake in moderate oven, 350 degrees for 10 to 15 minutes.

Mrs. Robert Marks, Tipton

Chocolate Drop Cookie

Cream together

½ cup shortening (I use butter)   1 egg
1 cup sugar   2 squares melted chocolate

Sift together:

1¾ cups sifted flour   ½ teaspoon salt
              ½ teaspoon soda

Add dry ingredients to creamed ingredients.

Add:

¾ cup buttermilk   1 cup chopped nuts (black walnuts best)

Drop from teaspoon on greased cookie sheet. Bake at 400 degrees
12-15 minutes. Frost with chocolate icing. Yields 4 dozen.

Chocolate Icing for Cookies

1 tablespoon butter   3 tablespoons milk
1 square melted chocolate   1 cup confectioner's sugar
              ½ teaspoon vanilla

Thin with milk to make glossy and easy to spread. Makes a
frosted cake like cookie. A real favorite of ours.

Mrs. Evan Hultman, Waterloo
Wife of Iowa Attorney General

Easy Coconut Macaroons

2⅔ cups coconut (flaked)   1 egg
¾ cup sweetened condensed milk   ¼ teaspoon almond extract

Combine ingredients and mix. Let mixture stand for 2 or 3 minutes. Drop by heaping teaspoonfuls on a greased baking sheet.

Flatten slightly. Bake in slow oven 325 degrees for 25 minutes.

Makes 2 dozen.

Mrs. Paul Hutchens, Tipton

Criss Cross Cookies

Mix together:

½ cup shortening
¾ cup sugar
1 egg

Stir in:

1 tablespoon milk
½ teaspoon lemon extract

Sift together and add:

1¾ cups flour
¾ teaspoon cream of tartar
¾ teaspoon soda
¼ teaspoon salt

Stir in ½ cup nuts or raisins. Roll into balls. Place on ungreased cookie sheet. Flatten with fork dipped in flour. This forms the criss cross look. Bake in 400 degree oven for 8 to 10 minutes.

Bessie Brinkman, Oxford Junction

Chocolate Covered Cookies

1 cup peanut butter
1 cup dates, cut or ground

1 cup powdered sugar
1 cup nuts, chopped fine

Mix and form into balls.

1 package chocolate chips
2 squares dot chocolate
3 tablespoons shaved paraffin

Melt in double boiler and dip balls in this mixture.

Mrs. Amos C. Borkland, Cylinder

Pecan Creams

3 cups pecans, ground
1 can coconut, ground

¼ pound butter
1 can Eagle Brand milk
Vanilla or maple flavoring

Mix and knead, then shape into desired size balls.

Melt in double boiler: 12-ounce package chocolate chips and 2 tablespoons chipped paraffin. When melted, remove from heat and dip balls to coat. Place on wax paper to harden. Use fork for dipping.

Mrs. Hans Henriksen, Clear Lake

Toffee Cookies

½ cup butter
½ cup margarine
1 cup brown sugar

1 egg yolk
1 teaspoon vanilla
1 cup flour

Cream shortening and sugar, then add remaining ingredients.

Beat until smooth and spread out thin on 12x18-inch cookie sheet.

Bake at 325 degrees for 20 minutes. **Don't overbake.** While still hot, break 6 plain Hershey bars over the top and spread when melted. Sprinkle with nuts. When cool, break or cut into squares.

Martha Gaul, Tipton

Molasses Sugar Cookies

¾ cup shortening
1 cup white sugar
¼ cup molasses
2 teaspoons soda
1 egg

2 cups flour
½ teaspoon cloves
½ teaspoon ginger
1 teaspoon cinnamon
½ teaspoon salt

Melt shortening in a 3 or 4 quart saucepan over low heat. Remove from heat and let cool. Add sugar, molasses and egg; beat well.

Sift together flour, soda, cloves, ginger, cinnamon and salt. Add to first mixture. Mix well and put dough in refrigerator to chill.

When ready to bake, form in 1-inch balls. Roll in granulated sugar and place on greased cookie sheets 2 inches apart. Bake in 375 degree oven 8 to 10 minutes.

Mrs. Robert Novak, Cedar Rapids

The word cookie comes from the Dutch word "koe kje", meaning cake. The first cookies were small portions of cake batter used to test the oven heat.

Chocolate Marshmallow Cookies

Sift together: 1½ cups flour
                               ½ teaspoon soda
                               ½ teaspoon salt

Cream together: ⅔ cup brown sugar
                               ½ cup shortening
                               1 egg

Add ½ of dry ingredients to the creamed mixture.

Add: ¼ cup maraschino cherry juice
                               2 tablespoons milk

Add the rest of the dry ingredients.

Add: 2 squares chocolate, melted
                               ½ cup walnuts, chopped
                               ¼ cup maraschino cherries,
                                   chopped

Drop by teaspoonfuls on ungreased baking sheet. Bake in 350 degree oven 12 to 15 minutes. Cut marshmallows in half and put cut side down on cookie to melt. Frost with powdered sugar frosting. Put cherry or nut on top.

                                         Mrs. Cora Phillips, Tipton

Mince Meat Cookies

1 cup lard	3¼ cups flour
1½ cups sugar	1 teaspoon soda
3 eggs	1⅓ cups mince meat
1 teaspoon salt	

Cream lard, sugar, salt and eggs together until light. Add mince meat. Sift flour and soda together and add to first mixture. Drop from teaspoon on greased cookie sheet. Bake 8-10 minutes in 425 degree oven.

                                         Mrs. Louis Thordsen, Tipton

Lace Cookies (no flour)

1 egg well beaten

Add:

½ cup sugar
½ cup chopped nuts

½ cup oatmeal
½ cup coconut
Pinch of salt

Drop on foil paper and bake at 350 degrees 10-12 minutes until golden brown. When cool, peel off paper.

Mrs. George Janssen, Eldora

Lemonchip Cookies

I — Mix:
½ cup sugar
½ cup shortening
1 egg
1 tablespoon milk
1 teaspoon lemon extract

II — Sift together:
1¾ cup flour
¾ teaspoon soda
¾ teaspoon cream of tartar
¼ teaspoon salt

Combine I and II. Add ½ cup raisins and 1 package lemon custard chips. Form small ball in hand — dip fork in flour and mark balls crisscross. Bake on ungreased cookie sheet in 400 degree oven 9-10 minutes.

Grace Vincent, Keota

Pumpkin Cookies

½ cup shortening
1 cup sugar
1 cup strained pumpkin
1 cup raisins
½ cup chopped nuts

2 cups flour
1 teaspoon soda
1 teaspoon baking powder
1 teaspoon vanilla
1 teaspoon cinnamon

Cream shortening and sugar. Add pumpkin, raisins and nuts.

Sift and add dry ingredients. Drop from spoon on greased cookie sheet. Bake in 350 degree oven 12-14 minutes. When cool frost with powdered sugar frosting flavored with maple flavoring.

These cookies freeze well.

Mrs. Harold Eiler, Tipton

68

White Christmas Cookies

1 cup butter
1 cup lard
2 cups sugar

4 cups flour
2 eggs
⅓ teaspoon soda

1 teaspoon vanilla

Cream butter, lard, and sugar. Add eggs to mixture. Add the combined soda and flour. Mix well and add vanilla. Shape into rolls.

Place in refrigerator or freezer. May be sliced anytime after they are chilled. Bake until done, 12-15 minutes at 325 degrees.

Mrs. Robert H. Agne, Tipton

Unbaked Peanut Butter Cooky

¼ cup brown sugar

¼ cup white sugar

½ cup white Karo

Bring to boil; boil until sugar is dissolved. Remove from heat and add:

¾ cup crunchy peanut butter

1 teaspoon vanilla

2 cups special "K" cereal

Drop by teaspoon on wax paper. Very tasty and easy to do.

Constance Cottingham, Iowa City

Potato Chip Cookies

1 cup margarine
1 cup white sugar
1 cup brown sugar
2 eggs well beaten

2 cups flour
1 teaspoon soda
2 cups crushed potato chips
6 ounces butterscotch chips

Cream shortening with sugar and add remaining ingredients. Roll in balls and put on greased cookie sheet. Bake in a 325 degree oven 10 minutes. Makes about 60 cookies.

Mary Kipp, Tipton

Raisin Cookies

Cook ½ box of white raisins in 1 cup water until soft. Cool.
Add:

1 cup shortening
1 pound brown sugar
1 teaspoon soda
3 eggs

1 cup nut meats
½ pound flake coconut
4 cups flour

Drop from teaspoon onto cookie sheet and bake at 350 degrees from 12 to 15 minutes. These freeze well.

Ethel M. N. Nebergall, Tipton

Sour Cream Cookies

2 cups sugar
1 cup butter
2 egg yolks
1 teaspoon lemon extract

¼ teaspoon salt
1 teaspoon soda
1 teaspoon baking powder
5 cups flour

1 cup sour cream

Mix and roll thin. Bake in 325 degree oven 15 minutes. Sliced and split almonds may be placed on each cookie before baking.

Christine Sondergard, West Branch

Sugar Cookies

1¼ cups white sugar
1 cup shortening
3 eggs

1 teaspoon vanilla
3 cups flour
1 teaspoon baking powder

¼ teaspoon salt

Cream butter and sugar and add eggs and vanilla. Add baking powder and salt to one cup of flour. Add flour to first mixture one cup at a time. Roll to ¼ inch thick and cut with cookie cutter. Bake at 325 degrees for 10-12 minutes.

Mrs. Robert M. L. Johnson, Cedar Rapids

To give rolled cookies a sparkle — roll the dough on a board sprinkled with a mixture of one part sugar to two parts flour. Use the mixture on the rolling pin too.

70

Molasses Cookies

1 cup sugar
1 tablespoon soda
1 tablespoon ginger
1 teaspoon salt

1 cup molasses
1 cup minus 2 tablespoons water
1 cup plus 2 tablespoons unmelted lard
1 egg
Flour to form soft dough

Cream sugar and lard, add beaten egg and other ingredients. Add enough flour to roll, not too stiff. Use cutter. Bake 12 minutes in 350 degree oven.

Frosting

1½ cups sugar
5 tablespoons water

1 tablespoon vinegar
2 egg whites

Cook as for seven minute frosting. After beating a few minutes, add 8 marshmallows and flavoring.

Mrs. Marvin W. Smith, Paullina
Wife of State Representative

Rolled Ginger Cookies

Boil for 5 minutes:
1 cup sugar
1 cup sorghum or molasses

½ cup strong coffee
1 cup shortening

Remove from stove and add:

2 cups sifted flour
2 well beaten eggs

1 tablespoon soda
½-1 tablespoon ginger
½ teaspoon salt

Let cool, then add 3 more cups flour. Chill well. Roll and cut. Bake at 375 degrees 8 to 10 minutes.

Mrs. Gladys Reed, Manchester

Oh weary mothers rolling dough
Don't you wish that food would grow?
How happy all the world would be
With a cookie bush, and a doughnut tree.

Apriscotch Bars

Prepare filling as follows. Cook, stirring 1 cup apricot pulp, ½ cup sugar, 1 tablespoon flour, 1 tablespoon lemon juice, 2 tablespoons orange juice, 2 teaspoons butter. Set aside.

Sift together 4½ cups flour, 2 teaspoons cream of tartar, 1 teaspoon soda, 1 teaspoon salt. Cream well 1½ cups brown sugar, ¾ cup vegetable shortening. Add 2 eggs and mix well.

Put ½ the crumbly dough in a greased 9x13-inch pan. Spoon on the filling and sprinkle remaining dough on top. It will spread in baking. Bake in 350 degree oven for 25 to 30 minutes or until brown. Cool slightly. Cut in bars and roll in powdered sugar. May be cut in squares and served with whipped cream as a dessert.

This is an original recipe, tested many times and a winner in a cookie contest.

Vern Berry, Tipton

Brazil Nut Strips

1 cup butter
1 egg
1 egg separated
1 cup chopped Brazil nuts

2 cups flour
1 teaspoon baking powder
1⅓ cup sugar
4 teaspoons cinnamon

Sift flour, baking powder, 1 cup sugar, and 3 teaspoons cinnamon.

Add butter, egg and egg yolk. Mix well. Turn into greased 15½x10½-inch jelly roll pan. Spread with spatula. With fork, beat egg white slightly. Brush over dough.

Combine remaining ⅓ cup sugar, 1 teaspoon cinnamon, and nuts. Sprinkle over dough. Bake at 350 degrees for 25 minutes or until golden brown. Cool in pan and cut into 2x1-inch bars. Yield 75 bars.

Nice to serve at a tea or coffee.

Mrs. Theodore Nelson, Cylinder

Apricot Squares

Mix together:
½ cup butter
1 cup all purpose flour

1 teaspoon baking powder
1 egg well beaten
1 tablespoon milk

Place in 9 inch square ungreased pan. Spread **exactly** 8 level tablespoons of apricot jam carefully over the above ingredients then spread the following topping over jam.

1 egg well beaten
4 tablespoons melted butter

1 cup sugar
1 teaspoon vanilla

2 cups shredded coconut

Bake at 350 degrees 30 minutes or until nicely browned.

Mrs. H. N. Struve, Clinton

Bran Apricot Squares

Tasty and nutritious.

1 cup dried apricots, diced

1 cup water

Simmer 10 minutes, drain and cool.

Bran crust:

1 cup shortening
½ cup sugar

1 cup sifted flour
1½ cups 100% bran

Cream shortening and sugar. Add flour and bran. Press into jelly roll pan and bake 15 minutes at 350 degrees.

Topping:

4 eggs
2 cups brown sugar
1 teaspoon vanilla
1 teaspoon baking powder

1 teaspoon salt
1 cup flour
Cooled apricots
1 cup chopped nuts

Beat eggs, brown sugar and vanilla. Add other ingredients.

Pour topping over bran layer. Bake 25 to 30 minutes at 350 degrees. Sprinkle with powdered sugar.

Ethel Fields, Webster City

73

Old Fashion Raisin Bars

1 cup raisins
1 cup water
½ cup oil
1 egg
1 cup sugar
1¾ cups flour

1 teaspoon soda
½ teaspoon allspice
⅛ teaspoon salt
¼ teaspoon cloves
½ teaspoon cinnamon
½ teaspoon nutmeg

Bring raisins and water to a boil, cool and add oil. Cream egg and sugar. Sift dry ingredients together. Add alternately with liquid to egg mixture. Pour into a greased 9x13-inch pan. Bake at 350 degrees for 20 to 30 minutes. Cool and dust with powdered sugar. Cut in bars.

Mrs. J. A. Waddell, Tipton

Orange Date Squares

2 cups flour, sifted
1 teaspoon baking powder
1 teaspoon salt
⅓ cup butter
⅔ cup sugar

2 eggs
1 orange rind grated
½ cup orange juice
½ cup pecans
1½ cup chopped dates

Sift flour, baking powder, and salt. Flour dates in portion of mixture. Cream butter and sugar and blend in eggs and orange rind. Beat until creamy. Add dry ingredients and orange juice alternately to creamed mixture. Fold in dates and nuts. Pour in greased 8x8x2-inch pan. Bake at 350 degrees for 1 hour. Invert to cool.

Icing for Orange Date Squares

1 tablespoon butter   1¼ cups sifted powdered sugar
             2 teaspoons orange juice

Melt butter and add powdered sugar and juice. Blend.

Suzie Schafer, Tipton

Maraschino Cherry Bars

Base:

½ cup sifted flour	½ cup firmly packed brown sugar
¼ teaspoon soda	1 cup uncooked rolled oats
⅛ teaspoon salt	⅓ cup melted butter

Topping:

¼ cup sifted flour	2 eggs, beaten
¾ cup sugar	¾ cup cut-up maraschino cherries
½ teaspoon salt	½ cup flaked or shredded coconut
	½ cup chopped nutmeats

For base, sift together flour, soda and salt. Add brown sugar, oats and butter, mixing well. Firmly press mixture into a greased 9-inch square pan. For topping, combine all ingredients thoroughly.

Spread mixture over base. Bake at 350 degrees about 30 minutes. Cool and cut into bars.

Mrs. Alfred Paustian, Tipton

Heath Candy Bar Cookies

Blend together:

2 cups brown sugar	½ cup butter or margarine
	2 cups sifted flour

Reserve one cup of the above. Then add altogether

1 egg	1 cup milk
½ teaspoon salt	1 teaspoon soda
	1 teaspoon vanilla

Beat well. Pour into greased 9x13-inch pan. Crush 6 Heath candy bars and add ½ cup chopped pecans and mix with the 1 cup of reserved mixture. Sprinkle mixture over the batter in the pan. Bake at 350 degrees for 35 to 40 minutes. Cut in bars.

Mrs. Orville Nicol, Emmetsburg

Chocolate Bars

2 squares of chocolate
3 eggs, beaten
¾ cup flour
½ teaspoon salt

½ cup butter or margarine
1 cup sugar
½ teaspoon baking powder
1 teaspoon vanilla
½-1 cup nuts

Melt chocolate and add butter. Let stand until butter melts. Mix other ingredients and add butter and chocolate mixture last. Bake in greased floured sheet (9x13-inch pan) for 20 minutes at 350 degrees. Immediately, when removed from oven, cut into bars and roll in powdered sugar.

Marie Richards, Tipton

Three Layer No-Bake Cookies

First layer:

Place in top of double boiler and cook until blended, about 5 minutes:

½ cup butter
¼ cup sugar

¼ cup cocoa
1 egg slightly beaten

Add 1 teaspoon vanilla, 2 cups finely crushed graham cracker crumbs, 1 cup flaked coconut, and ½ cup chopped nuts. Press mixture into a 9x13-inch pan. Cool.

Second layer:

Cream ½ cup butter until light and fluffy. Mix 3 tablespoons milk and 2 teaspoons instant vanilla pudding. Add to butter and mix well. Add 2 cups confectioner's sugar and beat until smooth. Spread over first layer, let stand until firm.

Third layer:

Melt one 6-ounce package chocolate bits and 1½ tablespoons butter in top of double boiler. Spread over second layer. Cut in squares or small bars before chocolate becomes hardened. Store in refrigerator.

Dorothy Crock, Tipton

76

Marshmallow Fudge Bars

Sift:

¾ cup flour   2 tablespoons cocoa
¼ teaspoon salt   ¼ teaspoon baking powder

Cream:

½ cup butter   ¾ cup sugar
2 beaten eggs   1 teaspoon vanilla
            (scant) ¼ teaspoon red food coloring

Add sifted dry ingredients to cream mixture. Bake in 12x8-inch greased pan in 350 degree oven 25 minutes. Remove from oven and cover top with tiny marshmallows. Return to oven for 3 minutes. Remove and push marshmallows together by pressing each one with finger. Cool and frost.

Frosting

½ cup brown sugar   ¼ cup water
            1 square of chocolate

Boil slowly for 3 minutes and add 3 tablespoons butter, 1 teaspoon vanilla and 1½ cups powdered sugar.

Alta Wuestenberg, Bennett

Mound Bars

2 cups graham cracker crumbs   ¼ cup sugar
            ½ cup melted butter

Mix and spread in 9x13-inch pan. Bake 10 minutes at 350 degrees.

1 package flaked coconut   1 can sweetened condensed milk

Mix and spread over first layer. Bake 10-12 minutes at 350 degrees. Remove from oven and while still warm frost with 1 12-ounce package chocolate chips and 1 teaspoon peanut butter that have been melted together.

Doris Davis, Tipton

77

Orange Slice Cookies

Beat together:

3 eggs   2 cups brown sugar

Add:

1½ cups candy orange slices, cut up
1¼ cups coconut
½ cup nuts
2 cups flour
¼ teaspoon salt

Pour into jelly roll pan and bake in 350 degree oven for 18 to 20 minutes.

Mrs. LeRoy Louer, Mallard

Tea Time Tassies

1 3-ounce package cream cheese   ¾ cup brown sugar
½ cup butter or margarine   1 tablespoon soft butter
1 cup sifted flour   1 teaspoon vanilla
1 egg   Dash of salt
                ⅔ cup coarsely broken pecans

Cheese pastry: Let cream cheese and ½ cup butter soften at room temperature; blend. Stir in flour and chill well. Shape in 2 dozen 1 inch balls. Place in tiny ungreased 1¾-inch muffin cups.

Press dough on bottom and sides of cups.

Pecan Filling: Beat together egg, sugar, 1 tablespoon butter, vanilla and salt just until smooth. Divide the pecans among the pastry lined cups; add egg mixture. Bake in a slow oven (325) degrees for 25 minutes or until filling is set. Cool; remove from pans.

Mrs. Earl M. Kelley, Waukon

Oatmeal Cookie Mix

3 cups sugar   3 cups uncooked rolled oats
4½ cups sifted flour   2¼ cups soft shortening
2 tablespoons baking powder   1½ teaspoons salt

Sift together flour, baking powder and salt. Cut in shortening until mixture resembles coarse crumbs. Blend in rolled oats. Store in tightly covered container.

4 cups of mix, 1 egg and scant tablespoon of milk makes 30 cookies.

Variations:

ROLLED: Combine

4 cups mix   ½ teaspoon mace
1 egg   1 teaspoon vanilla
         1 tablespoon milk

Roll on board dusted with powdered sugar. Cut into rounds and bake on ungreased sheet at 350 degrees 12-15 minutes.

CHOCOLATE DROPS:

4 cups mix   2 squares melted baking
1 egg   chocolate
1 teaspoon vanilla   3 tablespoons milk

Drop onto ungreased cookie sheet, top with ½ pecan. Bake at 350 degrees, 15 minutes.

GUMDROPS: Add

1 egg   1 tablespoon milk
4 cups mix   1 teaspoon vanilla
       Mix in 1 cup cut gumdrops

Shape dough into small balls and roll in flake coconut. Bake on ungreased sheet at 350 degrees for 12-15 minutes.

Barbara Ann Grassley, New Hartford
Wife of State Representative

Candies

Butter Crunch

1 cup sugar
¼ cup water
1½ cups walnuts
  finely chopped

½ teaspoon salt
½ cup butter
2 6-ounce packages,
  chocolate bits, melted

Combine sugar, water, salt, and butter. Cook to light crack stage (285 degrees). Add ½ cup finely chopped nuts. Pour onto well greased cookie sheet. Cool, then spread half of chocolate mixture and ½ cup of chopped nuts on top. Let stand until chocolate is set; turn and spread with remaining half of chocolate and nuts.

Break into pieces to serve. Makes about two dozen pieces.

LaVonne Maurer, Tipton

Fruit Balls

½ pound butter or margarine
1 cup nut meats, chopped fine
25 maraschino cherries

1 pound powdered sugar
1 cup coconut
½ cup crushed pineapple

(After grinding up cherries and pineapple, squeeze out the juice)

Mix well and shape into small balls. Place on waxed paper trays in the refrigerator until firm.

Melt 4 4-ounce Hershey chocolate bars and ½ bar of paraffin and keep over hot water while covering the balls. Some people use tooth picks in each ball for dipping, but I use a nut pick, then touch up the hole.

Mrs. Paul Hutchens, Tipton

80

Divinity

Part I

½ cup water   1 cup sugar

   Cook until it threads, (242 degrees)

Part II

3 cups sugar   ½ cup water
1 cup corn syrup

   Cook until hard ball stage, (250 degrees)

Method:

Beat the whites of 3 eggs until stiff. Add part I and then add part II to beaten egg mixture. Beat it until it loses its shine. Add 1½ cups nuts. Drop by spoonfuls onto waxed paper.

Florence Walker, West Branch

Cream Nut Candy

3 pints nuts   3 pints cream
3 pints white sugar   1 cup white syrup
                 Pinch of salt

Mix above ingredients in a large pan and cook until firm ball stage is reached. Stir frequently. Remove from heat and beat until candy loses its gloss. Pour into two loaf pans and cool before cutting. Makes ten pounds.

Mrs. Dan Sweeney, Mediapolis

Taffy

2 cups white sugar   1 cup water
1 cup white syrup   ½ cup vinegar

Boil until mixture threads from spoon or reaches 260 degrees. Add color and flavor to taste. Pour on buttered platter to cool. Grease hands and pull with a twisting motion. After pulling, stretch into a long rope and break into pieces.

Kevin Nebergall, Tipton

Fudge

4 cups sugar   ¼ cup butter
         1 14½-ounce can evaporated milk

Boil above mixture 5 minutes; stir while boiling.

Break into large bowl: One pound Hershey bars
                              2 packages chocolate chips (6 oz.)
                              1 pint marshmallow creme
                              1 cup nut meats chopped
                              2 teaspoons vanilla

Pour boiled mixture onto this and stir until well blended. Pour into
well buttered 10x13-inch pan. Cut into squares when cold.

This keeps very well when kept in a tightly covered pan. Makes
five pounds.

Mrs. Hans Henricksen, Clear Lake

Chocolate Fudge

2 cups sugar   2 tablespoons butter
⅔ cup milk   1 teaspoon vanilla
2 squares chocolate   ½ cup nuts
         2 tablespoons light corn syrup

Break chocolate into small pieces so it will melt easily. Put sugar,
milk, chocolate, and syrup into a sauce pan and cook slowly, stirring until sugar is dissolved. Continue cooking, stirring often to
prevent burning, until temperature of 236 degrees F. Remove from
fire; add butter; cool, without stirring, to lukewarm. Add vanilla
and beat until fudge loses its shiny look and will hold its shape.

Add nuts. Pour into greased pan or shape into rolls.

Olivette Werling, Tipton

Five-Minute Cherry Nut Fudge

1 small can evaporated milk
½ teaspoon salt
1½ cups chocolate chips
1 teaspoon vanilla
⅔ cups sugar
1½ cups miniature
   marshmallows
½ cup chopped nut meats
½ cup maraschino cherries
(cut in pieces)

Mix evaporated milk, sugar and salt. Heat over low heat to boiling, then cook five minutes, stirring constantly. Remove from heat and add marshmallows, chocolate, vanilla, nut meats and cherries. Stir until marshmallows are melted. Pour into buttered 8-inch square pan. When cool cut into squares. Makes about two pounds.

Mrs. Homer Burgess, Clarence

Frieda's Peanut Butter Fudge

2 cups sugar
⅔ cup milk
1 cup marshmallow creme
1 cup crunchy peanut butter

Combine sugar and milk. Boil to firm, soft-ball stage (234 degrees).

Take off fire and add the peanut butter and marshmallow creme.

Stir — (don't beat) — until ready to pour. Spread in buttered pan (9x9-inches).

Grace Hutchison, Tipton

Molasses Fudge

3 cups sugar
½ teaspoon soda
Few grains of salt
3 tablespoons molasses (or I
   use dark or white syrup)
1 cup milk
Butter, size of walnut

Boil in a large pan to soft ball stage, 236 degrees. Add flavoring, butter, and nutmeats and beat. Pour into pan. When cool, cut into squares.

Mrs. Norwin Martens, Tipton

Nougat Nut Roll

In a sauce pan combine: 2 cups granulated sugar
½ cup white corn syrup
½ cup water

Stir well. Bring mixture to a boil and boil one minute, covered, or until all sugar crystals on sides of pan have melted. Remove cover. Continue cooking over gentle heat, without stirring, to 265 degrees F. or until a little mixture in cold water forms hard, almost brittle ball.

Meanwhile, in large mixer bowl, beat 2 egg whites until stiff. Then slowly pour the syrup over whites, while beating, and continue beating until mixer has difficulty turning. Add vanilla. Let stand at room temperature, occasionally beating with spoon until mixture has consistency of soft dough.

With greased hands, form into about 7 rolls about 3"x½". Chill until firm and dry, about 3 hours, or it can be wrapped and stored in refrigerator for several days.

Combine: 1 can sweetened condensed milk
¼ teaspoon salt
½ cup corn syrup

Cook over low heat, stirring often, 20 minutes or until a little mixture in cold water forms a soft ball, 236 degrees. Drop rolls, one by one, into the mixture; turn to coat. Remove with fork and spatula; roll in nuts. (3 cups chopped walnuts, peanuts, or pecans). Chill 1 hour or until set. Slice.

Mrs. Lee Scott, Mechanicsville

84

Martha Maries

5 cups sugar
2 cups milk
½ teaspoon salt

1 teaspoon vanilla
2 teaspoons shaved paraffin
1 cup broken nuts

4 squares bitter chocolate

Combine chocolate, sugar, milk and salt. Cook to 236 degrees.

Cool. Add vanilla and stir until creamy. Knead and add broken nuts. Form into balls.

Chocolate Coating: Melt 2 squares of bitter chocolate over hot water. Add 2 teaspoons shaved paraffin.

Dip the fudge balls in the chocolate. Put on wax paper to harden.

Cool. Wrap in wax paper for storing. This amount of candy will take quite a lot of chocolate but it is better to melt a small amount at a time.

Verda Wilson, Tipton

Peanut Butter Logs

1 cup peanut butter
½ cup powdered milk
2 tablespoons water

⅔ cup powdered sugar
1 tablespoon honey
⅓ cup peanuts

Mix and work into two rolls. Roll in additional ½ cup peanuts.

Chill and slice.

Mrs. W. Conrad, Tipton

Penuchi Nut Roll

½ cup light corn syrup
1 cup evaporated milk

2 cups sugar
1 cup brown sugar

Method: Cook until soft ball (235 degrees) stirring until sugar is dissolved. Cool at room temperature, without stirring, until luke warm (110 degrees). Beat until it holds its shape. Knead cooled mixture until firm. Keep hands greased. Shape into 2-1½ inch rolls. Roll in 1½ cups finely chopped pecans. Wrap in aluminum foil or waxed paper.

Norma Horn, Tipton

Peanut Brittle

2 cups sugar
1 cup white syrup
½ cup water
1 pound raw Spanish peanuts

Butter, size of walnut
Scant teaspoon of salt
1 teaspoon vanilla
2 scant teaspoons of soda

Boil sugar, syrup and water until it forms a very hard piece when dropped in cold water, 240 degrees (piece should be brittle). Add peanuts and stir constantly. Cook 10 to 12 minutes or until the mixture begins to turn brown. Then add the salt, butter, and vanilla. Cook a little longer or until mixture becomes a little darker, 280 degrees. Then add the soda. Mixture must be stirred quickly as it is removed from the stove as it will foam up and boil out of the cooking vessel. Pour on a buttered cookie sheet. As it begins to harden, loosen with a spatula. It is well to have the soda measured out in a small dish so it can be poured in all at once.

Ina Barewald, Tipton

Nut Brittle

2 cups sugar
Butter, size of walnut

Melt slowly, stirring constantly, about 20 minutes.

Heat 2 cups salted nuts at 250 degrees, until warm.

Have cookie sheet well buttered. After sugar is melted add a generous pinch of soda. Stir quickly and add nuts. Pour onto cookie sheet and spread very thin. Cool, loosen, and break with knife handle.

Grace Hutchison, Tipton

Desserts

Some, frankly fancy
For party or tea—

Some, very simple,
But——good as can be.

Apple Torte

2 cups flour
½ cup oatmeal
1 cup brown sugar
3 tablespoons cornstarch
1 cup white sugar
Juice of 1 orange plus
    water to make 1 cup

½ teaspoon cinnamon
½ teaspoon nutmeg
¾ cup shortening
¼ teaspoon salt
1 teaspoon vanilla
1 quart sliced apples, peeled
Grated rind of 1 orange

Method: Mix flour, oatmeal, brown sugar and shortening as for a pie crust. Reserve 1 cup of mixture and pat remaining mixture into a 9-inch pie plate or 8x12-inch cake pan.

Combine the white sugar, salt, cornstarch and orange juice and cook until it thickens. Add vanilla, apples and spices and mix well. Pour into crumb lined pan. Sprinkle with the 1 cup reserved crumbs and bake in 350 degree oven for 45 minutes or until apples are tender. Serve with whipped cream.

Mrs. Don Dallas, Stanwood

Apple Torte

2 eggs
1 cup white sugar
¼ cup brown sugar
½ cup flour

1 teaspoon baking powder
½ teaspoon salt
2 medium apples
1 cup chopped nuts

½ pint cream

Beat eggs until stiff. Add sugar gradually, continuing to beat. Fold in sifted dry ingredients. Add finely cut apples and nuts. Pour into buttered 9-inch square pan or deep 10-inch pie pan. Bake 25 minutes at 375 degrees. Serve with whipped or ice cream.

Ruth Schneekloth, Tipton

For something special in baked apples, use honey for sweetening. Add raisins, dates, or nuts with cinnamon, according to family tastes.

Apricot Torte

Roll enough vanilla wafers very fine to make 1½ cups wafer crumbs. Add enough butter to hold together. Spread in pan, saving ½ cup for top.

Drain one No. 2½ can peeled apricots

Mix and beat: ½ cup butter
                  1 cup brown sugar
                  1 teaspoon vanilla
                  2 egg yolks

Beat: 2 egg whites

Add: ½ teaspoon salt

Fold into above mixture.
Pour above mixture into crust. Add the apricot halves and ½ pint cream, whipped. Sprinkle on the remainder of crumbs. Refrigerate.

Bernice Wright, Bennett

Coconut Crunch Torte

1 cup graham cracker crumbs
½ cup shredded coconut
½ cup chopped nuts
    (walnuts or pecans)
1 pint butter brickle ice cream

4 egg whites
¼ teaspoon salt
1 teaspoon vanilla
1 cup sugar

Method: Combine graham cracker crumbs, coconut and nuts. Beat egg whites with salt and vanilla until foamy. Gradually add sugar and continue beating until egg whites form stiff peaks. Fold graham cracker mixture into egg white mixture. Bake in 350 degree oven about 30 minutes. Cool. Cut in wedges and serve with the ice cream. A 9-inch pie plate or an 8 or 9-inch square cake pan may be used. Be sure to grease well.

Mrs. Lester Engler, New Liberty

Chocolate Torte

Meringue layers:

6 egg whites
1 cup sugar
1½ teaspoons vinegar

Method: Beat egg whites until frothy; gradually beat in sugar and vinegar, adding alternately. Beat until stiff and glossy.

Draw five 8-inch circles on pieces of brown paper and spread mixture evenly inside the circles. Bake at 275 degrees for 30 minutes. Turn off oven and leave in until cool.

Filling:

9 ounces chocolate morsels
1 8-ounce package cream cheese
1 tablespoon milk
¾ cup brown sugar, packed in cup
1 cup heavy whipping cream

Method: Melt chocolate over hot, not boiling water. Blend cream cheese with milk and blend this mixture with chocolate. Beat in gradually the brown sugar and dash of salt. Fold in the whipped cream. The boxed whipped topping may be used. Spread between the meringue layers and chill.

Mrs. A. Anthes Smith, Fort Madison

Chocolate Chip Torte

1¾ cups flour
½ teaspoon salt
1 cup boiling water
1 cup oil (salad)
2 beaten eggs
6-ounce package chocolate chips

2 tablespoons cocoa
1 teaspoon soda
1 cup cut dates
1 cup sugar
1 teaspoon vanilla
¾ cup nuts

Method: Pour boiling water over dates. Cream sugar, oil and eggs and add vanilla. Stir in dates. Add the dry ingredients. Spread in greased 13x9-inch pan. Put chocolate chips and nuts on top. Bake in 350 degree oven for 45 minutes. Serve with whipped cream.

Mrs. Charles Towle, Davenport

Raspberry Torte

1 cup drained raspberries   ½ pound marshmallows
½ pint whipping cream   ¼ cup milk
12 graham crackers, crushed   3 tablespoons melted butter

Method: Melt marshmallows in milk in double boiler. Cool. When cooled, fold in whipped cream and the fruit. Pour in crumb crust.

Pineapple, bananas, strawberries or fruit cocktail may be substituted.

Mrs. Don Hegarty, Tipton

Supreme Torte

Cream: ½ cup butter

Add: 1½ cups powdered sugar gradually

Add: 2 eggs, one at a time. Continue beating.
           This mixture will be smooth and light

Crush: 1 pound vanilla wafers

Chop: 1 cup nut meats coarsely

Drain: 1 No. 303 can crushed pineapple

Whip: ½ cup cream

Method: Butter 9x12-inch pan, place one half the crumbs on bottom of pan. Add in layers, creamed mixture, pineapple, whipped cream, nut meats. Sprinkle remaining crumbs on top. Place in refrigerator over night or let stand at least 3 to 4 hours before serving. Cut in squares. May be served plain or with a dash of whipped cream on top, topped with a cherry.

Mrs. Hans Henricksen, Clear Lake

Cherry Crisp Dessert

1 can cherry pie filling
½ package or 1¾ cups
   yellow or white cake mix

½ cup melted butter
  or margarine
½ cup chopped pecans

Turn pie filling into 8x8x2-inch pan. Sprinkle dry cake mix over top. Pour butter over cake mix and cover with nuts. Bake at 350 degrees for 45 minutes. Serve warm or cold with whipped cream or ice cream.

Mrs. A. W. Kemmann, Tipton

Cherry Crisp

1 cup flour
1 cup brown sugar

½ cup rolled oats
1 can cherry pie filling
½ cup butter or margarine

Method: Spoon flour into cup, level and pour into mixing bowl.

Stir in brown sugar. Cut in butter with a pastry blender. Add rolled oats and mix well. Spread half the crumb mixture in greased 8-inch square pan. Pour in the pie filling. Sprinkle remaining crumb mixture on top. Bake at 350 degrees for 40 to 45 minutes. Serve warm or cold with ice cream or whipped cream. Other fruits may be used. Will make 8 or 9 servings.

Mrs. C. W. Norton, Davenport

Ozark Pudding

2 eggs
1½ cups sugar
¾ cup flour
2½ teaspoons baking powder

¼ teaspoon salt
1 cup chopped nuts
  (may be omitted)
2 cups raw chopped apples
2 teaspoons vanilla

Beat eggs and add sugar. Add dry ingredients and mix well. Stir in nuts, apples and vanilla. Pour into buttered pan and sprinkle with cinnamon. Bake in 350 degree oven for 45 minutes.

Rhubarb or raw peaches may be used in place of apples but omit cinnamon.

Sarah Davis, Wyman

Rhubarb Crisp

Mix together the following ingredients and pour into a shallow glass cake pan 8x8x2-inches.

3 cups cut rhubarb	1¼ cups sugar
3 eggs, slightly beaten	2 tablespoons flour

Sprinkle over this a topping consisting of the following ingredients which are blended together:

⅔ cup brown sugar   ½ cup flour
3 tablespoons butter

Bake at 350 degrees for about 1 hour. Serve either warm or chilled with whole milk or cream. Also goes very well with ice cream.

Mrs. Frank Miller, Decorah

Quick and Easy Rhubarb Shortcake

Enjoy fresh rhubarb in this quick to bake shortcake.

1 cup sugar	2 cups flour
1 cup sour cream	Pinch of salt
1 teaspoon soda	Dash of nutmeg

2 cups fresh rhubarb, cut up

Mix sugar and cream together, add soda and stir. Stir in flour and rhubarb. Spread in a greased pan. Sprinkle with nutmeg. Bake at 350 degrees for 30 minutes. Serve warm with cream.

Note: We like it cold too. I use sweet or sour cream.

Mrs. Chalmers Keller, Tipton

Any woman who has delighted her husband and family with a perfect dish does not need to be told how sweet culinary compliments are to the soul.

Rhubarb Roll

3 cups finely diced rhubarb

Prepare dough: 2¾ cups flour
4 teaspoons baking powder
⅓ cup cream
½ teaspoon salt
⅔ cup milk

Sift flour, baking powder and salt together. Mix milk and cream.

Add gradually to flour mixture. Knead a little. Roll out ¼ inch thick. Spread diced rhubarb over dough.

Roll and cut in slices. Place rolls in flat pan and cover with syrup made of: 1½ cups sugar
1¼ cups water

Mix and heat. Pour over rolls. Bake in hot oven at 400 degrees for 30 minutes. (Very good. My family thinks they are delicious.)

Esther Rupe, Cedar Rapids

Bridge Club Dessert

Blend together: 1 cup butter
1½ cups flour
2 tablespoons sugar

Pat lightly in 9x12-inch pan. Bake 15 minutes at 350 degrees.

Boil: 1 cup pineapple tidbits
¾ cup sugar
2 tablespoons cornstarch

Pour on the baked crust.

Beat 4 egg whites very stiff. Gradually add 1 cup sugar and put on top of pineapple filling. Bake at 300 degrees for 1 hour.

Mrs. J. Henry Lucken, LeMars
Wife of State Senator

Delicious Peach Pudding

Cream 1 cup sugar with ½ cup butter;

Add 1 beaten egg and 1¼ cups mashed, cooked peaches and juice.

Sift 2 cups flour, 3 teaspoons baking powder and ¼ teaspoon salt.

Add to first mixture along with 1 teaspoon vanilla.

Mix until smooth.

Bake in shallow, greased and floured loaf pan at 350 degrees for 30 to 45 minutes.

Sauce:

Cook together until smooth and thick, then cool:

½ cup sugar   ⅛ teaspoon salt
1½ tablespoons cornstarch   ½ teaspoon vanilla
1 cup scalded milk   2 beaten egg yolks

Spread over pudding; top with a meringue made from the two egg whites and 4 tablespoons of sugar. Arrange thin slices of cooked, drained peaches over the meringue and bake in a slow oven until lightly browned. Serve hot or cold.

This is a very moist dessert. The little homegrown peaches are especially tasty this way.

Mrs. Norwin Martens, Tipton

Tapioca Grapenut Pudding

4 tablespoons minute tapioca   ¾ cup brown sugar
2 cups water   ¼ teaspoon salt
½ cup raisins
Cook all until clear. Cool. Add

½ cup grapenuts   4 tablespoons chopped nuts
                1 small apple cut fine

Serve with whipped cream.

Mrs. Claude Mitchell, Tipton

95

Apricot Dessert

½ cup butter
1 cup confectioner's sugar
2 eggs, beaten
1½ packages vanilla wafer crumbs

2 cups cream, whipped
2 No. 2½ cans apricots, halved
1 cup chopped pecans

Melt butter in top of double boiler. Add sugar and eggs; blend. Cook over boiling water, stirring constantly, until mixture thickens, about 4 minutes. Gently pack three-fourths of the crumbs in a 15x10x1-inch pan. Spread cooked filling over crumbs. Spread half of whipped cream over filling. Arrange apricot halves on cream. Sprinkle nuts over apricots. Spread on remaining whipped cream. Top with remaining wafer crumbs. Chill at least 24 hours. This serves 16-20 people.

Mrs. J. H. Hamiel, Adel

Cherry Dessert

6 tablespoons butter
3 tablespoons sugar
1¼ cups graham cracker crumbs

Combine ingredients. Line glass baking dish. Chill for 1 hour or bake 8 minutes at 350 degrees.

1 cup cream, whipped   1 package miniature marshmallows
1 can prepared cherry pie filling
Nuts if desired

Fold above ingredients together and pour into crust. Let stand a couple of hours before serving. Other fruits may be used if desired.

Mrs. Coover Pressel, Arnolds Park

Cherry Dessert

1 pound vanilla wafers
1 cup powdered sugar

1 egg
¼ pound butter

Crush vanilla wafers and place half of them in a buttered 9x13-inch pan. Cream butter, powdered sugar well. Add egg and beat well. Spread mixture over crumbs. Top with 1 can prepared cherry pie filling. Whip 1 cup cream and spread over the cherries. Top with remaining crumbs. Chill 6 hours or overnight. Serves 15.

Mrs. Austin Ford, Tipton

96

Choc-O-Date Dessert

12 packaged cream-filled chocolate cookies, crushed
1 8-ounce package (1cup) pitted dates, cut up
¾ cup water
2 cups tiny marshmallows
 or 16 marshmallows
½ teaspoon vanilla
¼ teaspoon salt
½ cup walnuts
1 cup heavy cream
Walnut halves

Reserve ¼ cup cookie crumbs; spread remainder in 10x6-inch baking dish. In saucepan, combine dates, water and salt; bring to boiling, reduce heat and simmer three minutes. Remove from heat, add marshmallows and stir until melted.

Cool to room temperature; stir in chopped nuts. Spread date mixture over crumbs in dish. Whip the cream and add vanilla; swirl over dates. Sprinkle with reserved crumbs; top with walnuts. Chill overnight. Cut in squares. Makes 8 servings.

Mrs. Earl M. Kelley, Waukon

Toffee Refrigerator Dessert

½ cup margarine or butter
1 cup confectioner's sugar
1 square unsweetened chocolate (melted)
½ teaspoon vanilla
3 eggs
¼ pound vanilla wafers (crushed)
½ cup nut meats (finely chopped)

Cream margarine and sugar together thoroughly. Beat in slightly beaten egg yolks and melted chocolate. Cool slightly and fold in stiffly beaten egg whites and vanilla. Add nuts. Sprinkle half the wafer crumbs on bottom and half on top of chocolate mixture. Put in freezing compartment to chill for 24 hours.

Frances Langley, Tipton

Pineapple Icebox Dessert

¾ box vanilla wafers
2 eggs
½ cup melted butter
1½ cups confectioner's sugar
1 cup whipping cream
1 No. 2 can crushed pineapple, drained

Crush cookies and put half of crumbs in freezing tray. Beat eggs, add butter and sugar and pour over crumbs. Whip cream, fold in pineapple and pour over egg mixture. Sprinkle balance of crumbs on top. Chill.

Beatrice B. Dunn, Iowa City

Fruit Marshmallow Dessert

1¼ cup flour
½ cup brown sugar

½ cup butter or margarine
¼ teaspoon salt

Mix together until real fine. Pat mixture into a shallow pan and bake in a 275 degree oven 10 to 15 minutes. Cool and break into crumbs.

Melt ½ pound large marshmallows with 1 cup milk in double boiler. Chill this until cold and slightly thickened.

Whip 1 cup cream and ¼ teaspoon almond extract. Fold marshmallow mixture into whipped cream.

Reserve one half of the crumbs. Press the rest firmly into a 13x9-inch pan, spread ⅔ of marshmallows over crumbs. Then spread 1 can pie filling of any kind over the marshmallow mixture; then spread the rest of the marshmallow mixture over the pie filling.

Sprinkle with the reserved crumbs. Chill six hours or over night.

Mrs. Adah Agne, Tipton

Cheesecake

4 eggs
1 cup sugar

24 ounces cream cheese
1 teaspoon vanilla

Using an electric beater, beat eggs and sugar for 10 minutes, until real creamy. Break in cheese and add vanilla. Beat for a full 20 minutes until texture is like velvet. Pour into a graham cracker crust in a spring pan and bake for 20 minutes in a 375 degree oven. Remove from oven and cool for 20 minutes. Then pour Sour Cream Icing gently on top of cheesecake. Return to oven for 6 minutes at 425 degrees. Take cake out and let it cool for at least 1½ hours before putting in ice box. Cake must be in ice box at least 8 hours before serving.

Graham Cracker Crust:

Use about 15 crackers and ⅓ cup melted butter or margarine.

Mix together and press in pan.

Sour Cream Icing:

Beat together:
1 pint sour cream

4 tablespoon sugar
1 teaspoon vanilla

This cheesecake may be served topped with cherry, blueberry, or strawberry pie filling to be extra fancy.

Serves 14 to 16.

Mrs. M. Telpner, Council Bluffs

Brown and Green Dessert

1 package of lime gelatin
½ cup hot water
½ cup sugar
Grated rind and juice of 1 lemon
1 can (14½ ounces) evaporated milk (frozen crystals)
Chocolate cookie crumbs

Mix water and gelatin; add sugar, lemon rind and juice. Let partially set and then whip. Whip milk. Combine two mixtures and pour over chocolate crumbs. Top with some of the crumbs. Chill.

Mrs. Charles Thomson, Stanwood

Philadelphia Cream Cheese Cake

Chill 1 14½-oz. can evaporated milk.

Drain one No. 2 can of crushed pineapple.

Heat the pineapple juice, add ¼ cup of hot water and add to one package of lemon gelatin. Cool.

Cream one 8-ounce package of Philadelphia cream cheese and add to the gelatin mixture along with ⅓ cup sugar, 1 tablespoon of lemon juice and a pinch of salt.

Whip the chilled milk, add the drained pineapple and fold in the gelatin mixture.

Press graham cracker crust in a large pan, reserving one cup for top. Pour gelatin mixture over cracker crumb crust. Sprinkle rest of crumbs on top. Chill.

Graham Cracker Crust: Mix together

> 36 graham crackers, crushed
> ½ cup sugar
> 1 stick melted margarine
> ½ teaspoon salt

> Hazel Daugherty, Burlington

Ritz Cracker Dessert

Crush 40 Ritz crackers and mix with ¼ cup melted butter. Put into a 12x7½-inch pan. Beat 4 egg yolks well, add ¼ cup sugar and a small can of crushed pineapple. Cook until thick and stir in ½ package lemon gelatin. When cool and it starts to set, add 4 beaten egg whites to which ½ cup sugar has been added. Serve with whipped topping and a few Ritz crumbs.

Apricots and orange gelatin can be used in the same way if desired.

> Alta Wuestenberg, Bennett

Strawberry Dessert

Spread 1 cup crushed graham crackers in a 7x11-inch cake dish.

Mix together: 1 cup powdered sugar
½ cup butter
2 egg yolks

Beat 2 egg whites and add to above. Spread this over crumbs.

Dissolve one package strawberry gelatin in one cup boiling water.

Add one package of frozen strawberries or 3 cups fresh berries (sweetened) to cooled gelatin. When fruit begins to thicken spread over sugar, butter and egg mixture. Chill several hours. Top with whipped cream with few graham cracker crumbs on top.

Mary A. Henderson, Tipton

Strawberry Swirl

1 cup graham cracker crumbs   1 tablespoon sugar
¼ cup butter or margarine
2 cups fresh sliced strawberries   2 tablespoons sugar
1 3-ounce package strawberry   1 cup hot water
gelatin   ½ cup milk
½ pound marshmallows
1 cup whipping cream, whipped

Mix crumbs, sugar and butter; press firmly over bottom of 9x9x2-inch baking dish. Chill until set.

Sprinkle 2 tablespoons sugar over sliced berries; let stand ½ hour. Drain, reserving juice.

Dissolve gelatin in the 1 cup hot water; add cold water to juice to make 1 cup. Add to gelatin mixture. Chill until partially set.

Meanwhile, combine marshmallows and milk, heat until marshmallows melt. Cool, then fold in whipped cream. Add berries to gelatin, then swirl in marshmallow mixture to marble. Pour into crust. Chill to set. Cut in 9 or 12 squares.

E. Fife, Cedar Rapids

101

Gingersnap Icebox Dessert

1 box gingersnaps (roll to make fine crumbs)

Add one stick margarine, melted. Mix well.

½ cup butter	2 cups powdered sugar
2 eggs	1 cup pineapple
½ cup nuts	3 bananas
1½ cups whipped cream	

Cream powdered sugar, eggs and butter until creamy.

Combine fruits, nuts and whipped cream. Grease pan with butter and cover bottom of pan with crumbs. Put a layer of powdered sugar, eggs and butter mixture. Sprinkle crumbs over this, then add fruits, nuts and whipped cream mixture. Put rest of crumbs on top. Let stand over night. Garnish with whipped cream.

LaVaughn Eaton, Tipton

Marshmallow–Mint Dessert

Whip one pint of cream and sweeten with ¼ cup sugar. Add ¾ package of colored, miniature marshmallows and 1 package of small colored mints.

Crush 1 package vanilla wafers. Line pan, saving some for the top. Spread on whipped cream mixture. Put remaining crumbs on top. Chill at least 24 hours.

Mrs. Bruce Cheney, Cedar Falls

Instead of chopped nuts in a recipe, try adding crisp, dry rice, corn or oat cereal for a new flavor and texture.

Orange Over-Night Pudding

1 cup orange juice
1 cup sugar
2 tablespoons butter
3 egg yolks (lightly beaten)

3 tablespoons flour
3 egg whites
½ teaspoon lemon extract
1 pound vanilla wafers

Method: Mix juice, sugar, flour, butter and egg yolks and cook until thick. Cool. Add egg whites, beaten until stiff, and lemon extract. Put one-half of crushed wafers on bottom of pyrex dish, fill with custard, and put the other half of crushed wafers on top.

Serve with whipped cream.

Ruth Hamilton, Tipton

Chilled Raspberry Creme

2 cups vanilla wafer crumbs
1 cup powdered sugar
½ teaspoon salt
2 pints raspberries (fresh)

1 cup whipping cream
½ cup soft butter
1 teaspoon vanilla
2 eggs

Method: Line an 11x7x2-inch glass baking dish with half the crumbs. Cream butter, gradually add sugar. Add vanilla and salt and beat until very fluffy. Add eggs one at a time, beating well after each addition; spread mixture carefully over crumbs on dish.

Arrange raspberries over creamed mixture; whip cream and spread over berries. Do not sweeten cream. Sprinkle remaining crumbs over whipped cream. Refrigerate at least 3 hours, preferably over night. Cut in squares and top each square with a berry.

(This recipe is very good with fresh strawberries also.)

Mrs. Harry Dodds, Tipton

103

Chocolate Meringue Dessert

6 egg whites   ½ cup sugar
½ teaspoon cream of tartar

Method: Beat together as for a meringue. Put in a 9-inch pie pan and place in preheated oven, 375 degrees. Turn off heat and leave in over night.

Filling:

2 bars German chocolate   1 pint whipping cream
1 cup nut meats in broken pieces

Method: Melt chocolate and cool. Whip the cream. Add cooled chocolate and broken nut meats to whipped cream.

Fill shell next morning with above mixture.

Mrs. Fred E. Wier, Letts
Wife of State Representative

Forgotten Dessert

Beat: 5 egg whites until frothy

Add   ¼ teaspoon salt
                ½ teaspoon cream of tartar
                Beat until stiff

Add: 1½ cups sugar, gradually
                1 teaspoon vanilla
                Beat for 15 minutes

Method: Heat oven to 450 degrees. Turn off the heat when the dessert is placed in oven and leave over night.

Whip: 1 cup of cream

Spread over top of the dessert in the morning. Refrigerate at least 1 hour. Serve with fruit garnished whippd cream. Excellent with strawberries.

Mrs. Rhea Hambright, Davenport

104

Cottage Pudding

1¾ cups sifted flour
2 teaspoons baking powder
½ teaspoon salt
¼ cup shortening

1 cup sugar
1 egg
¾ cup milk
1 teaspoon vanilla

Cream shortening and sugar; add egg and mix well. Add sifted dry ingredients alternately with liquid. Beat until smooth. Pour into greased and floured 9-inch square pan. Bake 25-30 minutes in 350 degree oven. Serve warm with hot nutmeg sauce.

Nutmeg Sauce

2 cups hot water
2 tablespoons butter
1⅓ cups brown sugar

3 tablespoons flour
¼ teaspoon salt
½ teaspoon nutmeg

Boil water, butter and half of sugar together. Mix flour, salt and remaining sugar; add to first mixture. Cook until thick and smooth, stirring constantly. Add nutmeg and serve hot.

Edna Martin, Tipton

Ritz Cracker Dessert

Mix together: 22 Ritz crackers, crushed
1 teaspoon baking powder
½ cup chopped nuts
Beat: 3 egg whites
Add: 1 cup sugar, gradually, beating until very stiff.

Method: Add above ingredients to crackers. Pour into greased 9-inch pan and bake in 350 degree oven for 30 minutes. Cool thoroughly.

Filling: Pour ½ pint whipping cream over 60 small marshmallows.

Let stand in refrigerator over night, covered. Beat and spread over cracker crust. Put chocolate shavings on top.

Mrs. Julius Petersen, Davenport

Black John Pudding

½ cup butter
½ cup sugar
½ cup molasses
½ cup sour milk
1 teaspoon soda

¼ teaspoon ginger
¼ teaspoon cloves
1 teaspoon cinnamon
⅛ teaspoon salt
2 cups flour, sifted

Method: Cream sugar and shortening. Dissolve soda in sour milk, sift spices into flour.

Add the liquid and the dry ingredients alternately. Beat well. Turn into a well greased 6x12-inch pan. Bake at 350 degrees for 35 minutes. Cut into squares and serve with the following sauce.

Sauce:

Mix and cook 1 cup sugar and 3 eggs in double boiler, stirring with fork while sugar is melting. Keep flame low to prevent whites of eggs from coagulating. Sauce should be smooth. Serve warm over pudding squares.

Note: This has been a favorite dessert in the family and has been handed down from one generation to another.

Mrs. R. O. Burrows, Sr., Belle Plaine
Wife of Iowa Senator

Chocolate Pudding

1 pint milk
1 pint bread crumbs

Yolks of 3 eggs
5 tablespoons grated chocolate

Scald milk; add bread crumbs and chocolate. Take from fire; add ½ cup sugar and the beaten egg yolks. Put in baking dish and bake 15 minutes at 350 degrees or until it is well thickened.

Beat the 3 egg whites; add 3 tablespoons of sugar; spread over top of hot pudding and brown in oven.

Beulah Dodds, Tipton

Brownie Pudding

½ cup sifted flour

1 teaspoon baking powder

½ teaspoon salt

⅓ cup granulated sugar

1 tablespoon cocoa

¼ cup milk

1 tablespoon melted shortening

½ teaspoon vanilla

¼ cup chopped nut meats

½ cup brown sugar, firmly packed

2 tablespoons cocoa

¾ cup boiling water

Sift flour once, measure, and add baking powder, salt, sugar and cocoa. Sift together into bowl. Add milk, shortening and vanilla.

Mix only until smooth. Add nuts. Turn into greased casserole.

Mix together brown sugar and other 2 tablespoons of cocoa and sprinkle over batter.

Then pour boiling water over top of batter. (This forms a sauce in the bottom of pan after pudding is baked.)

Bake in moderate oven (350 degrees) 30 to 40 minutes. Serves 6 to 8.

Marion Jones, Tipton

Brown Sugar Pudding

Syrup:

1 cup brown sugar

2 cups water

2 tablespoons butter

Batter:

½ cup sugar

1 cup sifted flour

2 teaspoons baking powder

½ cup water

½ cup seedless raisins

Mix brown sugar and water in sauce pan and boil for 10 minutes.

Remove from fire and add butter. Pour into greased one and one-half quart baking dish. Combine batter ingredients and pour over the hot syrup. Do not stir. Bake for 25 minutes at 400 degrees.

Serve hot or cold.

Mrs. Roy Jarrett, Red Oak

107

Refrigerator Dessert

2 4-ounce cakes German sweet chocolate, melted

Add: 3 tablespoons sugar and 3 tablespoons water. Cook until smooth, stirring constantly. Remove from heat.

Stir in: 3 egg yolks, ½ teaspoon vanilla and a few grains of salt. Cool.

Fold in 3 egg whites, beaten stiff and 1 cup cream, whipped.

Tear one angel food cake into bite size pieces. Drop into 1 large angel food cake pan, alternately with chocolate mixture.

Refrigerate 24 hours. Serves 15.

"I like to top with salted almonds before serving."

Mrs. Harold Hughes
Wife of Governor of Iowa

Chocolate Angel Dessert

1 10-inch angel cake
⅔ cup fudge or chocolate sauce

2 cups whipping cream (1 pint)
½ pound English toffee

Cut cake into two layers. Whip the cream; fold in the fudge sauce.

Frost bottom layer, sprinkle with toffee. Add second layer and frost top and sides, sprinkle with the rest of the toffee. Refrigerate 8 hours. 16 servings.

Mrs. Wayne Miller, Tipton

The 100% Home
Economically sound
Mechanically convenient
Physically healthful
Morally wholesome
Mentally stimulating
Spiritually inspiring
Socially responsible
A center of unselfish love.

Angel Food–Lemon Icebox Cake

¾ medium sized angel food cake (from store)
1 can sweetened condensed milk
¼ cup lemon juice
Grated rind of 1 lemon
Juice of 1 orange
2 eggs

Break cake in 1-inch pieces into a glass tray; mix milk and juices together; beat eggs well and mix with milk mixture; put over cake pieces, mix well, and let stand in ice box overnight. Serve with whipped cream.

If preferred, spread with whipped cream one hour before serving; a maraschino cherry may be put on each piece for added color. This makes about 10 servings.

Erma Kier, Tipton

Strawberry Angel Food Dessert

Pour 3 cups hot water over 2 packages of strawberry gelatin. Stir until dissolved and chill until partly set. Stir in 1 cup of whipped cream. Add 2 packages of thawed, frozen strawberries (juice also), 1 banana sliced, and ½ cup nuts. Stir together.

Crumble one-half an angel food cake into a 9x12-inch cake pan. Pour half the above mixture over this. Crumble other half of cake and spread over this. Then add the rest of the whipped cream-gelatin mixture. Put in freezer. Will keep several days.

Mrs. Albert Heiserman, Manchester

Cranberry Ice

Cook 3 cups cranberries in enough water to cover. Run through sieve. Add 3 cups sugar, juice of 2 lemons and enough water to make 1¾ quarts. Freeze. Serve in sherbet dishes.

Darlene Donohue, Tipton

Frosty Orange Angel Cake

1 large package angel cake mix
3 pints orange sherbet, softened
2 cups heavy cream

Yellow liquid food coloring
Grated lemon rind

Make angel cake according to directions on package. Bake in a loaf pan 15½x4½-inches.

When cake has completely cooled, invert, and using sharp knife, split lengthwise into three equal layers. Place top layer of inverted cake, with bottom side down, in bottom of loaf pan.

Carefully spoon 1½ pints orange sherbet on top of this cake layer. Top with middle layer, then spread with remaining sherbet.

Top with last layer.

Cover with foil; place in freezer. About 1½ hours before serving time, quickly dip angel cake loaf pan in and out of hot water, dry pan, and gently loosen cake with spatula. Place oblong serving plate or tray on top of cake pan, invert, and shake gently until cake comes out of pan. Return to freezer.

Whip heavy cream stiff, tint it pale yellow with food coloring. Use to frost entire cake. Sprinkle top and sides with grated lemon rind.

Refrigerate until served. Note: Layered cake may be made days ahead and frozen.

Mrs. W. L. Mooty, Grundy Center
Wife of Lieutenant Governor of Iowa

Cranberry Ice

(No stirring — just mix — pour into two ice cube trays and freeze. Don't take out to restir.)

Cook 1 quart cranberries in 2 cups water and run through sieve.

Add 3 cups sugar, 2 tablespoons lemon juice and 2 cups milk.

It will be curdly when mixed, but it is "fool proof" and creamy.

Not rich, but a favorite.

Frances Forster, Mason City

Ice Cream Wich Sundae

(9 servings)

¼ cup brown sugar
¼ cup melted butter
½ cup nuts
1 cup flaked coconut

1½ cups rice flakes or
    krispies (crushed)
1½-2 quarts ice cream,
    softened

Combine first 5 ingredients. Place one-half of mixture in 9 inch pan, then ice cream, and the remainder of the mixture on top. Freeze.

This may be garnished with strawberries or any prepared fruit pie fillings when served.

Elnora Suchomel, Tipton

Ice Cream Dessert

Blend ½ cup soft butter into 2 squares melted semi-sweet chocolate.

Add:

2 cups powdered sugar   3 beaten egg yolks

Beat all together until fluffy.

Add ½ teaspoon vanilla and fold in 3 stiffly beaten egg whites and ½ cup nuts.

Line pan with crushed graham crackers or vanilla wafers. Pour one-half of chocolate sauce into pan. Spread this with ½ gallon ice cream and cover with remaining chocolate sauce. Sprinkle some graham crackers on top. Store in freezer.

Mrs. Kenneth Wagner, Tipton

Fruit Ice

1 No. 2 can shredded pineapple   4 bananas
1 No. 2½ can apricots, sliced   1 large box frozen strawberries

Drain juice from apricots and pineapple. Add 1½ cups sugar and bring to a boil. When cool, add fruit and put into molds to freeze. Makes about 18 molds.

Edna White, Tipton

111

Date Nut Roll

2 cups vanilla wafers, or if you prefer, graham crackers, rolled
1 cup chopped dates   ½ cup nut meats
1 cup diced (very small) marshmallows
1 teaspoon cream   1 teaspoon salt
1 teaspoon vanilla

Mix and form into a roll and refrigerate. (Wrap in wax paper and foil — keep cold but not frozen). Slice and serve.

Requires no baking. (We like this very much.)

Dorothy B. Christianson, Boone

Steamed Pudding

Beat: 2 eggs

Add: ½ cup melted butter
              1 cup country sorghum
              1 cup sweet milk

Sift together and add:
              1 teaspoon soda
              ½ teaspoon baking powder
              ½ teaspoon salt
              3 cups flour

Add: 1 teaspoon vanilla
              1 cup raisins, dates, or candied fruit
              Nuts

Steam 2 hours in greased No. 2 cans. This is also good to slice as bread or can be used with whipped cream or a sauce. Makes 3 No. 2 cans or 4 if more than 1 cup of fruit is used.

Mrs. John Greig, Clarence

Bananas Foster

This may be made in a chafing dish and flamed at the table.

6 large all-yellow bananas   ½ cup butter
2 lemons   Dash of cinnamon
1 cup brown sugar

Peel bananas and halve them lengthwise; brush with lemon juice.

Melt brown sugar with lemon juice (¼ cup) and butter in flat chafing dish. Add bananas. Serve with vanilla ice cream. Give each serving a dash of cinnamon. Serves 6.

Mrs. R. S. Hummel, Tipton

Northern Lights

Beat up as many egg whites as people to serve and maybe one extra for good measure Beat until very, very stiff, then add a teaspoon of powdered sugar and a tablespoon of orange marmalade for each egg white.

In a double boiler, melt 2 tablespoons butter for each egg white.

Pour the egg white mixture right on top of the melted butter and leave it alone on the stove with moderate heat while you are serving and eating the first course of your luncheon. By the time you are ready for dessert, the meringue will be ready.

Spoon it into parfait glasses. Then spoon melted butter and Creme de Menthe over it.

This is definitely a ladies' dessert, very easy to make, pretty to look at and delicious!

Mrs. Milo T. Sorden, Washington

Butter Sauce

1 cup butter   2 cups granulated sugar

Heat until smooth. Add one cup cream slowly over heat. Add 1 teaspoon vanilla.

Mrs. Duane Forest, Tipton

Cinnamon Syrup

1 cup sugar   ½ cup butter
1 teaspoon cinnamon   1 cup boiling water
              1 tablespoon flour

Mix together and cook until thick. Very good on pancakes or ice cream.

Margaret Daugherty, Tipton

Chocolate Sauce

Mix together and place over low heat:

½ cup melted butter or margarine   ½ teaspoon salt
½ cup cocoa   ¼ cup white syrup

Add slowly 3 cups white sugar.

Then add:

1 14½ oz. can condensed milk   1 teaspoon vanilla

Mix and heat until sugar is dissolved.

Put in jar and refrigerate. Serve warm or cold on ice cream. Very good.

Mrs. Vernon Kimberling, Tipton

Hot Fudge Sauce

Melt together over low heat:

3 squares unsweetened chocolate   ¼ cup butter

Add:

1 cup evaporated milk   1 cup sugar

Bring to boil, stirring constantly and boil until mixture is thick. Remove from heat and add ½ teaspoon vanilla.

Mrs. Gene Gray, Tipton

114

Meats, Fish, Fowl
Casserole Dishes

Just add a dash of this or that

To be a real "gourmet"

A casserole fit for a king,

Can happen any day!

Deviled Crab

2 6½-ounce cans crab meat
2 hard cooked eggs
1 cup mayonnaise
1 teaspoon minced onion
1 teaspoon minced parsley
1 teaspoon Worcestershire sauce
1 teaspoon prepared mustard
2 teaspoons lemon juice
½ teaspoon salt
¼ cup sherry wine
Buttered crumbs

Chop eggs and add to the crab meat. Fold in mayonnaise, onion, parsley, Worcestershire sauce, mustard, lemon juice, and salt.

Add wine. Spoon mixture into 4 lightly buttered baking shells and top with buttered crumbs.

Bake uncovered for 15 or 20 minutes at 400 degrees. Sometimes I serve this in patty shells. Then I bake it in a casserole.

Betty Higgins, Harlan
Wife of the president of the Iowa State Fair Board

Shrimp De Jonghe

1 cup melted butter
2 cloves garlic, minced
⅓ cup chopped parsley
½ teaspoon paprika
Dash cayenne
⅔ cup cooking sherry
2 cups soft bread crumbs
5-6 cups cleaned cooked shrimp

Add garlic to melted butter. Then add the parsley, paprika, cayenne and wine. Mix.

Add the bread crumbs and toss.

Place shrimp in a buttered 11x7½-inch baking dish. Spoon the buttered mixture over the shrimp.

Bake in a slow oven (325 degrees) for 20-25 minutes or until the crumbs brown. Sprinkle with additional chopped parsley before serving.

This serves 6-8 people. I also use it for hot hors d'oeuvres.

Betty Higgins, Harlan

Shrimp Casserole

5 slices of buttered bread, cut in cubes

2 cups fresh shrimp, cooked

1 can cream of celery soup

2 cups grated sharp cheddar cheese

3 eggs

In a buttered casserole, alternate layers of bread cubes, shrimp, and cheese. Pour over 2 cups of soup (add milk to make 2 cups) and 3 eggs, beaten together.

Place in a pan (shallow) of hot water and bake at 375 degrees for one hour.

Mrs. Max W. Kreager, Newton
Wife of Iowa State Representative

Shrimp Delight Casserole

2 strips of bacon, diced

1 small onion

Small piece of green and red sweet pepper, diced

1½ cups cooked shrimp, cut in pieces

⅔ cup undiluted canned tomato soup

6 tablespoons evaporated milk

¾ teaspoon salt

¼ teaspoon curry powder

Dash of pepper

2 cups cooked rice

2 tablespoons evaporated milk

Buttered bread crumbs

Cook bacon slightly, add chopped onion, green and red sweet pepper. Saute until tender. Add tomato soup and seasoning, the 6 tablespoons milk and rice. Mix. Add the shrimp. Stir only enough to mix evenly. Place in buttered baking dish. Pour the 2 tablespoons condensed milk on top, then cover with buttered bread crumbs. Bake 30 minutes at 350 degrees. Serves 6.

Edith Hass, Tipton

For an interesting casserole topping: Cut fresh bread slices in ½ inch cubes. Coat with melted butter and spread onto casserole before baking— or try broken potato chips added 15 minutes before casserole has finished baking.

117

Chicken-Tuna Casserole

1 cup macaroni
½ cup chopped onion
¼ cup chopped green pepper
3 tablespoons fat
3 tablespoons flour

1¼ cups milk
1 can cream of chicken soup
1 can tuna
¼ cup chopped pimento

Almonds or crushed potato chips or crumbs

Cook macaroni for 7 minutes, drain. Cook onion with green pepper in fat until tender. Add flour, blend, stir in milk, cook until thick. Stir in 1 can soup. Add tuna and pimento. Fold in macaroni and pour in greased 1½ quart casserole. Garnish with almonds, crushed potato chips or crumbs. Bake 30 minutes at 350 degrees.

Mrs. Fred Lamp, Tipton

Scalloped Oysters

1 cup bread crumbs
1 cup cracker crumbs
¼ pound butter

1 pint oysters
½ teaspoon salt
⅛ teaspoon pepper

2 cups light cream

Mix all ingredients, reserving some crumbs to put on top before baking. Pour into greased casserole. Bake 35 minutes at 400 degrees.

Mrs. Hans Freese, Tipton

Scalloped Oysters

1½ cups coarse cracker crumbs
8 tablespoons melted butter
1 pint oysters
½ teaspoon salt

⅛ teaspoon pepper
Dash nutmeg
2 tablespoons parsley, if desired
¼ cup oyster liquor

1 can cream of mushroom soup

Combine cracker crumbs and butter. Put thin layer in bottom of baking dish.

Alternate layers of oysters with crumb mixture, using 2 layers of oysters, 3 layers of crumbs. Pour oyster liquor and canned soup over top. Work soup down through mixture with knife. Bake 30 minutes at 450 degrees.

Sally Cobb Ingram, Storm Lake

118

Buffet Party Casserole

1 8-ounce package fine noodles
¼ cup salad oil
2 7-ounce cans tuna
2 4-ounce cans mushrooms
  (whole)
1 peeled garlic clove
1 minced small onion
1 tablespoon flour

1 teaspoon Worcestershire
  sauce
1 can condensed cream of
  chicken soup, undiluted
¼ cup sherry
1 5-ounce can shrimp
½ cup grated Parmesan
  cheese

Heat oven to 350 degrees. Cook noodles in boiling salted water as directed on package. Drain. Meanwhile put salad oil and oil from tuna into a skillet. Drain mushrooms, saving liquid, and put them into skillet; add garlic and onion.

Cook, stirring until onion is tender, but not brown. Remove garlic.

Blend in flour; stir in mushroom liquid and Worcestershire sauce.

Cook until thickened, stirring. Stir in wine and soup. Break tuna into bite size pieces and add with shrimp and noodles to sauce.

Place in 3 quart casserole. Sprinkle with cheese. Bake at 350 degrees for 40 minutes.

This may be prepared ahead of time and frozen. In that case, thaw for one hour, before baking. Serves 12.

Mrs. B. B. Hickenlooper, Washington, D.C.
Wife of U.S. Senator

Sea Food Casserole

1 medium green pepper, chopped
1 medium onion, chopped
1 cup celery, chopped
1 6½-ounce can flaked crab meat
1 6½-ounce can shrimp (whole)

½ teaspoon salt
Dash of pepper
1 teaspoon Worcestershire
  sauce
1 cup mayonnaise

1 cup buttered crumbs

Combine ingredients. Place in buttered baking dish with crumbs on top. Bake 30 minutes at 350 degrees. Serves 8.

Mary Ferguson, Tipton

119

Salmon Loaf

1 can salmon (drain off liquid) 3 eggs
½ cup cracker or bread crumbs 4 tablespoons butter

Chop salmon fine and add crumbs, eggs, and butter. Season highly with salt and pepper. Form in shape of a loaf and bake ½ hour at 350 degrees.

Sauce for above:

1 cup sweet milk 1 egg
1 tablespoon flour or corn starch 1 tablespoon of lemon juice
2 tablespoons of butter Liquid from the salmon

Let the milk come to a boil, add flour, butter, egg, lemon juice, and salmon liquid. Let boil 1 minute, pour over the loaf while hot.

Adah Agne, Tipton

Salmon Rounds

1 cup drained flaked salmon 1 egg, beaten
  (8-ounce can) 1½ cups sifted enriched flour
¼ cup enriched bread crumbs 2 teaspoons baking powder
¼ cup chopped celery ¾ teaspoon salt
¼ teaspoon salt ¼ cup shortening
1 tablespoon chopped onion ½ to ⅔ cup milk
1 tablespoon lemon juice

Combine salmon, bread crumbs, celery, salt, onion and lemon juice. Stir in egg. Set aside while preparing biscuit dough. Sift together flour, baking powder and salt. Cut or rub in shortening until mixture is crumbly. Add milk to make a soft dough. Turn out on lightly floured board or pastry cloth and knead gently 30 seconds. Roll out into a 9-inch square. Spread salmon mixture evenly over dough. Roll up like jelly roll, sealing edge securely. Cut into 1 inch slices. Place cut side down in lightly greased 8-inch square pan or 8-inch round baking dish. Bake in oven (425 degrees) 25 to 30 minutes. Serve hot with creamed peas.

Nita Conrad, Bennett

120

Wild Rice Casserole

1 cup wild rice	½ cup chopped onion
1 cup grated cheddar cheese	½ cup salad oil
1 cup canned tomatoes	1 teaspoon salt
1 cup mushrooms, sliced	¼ teaspoon pepper

1 cup hot water

Wash rice, cover with water generously and soak overnight. Drain rice, combine with other ingredients in ungreased casserole. Save some cheese to garnish top. Cover and bake 1 hour at 350 degrees. Uncover, sprinkle with rest of cheese and heat long enough to melt cheese. Should casserole seem dry, add small amount of water. If moist, bake longer. The rate of absorption in rice varies. Serves 8.

Elnora Suchomel, Tipton

Seafood-Wild Rice Casserole

1 can shrimp or crab meat	3 cups white sauce or 3 cans
1 can tuna	mushroom soup thinned with
½ cup wild rice	1 cup milk
½ cup brown rice (or white)	1 can mushrooms
½ pound grated cheese (optional)	1 cup chopped celery

1 onion, chopped

Wash wild rice thoroughly and cook according to directions on package. Cook other rice. Combine with remainder of ingredients and top with grated cheese. Bake ½ hour at 350 degrees. 2 cups Chinese noodles may be subsituted for the rice to make it a more economical dish.

Darlene Donohue, Tipton

Tuna Asparagus Hot Dish

3 cans tuna, cut	1 can chicken soup
2 cans asparagus, cut and drained	½ cup mayonnaise
1 can mushrooms, drained	1 cup grated American
1 can mushroom soup	cheese

Cashew nuts

Salt and cook 12-ounce package of noodles for 12 minutes. Mix with above ingredients. Place in casserole or pan. Sprinkle with nuts and bake 1 hour at 350 degrees. Serves 15.

Mrs. Henry Mente, Tipton

121

Braised Beef Cubes with Vegetables

2 pounds boneless beef for stew
3 tablespoons flour
1 teaspoon salt
⅛ teaspoon pepper
2 tablespoons lard or drippings
1 cup water
1 package (12 ounces) frozen green peas or 1 pound fresh peas
3 large potatoes, pared and quartered
6 medium carrots, cut in halves
6 small onions
6 large celery stalks, cut in half
¼ cup enriched flour

Mix flour, salt, and pepper. Dredge meat in seasoned flour, brown in lard or drippings, add water, cover tightly and cook slowly for 1½ hours. Add potatoes, carrots, onions and celery. Cover and cook 30 minutes. Add green peas and cook 30 minutes or until meat and vegetables are done. Remove meat and vgetables to serving platter. Add water to liquid in pan to make 2 cups. Thicken with ¼ cup flour for gravy.

Mrs. Jack Driscoll, Williamsburg

Good Casserole Dish

1½ pounds veal
1 pound pork
Small amount of shortening
2 small onions
1 package small noodles
1 number 2 can whole kernel corn
1 green pepper (cut fine)
Salt and pepper
1 can cream of chicken soup
1 small can pimentos
½ pound processed cheese
2 cups milk
Crushed corn flakes

Cut meat into small 1 inch squares; fry meat in shortening until brown. Add onions and brown. Cook noodles in salt water about 5 minutes and drain; add to meat and onion. Put in 2 quart casserole dish; add corn, green pepper, salt and pepper, soup, pimentos and cheese (cut in small pieces). Pour 2 cups milk over top, cover with crushed corn flakes. Bake in 350 degree oven one hour.

Serves 8 to 10.

Opal Sheetz, Davenport

Chop Suey

1 pound veal round
1 pound boneless pork loin
½ cup water
1 cup diced celery
1 diced medium onoin
1 tablespoon sugar
1 tablespoon bead molasses

2 tablespoons soy sauce
Salt and pepper to taste
1 can bean sprouts and liquid
1 small can mushrooms
1 can water chestnuts, optional
2 tablespoons corn starch
Cooked rice

Chinese noodles

Cut meat into bite size pieces and brown in pressure pan. Add water and pressure at 10 pounds for 10 minutes. Reduce heat and add celery, onion, sugar and molasses. Pressure for 7 minutes at 10 pounds. Reduce heat. Add soy sauce, salt, pepper, bean sprouts, mushrooms and chestnuts. Bring to boil and thicken with corn starch. Serve over cooked rice and top with Chinese noodles. Serves 10.

Mrs. James J. Bradley, Iowa City

Chinese Steak

1 pound round steak, cubed
2 medium onions, sliced
1 cup celery, diced
2 tablespoons fat
1 can mushroom soup

3 cups water
½ cup raw rice
3 tablespoons soy sauce
½ teaspoon salt
1 can bean sprouts

Lightly brown steak, onions and celery in fat. Add other ingredients. Pour into casserole. Bake 350 degrees for 1½ hours. Cover with slightly crushed potato chips and bake 15 minutes longer. Bean sprouts may be omitted, if desired.

Marjorie Cobb, Tipton

Rice — choose the correct type for the use to be made of it. Long grain is the best choice for use in a main dish or as a substitute for potatoes because it is plump and flaky when cooked. Regular grain rice is likely to be creamy or sticky and is more satisfactory in dishes such as rice pudding.

Even new brides know that rice swells when cooked. If you've forgotten the proportion of expansion, it is 1 cup rice — 2½ to 4 cups cooked. Variation depends on type of rice and method of cooking. Allow ¼ cup uncooked rice for each generous portion.

Beef Stroganoff

2 pounds beef for stew, cut in ½ inch strips. Dredge in mixture of 6 tablespoons flour, 1½ teaspoons salt and ¼ teaspoon pepper. Save remaining mixture for thickening the cooking liquid.

Brown meat in 1 tablespoon lard. Add 1 cup chopped onions and brown. Drain 4-ounce can mushrooms, saving liquid. Add enough water to make 2 cups. After meat and onions are browned, pour off drippings. Add 1 cup beef broth or bouillon and 1½ cups mushroom liquid. Add mushrooms, cover and cook slowly for 1½ hours.

Blend flour and remaining ½ cup liquid. Add to meat, stirring constantly until thickened. Fold in 1 cup sour cream. Serve over hot noodles or rice. Round steak may be used; shorten cooking time 30 minutes.

Norma Horn, Tipton

Hamburger and Noodle Casserole

1 pound hamburger	1 can cream of chicken soup
1 small onion, diced	1 can yellow, cream style corn
1 cup celery, diced	12 ounces noodles
2 tablespoons butter	1 teaspoon salt, (approximately)

Cook noodles in salted water and drain. Brown hamburger, onion and celery in butter. Combine with other ingredients and bake in a casserole 30 minutes at 375 degres.

Mrs. Lloyd Thien, Tipton

Sausage Apple and Sweet Potato Casserole

4 medium sized sweet potatoes	2 tablespoons sugar
6 apples	1 tablespoon flour
¾ pound sausage	½ cup cold water
½ teaspoon salt	1 tablespoon sausage drippings

Shape sausage into small balls and fry until brown. Pare and slice potatoes and apples. Arrange layers of apples, potatoes and sausage in casserole. Mix other ingredients and pour over top. Cover and bake 45 minutes at 375 degrees.

Mrs. Hans Freese, Tipton

Barbecued Spare Ribs

¾ cup water
¾ teaspoon chili powder
Small grated onion
2 tablespoons butter
2 tablespoons Worcestershire sauce
1 teaspoon paprika
¼ teaspoon red pepper
¾ cup catsup

1 teaspoon salt
½ teaspoon black pepper
2 tablespoons vinegar
2 tablespoons brown sugar
4 tablespoons lemon juice
½ teaspoon dry mustard
½ teaspoon celery salt
Ribs

Brown ribs. Mix all other ingredients and cook 5 minutes. Pour over ribs and bake in 350 degree oven for 1½ to 2 hours or until done. Keep basting ribs.

Mrs. Carl Thoresen, Tipton

Sweet and Sour Spare Ribs

3 pounds spare ribs
½ cup onion, chopped
½ cup celery, chopped
½ cup green pepper, chopped
1 tablespoon corn starch

1 cup pineapple juice
1 tablespoon soya sauce
4 tablespoons vinegar
1 cup chunk pineapple
Salt and pepper

Corn oil

Saute onion, celery and green pepper in corn oil. Mix corn starch, pineapple juice, soya sauce, vinegar and pineapple. Add and simmer a few minutes. Salt ribs and put in oven at 350 degrees for 30 minutes. Pour off grease, pepper ribs and pour sauce over them. Bake 80 minutes at 300 degrees.

Mrs. Don Safley, Tipton

Barbecued Pork Chops

4 pork chops
½ cup brown sugar
½ cup catsup

1 tablespoon salad mustard
1 cup water
Salt and pepper to taste

Place pork chops in baking dish. Mix remaining ingredients, pour over chops and bake about an hour at 350 degrees.

Mrs. Cyril Olson, Tipton

125

Deviled Pork Chops

6 rib pork chops (thick)
1 tablespoon shortening
½ cup water

Marinade:

3 tablespoons chili sauce
2 tablespoons lemon juice
1 tablespoon grated onion
½ teaspoon salt

½ teaspoon dry mustard
2 teaspoons Worcestershire
sauce
½ teaspoon paprika

Combine all ingredients for the marinade. Spread chops with the sauce and let stand overnight. When ready to cook, drain and brown chops on both sides in shortening. Drain fat. Add marinade drained from chops and the water. Cover and simmer until chops are tender, about 45 minutes. Uncover and cook until sauce thickens.

Mrs. W. L. Mooty, Grundy Center
Wife of Iowa's Lieutenant Governor

Orange Baked Pork Chops

6 pork chops, rather thick
½ cup orange juice
1 teaspoon salt

¼ teaspoon pepper
½ teaspoon dry mustard
¼ cup brown sugar

Cut fat from pork chops, if necessary. Place chops in large shallow baking dish; they don't need to be browned. Combine remaining ingredients, pour over chops and bake 350 degrees for 1 hour (depending on thickness of chops). Baste occasionally during baking.

Mrs. Austin Ford, Tipton

Skillet Pork Chops with Rice and Tomatoes

6 pork chops
⅓ cup rice

1 large onion, sliced
1 green pepper, sliced

1 No. 2 can of tomatoes

Use heavy medium large skillet. Brown chops well in fat, then pour off excess fat. Sprinkle rice around the chops. Place onion and green pepper over meat and rice. Pour tomatoes over all.

Cover and cook over low heat about 1 hour.

Mrs. Don Dallas, Stanwood

126

Ham and Asparagus

4 hard cooked eggs, sliced
1 package frozen, cut asparagus
1 cup cubed, cooked ham
2 tablespoons quick cooking
   tapioca
¼ cup grated American
   cheese
Topping:
½ cup dry bread crumbs

2 tablespoons green pepper
2 tablespoons chopped onion
1 tablespoon minced parsley
1 tablespoon lemon juice
½ cup light cream
1 can mushroom soup

2 tablespoons butter or
   margarine

Cook asparagus according to package directions, omitting salt. Drain thoroughly. Place in greased 1½ quart casserole. Combine ham, cheese, tapioca, chopped green pepper, onion, parsley and lemon juice. Place alternate layers of ham mixture and egg slices atop the asparagus. Stir cream into soup, mix until smooth and pour over casserole. Swirl topping on in a design. Bake in 375 degree oven for 25 to 30 minutes. Deck top with sprig of evergreen, ripe olive slices and asparagus tips to form star.

Viola Schroeder, Tipton

Ham and Broccoli Casserole

1 package frozen broccoli
4 slices pre-cooked ham
2 cups white sauce
½ cup shredded cheese

2 teaspoons prepared mustard
½ teaspoon salt
Dash of pepper
1 tablespoon minced onion

Partly cook broccoli. Butter casserole dish and place ham slices over broccoli. Prepare white sauce and add cheese (1 can of cheese soup diluted may be used instead of white sauce and cheese). Add remaining ingredients. Pour over meat and broccoli. Bake at 400 degrees for 20 to 25 minutes.

Eleanor Aker, Tipton

Freezing of ham — freeze uncooked, mild cured hams (most present day are mild cured) no longer than a month; the fat of salted meat tends to become rancid when frozen. Left over cooked ham may be kept frozen four to six weeks.

Ham Balls

2 pounds ground smoked ham
1 pound lean ground pork
2 cups cracker crumbs

1 cup milk
2 eggs
Dash of pepper

Mix above together. Shape into balls. Arrange in baking dish, single layer. Bake 45 minutes at 350 degrees and turn. Pour topping over balls, and bake 45 minutes longer, basting frequently.

Topping:

½ cup vinegar
½ cup water

1 cup brown sugar
1 teaspoon prepared mustard

2 teaspoons horseradish

Mix together and pour over meat.

Pearl Johnson, Cedar Rapids

Ham Loaf

1½ pounds ground ham
½ pound ground beef
½ pound ground lean pork
1 cup oatmeal or bread crumbs

3 eggs, well beaten
1 teaspoon salt
½ teaspoon pepper
1½ cups milk

Don't grind ham too fine. Combine all ingredients and form into loaf (or 2 small loaves) and bake in 350 degree oven for one hour.

Baste every 20 minutes with syrup made of 1 cup pineapple juice, ¼ cup brown sugar and ½ teaspoon ground mustard. Pickled peach juice is fine to use instead of pineapple syrup. This glazes the loaf and makes it juicy. Let stand 5 minutes before slicing.

Serve with pineapple chunks that have been browned in butter and brown sugar.

Gertrude Meacham, Iowa City

Ham Hawaiian

2 ¾-inch slices sugar
cured ham

2 cups crushed pineapple
½ cup brown sugar

Place slice of ham in baking dish. Cover with 1 cup crushed pineapple and ¼ cup brown sugar. Top with second slice of ham and remainder of pineapple and brown sugar. Put in cold oven. Set at 350 degrees for 1½ hours.

Mrs. Dwayne Drager, Tipton

Ham Biscuits

2 cups flour
4 teaspoons baking powder
½ teaspoon salt
4 tablespoons vegetable
   shortening
⅔ to ¾ cup milk
2 tablespoons melted butter
2 cups ground ham
1 teaspoon prepared mustard

1 tablespoon minced onion (optional)

Sift together flour, baking powder, and salt. Cut in shortening and add milk. Roll dough into rectangle as for jelly roll. Spread with melted butter, ham, mustard and onion. Form into roll. Cut slices about 1 inch wide and place cut side down in greased pan. Bake in very hot oven at 425 degrees for 15 to 20 minutes. Pour cheese sauce over top just before serving.

Cheese sauce:

2 tablespoons butter
2 tablespoons flour
1½ cups milk
1 teaspoon salt

½ cup grated sharp cheese

Make white sauce of butter, flour, milk and salt. Add cheese. Stir until melted. Makes 10 to 12 biscuits. This is a good way to use left-over ham.

Joyce Hamiel, Tipton

Hot Ham Mousse

3 tablespoons margarine
1 cup dry bread crumbs
   (not too fine)
1 cup milk
3 cups chopped ham
1 tablespoon grated onion
2 eggs (slightly beaten)
Pepper

Melt margarine, add crumbs, and cook until blended. Add other ingredients and pack into buttered baking dish. Pour over top the following sauce.

Sauce:

1 cup medium white sauce
½ teaspoon dry mustard
½ teaspoon paprika
1 cup grated cheese

Set baking dish in pan of hot water and bake at 350 degrees for at least 30 minutes.

Blanche Roland, Tipton

129

Ham Luncheon Dish

1 cup rice, cooked
1 cup diced ham
1 cup peas
1½ cups milk
1 cup grated cheese

Salt and pepper to taste
3 eggs, beaten
¼ cup melted butter
1 tablespoon chopped onion
1 tablespoon chopped parsley
Paprika

Mix all ingredients. Place baking dish in pan of warm water. Bake at 325 degrees for 75 minutes.

Mrs. Edward L. O'Connor, Iowa City

Ham and Egg Pie

2 cups cubed cooked ham
 (about ¾ pound)
2 tablespoons chopped onion
¼ cup chopped celery
3 tablespoons vegetable
 shortening or margarine
6 tablespoons flour

2 cups milk
½ teaspoon salt
Pepper to taste
2 hard cooked eggs
2 tablespoons chopped
 green pepper

Simmer onion and celery in fat. Add flour and blend. Add milk gradually, stirring until thickened. Add seasonings, ham, green pepper and eggs. Place in casserole and cover with rich biscuit dough cut in wedges and slightly separated. Bake 30 minutes at 400 degrees. Serves 5. Volume can be increased with more eggs.

Mrs. A. W. Kemmann, Tipton

Meat Timbales

½ cup milk
1 cup ground cooked meat
¼ teaspoon salt

⅓ cup soft bread crumbs
1 egg
¼ teaspoon paprika

Mix meat, salt, crumbs, and paprika. Add well beaten egg and milk. Pour into a buttered, shallow pan. Place in pan of hot water.

Bake in moderate oven about 30 minutes.

Katherine McKee, Tipton

130

Barbecued Beef Patties

1 cup bread crumbs
1 pound ground beef

½ cup milk
1 teaspoon salt

Pepper

Mix and make patties. Lay in 9x13-inch pan. Mix sauce and pour over patties. Bake at 375 degrees for 45 minutes to 1 hour.

Sauce:

1½ teaspoons Worcestershire sauce
⅓ cup vinegar
½ cup chopped green pepper

3 tablespoons sugar
½ cup catsup
½ cup chopped onion

Mrs. Kay Connelly, Allison

Hamburger Casserole

1 pound hamburger
4 ounces noodles

1 can cream of mushroom soup
1 can French fried onion rings

Cook noodles in salt water until done and drain. Put hamburger in skillet and cook until done, stirring often. Have casserole greased and put hamburger and noodles in it. Add soup and stir until mixed. Place onion rings on top. Bake at 400 degrees for about 15 minutes. Serves 6.

Ida Moreland, Tipton

Rice Porcupines

1 pound ground beef
1 cup minute rice
1 teaspoon salt

¼ teaspoon pepper
1 medium onion, chopped
1 can tomato soup

Mix and form into small balls. Place in sauce pan. Pour tomato soup over the meat balls; cover and cook on top of stove for 30 minutes or until done.

Mrs. Dale L. Stiff, Tipton

Hamburger Pie

1 pound ground beef
1 onion
2 cups whole tomatoes

1 can drained green cut beans
3 cups mashed potatoes (left overs
   or instant)
1 egg

Fry ground beef and onion together with seasonings until well done. Add tomatoes and beans and mix. Place in casserole and top with mashed potatoes in which the raw egg has been mixed.

Bake at 350 degrees for 25 minutes. This dish may be made ahead and refrigerated to be heated later.

Mrs. Ed Liercke, Tipton

Hot Dish

1½ pounds hamburger, browned
1 cup diced celery
½ cup onion, chopped

1 can cream of mushroom soup
1 small can mushrooms
1 can cream of chicken soup
1 large can chow mein noodles

Mix together in casserole. Do not dilute soups or use salt or any other seasonings. Bake 30 minutes at 350 degrees. May be frozen.

Alma Zutz, Hamburg

Rancho Baked Beans

1 pound ground beef
1 cup chopped onions
1 teaspoon salt
1 cup catsup

2 tablespoons prepared mustard
3 tablespoons brown sugar
1 pound can pork and beans
   in tomato sauce
1 can kidney beans

Brown beef and onions with salt; add catsup, mustard, and brown sugar. Put beans in bean pot; add other ingredients. Bake in a slow oven about 6 hours. If in a hurry, bake at 400 degrees about 1½ hours.

Mrs. Eugene Alcorn, West Union

Skillet Casserole Dinner

1 pound hamburger, browned
1 can tomato soup
1 soup can water
1 can red kidney beans
1 cup cut up celery
3 cups diced potatoes

½ cup diced onion
⅓ cup uncooked rice or
  ½ cup spaghetti
1 teaspoon salt
¼ teaspoon pepper
1 tablespoon Worcestershire
  sauce

Brown hamburger and add remaining ingredients. Cook for about 45 minutes on top of stove or in oven 1 hour at 350 degrees.

Mrs. John Greig, Clarence

Chop Suey Casserole

2 pounds hamburger
1 large onion, cut fine
1 cup celery, parboil 5 minutes

1 can cream of mushroom soup
1 can chicken rice soup
2 tablespoons soy sauce

1 package frozen mixed vegetables

Brown hamburger and onion. Mix well with other ingredients.

Bake 1 hour at 350 degrees. Serve with 1 can Chinese noodles spread over top.

Mrs. Claude Appleby, Monticello

Mock Chow Mein

1 pound ground beef
2 cups chopped celery
Small onion
1 cup instant rice

¼ cup soy sauce
½ teaspoon salt
2 cups water
1 can cream of mushroom soup

1 can cream of chicken soup

Brown meat and onions. Add remaining ingredients and bake at 350 degrees for 1½ hours.

Frances Hegarty, Tipton

133

Favorite Casserole

2 cups uncooked noodles
2 medium onions, sliced
1 tablespoon butter or
  margarine
1 pound ground beef

1 cup milk
1 cup mushroom soup
1½ teaspoons salt
½ cup grated cheese
1 cup cottage cheese

2 eggs, beaten

Cook noodles until tender, drain and rinse. Saute onion in butter until light brown; set aside. Cook ground beef until it changes color. Add onion and cottage cheese. In a 2 quart casserole, arrange ⅓ of the noodles and half of meat mixture. Repeat these layers, ending with layer of noodles. Combine milk, soup and salt and pour over casserole. Sprinkle grated cheese on top; pour beaten eggs over cheese. Bake uncovered in moderate oven, 375 degrees for one hour. Serves 6 to 8.

Mrs. Herman Hass, Tipton

Teta-Rena

1 pound hamburger
Salt and pepper to taste
1 small stalk celery, diced
5 or 6 carrots

2 large onions
3 or 4 potatoes
1 quart tomatoes
1 teaspoon chili powder

Brown hamburger and add other ingredients. Pour in a little water and let simmer until boiled down. When done, stir in a little flour and milk or cream to thicken. Boil 1 package spaghetti. Put spaghetti on platter, then hamburger and vegetable mixture and shake on grated cheese. You can put Worcestershire sauce on, if you like. Add a salad and you have a meal.

Mrs. Lester Engler, New Liberty

Unexpected guests are no cause for alarm to the hostess with a freezer. Most meats may be cooked while frozen (if pieces can be taken apart). Methods are the same as for fresh meat, but half again as much time should be allowed for cooking. Large cuts, as roasts, do cook more evenly when thawed.

Hamburger Noodle Casserole

1 pound ground beef	4 ounces noodles
2 tablespoons fat	Salt and pepper to taste
1 onion, chopped	2½ cups cream style corn
1 can cream of tomato soup	1 cup sliced mushrooms
1 cup water	1 cup shredded cheese

Brown meat and onions in fat. Add soup and water. Stir in uncooked noodles and season. Add mushroms and corn, place in casserole and top with cheese. Bake 45 minutes in 350 degree oven.

Mrs. Carl Kruse, Tipton

Covered Meat Dish

1½ pounds ground beef	½ pound diced American cheese
2 small onions	1 can cream of mushroom soup
1 4-ounce can mushrooms	1 cup milk
½ can stuffed olives	1 pound noodles, cooked

Brown beef and onions. Mix with other ingredients and put in casserole. Bake 40 minutes at 375 degrees. The last 15 minutes add 1 cup crisp chow mein noodles.

Mrs. Ray Buckman, West Liberty

Beef Rice Bake

½ pound ground beef	1 can condensed chicken soup
1 tablespoon fat	1 teaspoon salt
½ cup uncooked rice	½ cup chopped celery
1½ cups water	¼ cup chopped green pepper

Brown beef in hot fat. Add rice, soup, water, salt, celery and pepper. Mix thoroughly. Pour into 1½ quart casserole, cover, and bake in moderate oven for 1½ hours. At end of 1 hour, uncover, stir with fork. Top with crushed corn flakes and brown.

Mrs. Stan H. Maurer, Tipton

Italian Meat Sauce

2 pounds hamburger
2 quarts canned tomatoes
1 can mushrooms, stems and
   pieces
1 chopped green pepper
2 chopped medium onions
1 shake tabasco

2 shakes garlic salt
½ teaspoon oregano
¼ teaspoon thyme
½ cup chopped celery or
   flakes
Parsley, chopped or flakes
Salt and pepper to taste

Put hamburger in large kettle. Add tomatoes (3 No. 2 cans tomato sauce plus 1 can tomato paste may be used here instead of tomatoes). Add remaining ingredients. Seasonings may be increased or decreased according to family's liking. Cook all ingredients together 5 hours. Add water, if needed, to prevent sticking. This makes a delicious meat sauce that can be stored 2 weeks or more in refrigerator. Heat and serve on hot cooked spaghetti or macaroni. Rice may also be used. Can be baked 30 minutes in casserole with grated cheese over top. Serves 12 to 15.

Mrs. Elroy Maule, Onawa
Wife of State Legislator

Spaghetti and Meat Balls

¾ pound ground round steak
¼ pound ground pork
4 eggs
½ cup grated bread crumbs
½ cup grated cheese

2 pods garlic, cut up fine
Little parsley, chopped
Salt and pepper to taste
1 large onion, chopped
2 No. 2½ cans tomatoes,
   strained or 1 No. 5 can juice
1 can tomato sauce

Make meat, eggs, crumbs, cheese, parsley, 1 garlic pod and salt and pepper into small balls. Brown but do not cook through. Brown onion and other garlic pod. Add tomatoes and sauce. Combine with meat balls and put in large stew pan. Cook slowly for 2 to 3 hours. Serve on spaghetti. Cook spaghetti in boiling water. Have water boiling before adding spaghetti. Use long fine spaghetti and do not break but let fall into water as it softens.

Jeannette Platt, Davenport

Chicken Supreme

1 4-pound chicken, cooked
2 cups bread cubes
1 cup cooked rice

1½ teaspoons salt
1 small jar chopped pimento
3 cups liquid, milk and broth

4 beaten eggs

Combine all ingredients and pour into baking dish that has been buttered (9x12-inches). Don't overbake. Canned chicken may be used. Bake 1 hour at 350 degrees. Serves 8 to 10. Serve hot with mushroom sauce.

Sauce:

¼ cup butter
¼ cup flour
1 pint chicken broth

¼ pound mushrooms
¼ cup cream
1 tablespoon parsley

Blend butter and flour in double boiler and add chicken broth. Add mushrooms that have been sauteed in butter (or 1 can mushrooms). Add cream and parsley. Keep hot.

Marguerite Ashlock, Cedar Rapids
WMT Home Fare program

Country Captain

4 cups cooked chicken
1 can cream of mushroom soup
1 cup chicken broth
3 tablespoons chopped onion

1 cup chopped celery
1 can Chinese noodles
½ cup slivered almonds
Crushed potato chips

Cut chicken in chunks. Mix with next 6 ingredients and pour into casserole. Cover top with potato chips the last 10 minutes. Bake 1 hour at 350 degrees. 8 to 10 servings.

Mrs. William B. Anderson, West Branch
Wife of President Emeritus of Herbert Hoover Commission

137

Escalloped Chicken

4 cups cooked chicken

Dressing:

1½ quarts day old bread cut in half inch cubes
¾ cup melted butter
1¼ teaspoons powdered sage

¼ cup cream
¾ teaspoon salt
Few grains pepper
2 tablespoons chopped onion or chives

Gravy:

1 quart broth
4 tablespoons flour
4 tablespoons chicken fat

Mix dressing lightly with fork. Put 1½ inch layer of cooked chicken in flat pan or casserole. Cover with dry dressing. Pour gravy made of broth over top of dressing. Bake in oven until dressing is slightly brown, 35 minutes in 425 degree oven. This is a nice luncheon dish served with a salad, relish plate, rolls, and dessert. Serves 12.

Mrs. LeRoy Getting, Sanborn
Wife of State Senator

Delicious Chicken

Arrange a 2½ to 3 pound cut up frying chicken in a buttered shallow baking dish, large enough so that chicken is in a single layer. Mix together 1 can condensed cream of mushroom soup, 1 cup commercial sour cream and ½ packet dried onion soup mix. Pour mixture over chicken and bake uncovered at 350 degrees for 1 hour, or until chicken is tender.

Edna Hamilton, Tipton

Chicken-Rice

Place 1 cup raw rice in baking pan. Over rice pour 1 can onion soup and 1 can water. Place raw chicken over rice (8 or 9 legs or thighs are nice). Salt to taste. Pour 1 can cream of chicken soup over raw chicken. Bake covered at 350 degrees for 2 hours. Remove lid last ½ hour to brown and crisp chicken.

Margaret Ann Roland, Tipton

138

Oven Chicken Casserole

6 chicken breasts
¾ cup flour
1 teaspoon salt
1 teaspoon paprika
1 teaspoon pepper

1 teaspoon thyme
1 teaspoon garlic salt
1 tablespoon minced onion
2 cans cream of mushroom soup
1 tablespoon dried parsley flakes

Combine flour, paprika, salt, pepper, thyme and garlic salt in paper bag. Shake chicken in it to cover evenly. Lay pieces side by side in shallow bake pan. Sprinkle minced onion and then spread with soup (undiluted). Distribute parsley flakes over all. Bake uncovered at 400 degrees for 25 minutes or until browned. Cover and bake 1 hour at 325 degrees. Uncover and increase heat to 400 degrees to crisp. Serves 6. Instead of 2 cans cream of mushroom soup, you may use 1 can each of cream of mushroom soup and cream of chicken soup.

Gladys McCroskey, Tipton

Huntington Chicken

1 large chicken
2 7-ounce packages macaroni
1 teaspoon salt
1 8-ounce package Philadelphia
cream cheese

1 cup pimentos
1 quart chicken broth
4 tablespoons flour
1 pint cream, (half and half)
2 tablespoons butter

Cook chicken until tender, remove from bones. Cook macaroni. Make a sauce of broth, cream, flour and butter. Add cheese and season to taste. Pour over macaroni, pimento and chicken. Pour into buttered casserole and bake one hour at 350 degrees.

Lula Statts, Tipton

Chicken and Rice Casserole

Mix together in casserole:
1 can cream of chicken soup
1 can cream of celery soup

1 can cream of mushroom soup
¼ pound melted butter
1¼ cups quick rice

On top of this lay several pieces of chicken according to the size and taste of your family. Brush chicken with butter, salt, pepper and paprika. Bake 2½ or 3 hours (depending on amount) at 275 degrees.

Mrs. Russell Willer, Tipton

139

Chicken Casserole

1 can cream of chicken soup
½ cup milk
1 cup diced cooked chicken or a 5-ounce can of boned chicken
½ cup cooked lima beans or peas
1 cup noodles, cooked and drained

Mix all together in greased casserole. Top with potato chips and bake for ½ to ¾ hour at 350 degrees.

Mrs. Bernice K. Briceland, Iowa City

Chicken Loaf

1 chicken stewed and chopped (5 cups)
4 eggs, beaten slightly
2 to 4 cups broth
1 teaspoon salt

2 cups bread crumbs, rolled fine
1 teaspoon salt
¼ teaspoon pepper
2 tablespoons chopped parsley
2 tablespoons onion

Mix together and put buttered crumbs or crushed corn flakes on top. Bake in greased pan, set in pan of water, at 350 degrees for 1 hour or until done. Cut in squares. Serves 12.

Mrs. G. E. Grunewald, Iowa City

Hot Chicken or Turkey Salad

In casserole break 4 slices of bread.

Combine:

2 cups chicken or turkey, diced
1 cup celery
½ cup onion

½ cup salad dressing
¾ teaspoon salt

Spread over bread. Break 4 more slices of bread on top. Beat 3 eggs; add 3 cups milk. Pour over casserole and let stand over night, covered. Bake one hour at 350 degrees. Add one can mushroom soup. Sprinkle grated cheese on top. Bake 15 minutes more. Serves 6 to 8.

Mrs. C. R. Johnson, Shenandoah

Hot Chicken Salad

2 cups diced cooked chicken
1 can cream of chicken soup
¾ cup salad dressing
1 tablespoon lemon juice

3 hard cooked eggs, sliced
1 cup celery, chopped
½ cup chopped nuts, if desired
½ cup minced pimento
2 teaspoons minced onion

Mix all ingredients together Place layer of potato chips on bottom of baking dish and pour mixture over them. Cover with layer of potato chips. Bake 400 degrees for 15 minutes.

Catherine Kleese, Washington

Hot Chicken Salad En Casserole

2 cups diced chicken
2 cups chopped celery
½ cup chopped, blanched
  salted almonds
⅓ cup chopped green pepper
2 tablespoons chopped pimento

2 tablespoons minced onion
½ teaspoon salt
2 tablespoons lemon juice
2 cups crushed potato chips
1 cup mayonnaise
⅓ cup grated cheese

Blend chicken, celery, almonds, green pepper, pimento, onion, salt, lemon juice and mayonnaise. Put alternate layers of chicken mixture and crushed potato chips in buttered 1½ quart casserole. Top with layer of crushed potato chips and grated cheese. Bake in moderate oven 350 degrees for 20 to 30 minutes or until cheese is melted.

Mrs. A. L. Mensing, Lowden
Wife of State Representative

The best food in the world is a dish carefully prepared from good, wholesome ingredients, cooked just enough (not undercooked or overcooked) and attractively presented on a pretty table.

Chicken Grand Marnier

Dust pieces of chicken (breasts, thighs, or any pieces you like) with flour, salt, and pepper. Brown in liquid shortening and butter. Arrange chicken in baking dish. Pour over chicken a mixture of:

1 can frozen orange juice
2 cans water
¾ cup Grand Marnier

Sprinkle a pinch of crumbled rosemary over this.

Saute 1 can mushrooms and 1 tablespoon onion in 2 tablespoons butter and put over chicken. Bake 350 degrees for 1½ hours or until chicken is tender, basting occasionally with the sauce.

Mrs. Anthes Smith, Fort Madison

Turkey Supreme

2 cups cooked cut up turkey
2 cups diced celery
½ cup broken walnut meats
½ cup stuffed olives

1 tablespoon grated onion
2 tablespoons lemon juice
½ teaspoon salt
1 cup mayonnaise

Mix all and put in baking dish. Cover top with:

1 cup crushed potato chips
½ cup grated cheese

Bake 375 degrees for 20 minutes. This is a good way to use left over turkey.

Mrs. R. C. Moore, Dunlap

Let your guests wait for their steak, but never, never let a broiled steak wait for a guest.

For a special treat when broiling steak — place slices of bread or cooked rice in broiler pan under meat. Juices will give excellent flavor. Brown slightly before serving.

Family mealtime, with all its associations, is an American tradition that must not be lost.

Dried Beef Casserole

⅛ cup butter
¼ cup flour
1 pint milk
¼ pound Old English cheese
¼ pound or more noodles

¼ pound dried beef
1 cup celery
¼ medium onion
¼ can pimento
½ green pepper

Make white sauce of first three ingredients and blend in cheese. Cook noodles. Saute chopped celery, onion, green pepper and pimento. Combine all ingredients with white sauce. Cover with buttered crumbs. Bake 1 hour at 350 degrees. 6 to 8 servings.

Gertie Neessen, Tipton

Dried Beef and Potato Scallop

8 medium potatoes, cubed
2 cups dried beef
1½ tablespoons minced green
  pepper

1½ teaspoons minced onion
1 cup grated American cheese
½ teaspoon celery salt
2 cups white sauce

Pull dried beef apart. Combine with other ingredients using ½ the cheese. Pour into casserole and top with rest of cheese. Bake 350 degrees for 1½ hours or more. Serves 6.

White sauce:

3 tablespoons margarine
3 tablespoons flour
2 cups milk

1 teaspoon salt
¼ teaspoon pepper
¼ teaspoon dry mustard

1 tablespoon minced onion

Mrs. F. E. Fuller, Tipton

Gravy or white sauce should be velvet smooth if you blend flour and melted shortening in a heavy saucepan over low heat. Add milk slowly, stirring constantly.

The standard proportions for medium sauce are: 2 tablespoons fat, 2 tablespoons flour and 1 cup milk; for a thin sauce, reduce flour and fat to 1 tablespoon; for a thick sauce, increase flour and fat to ¼ cup each. Many cooks prefer cornstarch to flour for thickening because of its ease in blending with fat or cold liquid. Use only one-half as much cornstarch as flour to obtain the same degree of thickening. One tablespoon quick cooking tapioca equals 1 tablespoon cornstarch.

143

Corned Beef Casserole

2 stalks of celery
½ green pepper
1 can corned beef, cut up
1 tablespoon butter
1 can tomatoes, medium size

1 cup chopped ripe olives
1 can celery soup
1 tablespoon soy sauce
1 cup cooked rice
½ cup grated cheese

Brown celery, green pepper and corned beef in butter. Add tomatoes, olives, soup, soy sauce and rice. Pour into casserole and top with cheese. Bake 1 hour at 350 degrees.

Mrs. Warren Lyons, Le Claire

Corned Beef Casserole

6 ounce package macaroni
12 ounce can corned beef, chopped
¼ pound American cheese

1 can cream of chicken soup
1 cup milk
1 cup chopped onion
¾ cup buttered bread crumbs

Cook macaroni, drain and rinse in cold water. Combine all ingredients except bread crumbs. Put in 2 quart casserole. Top with buttered crumbs. Bake 1 hour at 375 degrees.

Mrs. Alfred Schluntz, Cedar Rapids

Corned Beef and Noodle Casserole

1 package (12 ounces) noodles
1 teaspoon salt
1 can (12 ounces) corned beef

1 can (10½ ounces) cream
of chicken soup
2 tablespoons chopped onion
¼ pound cheese

Cook noodles in salted water until tender. Drain; add other ingredients. Bake in a casserole at 325 degrees for one hour.

Mrs. Don Whitlach, Tipton

Macaroni and Luncheon Meat Loaf

1 cup macaroni, cooked
1 cup top milk
3 eggs, beaten
½ cup butter, melted
½ cup cheese, cut in cubes
1 can luncheon meat, cut up

1 cup bread crumbs
½ teaspoon salt
Little onion
1 can cream of mushroom
soup
½ cup milk

Scald top milk and pour over bread crumbs. Add melted butter, salt, onion, beaten eggs, cheese and meat. Add cooked macaroni.

Pour soup, diluted with milk, over loaf. Bake in flat pan 30 to 40 minutes at 350 degrees.

Mrs. M. C. Conrad, Winthrop

Macaroni and Cheese Squares

1½ cups scalded milk
1 cup soft bread cubes
½ cup melted butter or
margarine
¼ cup chopped pimento

1 tablespoon minced onion
1½ cups American cheese
½ teaspoon salt
⅛ teaspoon pepper
3 beaten eggs

1 cup cooked macaroni

Sauce:

1 can cream of mushroom soup   ¼ cup milk
Chopped parsley

Pour milk over bread cubes. Add butter, pimento, onion, cheese and seasonings and mix well. Add eggs and macaroni. Pour into greased 8x12-inch baking dish. Bake in oven at 325 degrees for 50 minutes. Cut in squares and serve with hot mushroom sauce.

Sprinkle with parsley.

Esther McCroskey, Tipton

Why are homemakers overweight? One reason — instead of using ingenuity in preparing leftovers, some good cooks stuff themselves with what is left and urge others to share in their gluttony.

Meat Loaf

1½ pounds ground beef
1 cup bread crumbs
1 medium onion, chopped
1½ teaspoons salt

½ of a No. 2 can tomato juice
1 egg, beaten
¼ teaspoon pepper

Sauce:

Rest of can of juice
1 cup water
2 tablespoons vinegar

2 tablespoons prepared
mustard
2 tablespoons brown sugar

Pour sauce over meat and bake 1 hour.

Mrs. Eli Stutsman, Washington

Meat Loaf

2 eggs, beaten lightly
⅓ cup catsup
¾ cup warm water

1 package onion soup mix
1½ cups soft bread crumbs
2 pounds ground beef

Mix ingredients well in order given. Bake in loaf pan, 350 degrees for 1 hour. Serves 6 to 8.

Martha Shaffer, Tipton

Meat Loaf

3 pounds hamburger
½ pound sausage
2 eggs, beaten slightly

½ cup crushed corn flakes
1 small onion, chopped fine
2 tablespoons barbecue sauce

2 teaspoons salt

Mix well. Bake 350 degrees for 1½ hours. Serves 10.

Mrs. E. H. Meyer, Burlington

Home dinner parties (Iowa's favorite way to entertain) lean heavily for success on the excellence of meat. The same healthy livestock which assures satisfaction at the table has made meat packing an important industry in Iowa.

Roast Supreme

3 to 4 pound beef roast (chuck or other less tender cut)
1 package dried onion soup
1 can cream of mushroom soup

Brown on both sides, salt, and add the soup. Cover and let simmer (325 degrees) for 2½ to 3 hours in oven or at 200 degrees in electric fry pan.

Mrs. Ray Schnack, Bennett

Pot Roast

3 or 4 pounds arm or blade pot roast
3 teaspoons lard
1 teaspoon salt
¼ teaspoon pepper
½ cup water
6 medium potatoes
6 medium carrots
6 medium onions
1 cup tomato puree
1 small head cabbage

Cut pot roast into 6 servings; cut cabbage into 6 wedges. Brown the pot roast slowly in hot lard, season. Add water, cover and simmer about 3 hours or until tender. When meat has cooked 2½ hours, add potatoes, onions, carrots and tomato puree. Cook 20 minutes and add cabbage. Cook 15 minutes longer or until meat and vegetables are done. Makes 6 servings.

Mrs. Louis Thordsen, Tipton

Veal Paprika

2 pounds veal steak
1 teaspoon salt
¼ teaspoon pepper
Small onion, diced
3 or 4 tablespoons butter
1½ cups vegetable soup
¾ cup cream
1½ teaspoons paprika

Cut veal into 2 inch pieces. Sprinkle with salt and pepper. Saute butter, onion and veal until brown. Add boiling soup. Cover and simmer 1 hour. Add cream and paprika. Do not let boil after adding cream. Serve over noodles.

Mary Michels, Tipton

147

Woodchuck

5 eggs, hard cooked
1 small can pimento
1 small green pepper
½ pound grated American
cheese

1 can mushrooms
⅛ pound butter
1 pint milk
2 tablespoons flour

Make white sauce of butter, milk and flour. Add cheese and then other ingredients. Serve on Chinese noodles or tea rusks.

Mrs. Leonard Hayes, Tipton

Caribbean Eggs

8 hard cooked eggs
½ teaspoon salt
Dash of pepper
1 teaspoon dry mustard
1 cup grated sharp
cheddar cheese

1 tablespoon cream
1 onion, minced
2 tablespoons butter
½ green pepper, thinly
sliced
2 8-ounce cans tomato sauce

Cut eggs in half, remove yolks and mash; add seasonings, half cheese and cream. Mix well and stuff the whites. Cook onion in butter 5 minutes; add green pepper and tomato sauce and heat.

Put in shallow baking dish. Put in eggs and sprinkle with cheese.

Bake 325 degrees for 10 minutes or until well heated. Serves 4.

Auro Lemkau, Tipton

Homemade Noodles

6 cups sifted flour
3 teaspoons salt

6 eggs
12 tablespoons milk

Beat eggs until light colored. Add other ingredients and mix well. For deeper yellow noodles add yellow food coloring. Roll out very thin, let dry and cut.

Lois Hein, Tipton

Stuffed Party Franks

1⅓ cups minute rice
1½ cups water
½ teaspoon salt
12 frankfurters
1 to 2 tablespoons prepared
    mustard

1 can cream of mushroom
    soup
2 tablespoons grated onion
2 tablespoons chopped
    pimento
⅓ cup grated cheddar
    cheese

Cook rice and let stand for 10 minutes. Slit frankfurters lengthwise and spread cut surface with mustard. Place in long shallow baking dish. Combine rice, mushroom soup, onion and pimento. Pile lightly in frankfurters. Sprinkle with grated cheese. Bake in moderate oven, 350 degrees for 30 minutes. Makes 6 servings.

Mrs. Fred Schwengel, Davenport
Wife of U. S. Congressman

Teriyaki

Cut round steak into one inch cubes. Marinate for one hour in the following: ⅓ cup soy sauce and ¼ cup cooking sherry. Place on skewers and grill over charcoal. Serve with hot garlic bread.

Mrs. Henry Geadelmann, Tipton

Chicken in Foil

Use 12 inch squares of heavy foil. Place 1 helping of cooked minute rice on each square. Sprinkle 1 tablespoon dry onion soup over rice. On top place 2 pieces of uncooked chicken and 2 tablespoons undiluted canned milk over chicken. On top of this put 2 more tablespoons of onion soup mix, distributing well. Wrap loosely for expansion, but air-tight. Bake 1½ hours at 350 to 375 degrees.

Ursula Bolton, Tipton

149

Chili

3 pounds hamburger
1 tablespoon fat
1½ teaspoons salt

2 quarts tomato juice
3 cans red beans
Chili powder to suit taste

1 medium sized onion

Brown hamburger and onion in fat. Add other ingredients and simmer. Better the day after made. May be frozen.

Edith Willer Eiler, Tipton

To add elegance to a dinner, try —

Curried Fruit

1 No. 303 can peaches (halves)
1 No. 2 can pineapple slices
1 No. 303 can pear halves

5 maraschino cherries
⅓ cup butter
¾ cup brown sugar, packed

4 teaspoons curry powder

Heat oven to 325 degrees. Drain fruits; dry well on paper towel and arrange in 1½ quart casserole. Melt butter; add brown sugar and curry. Spoon over fruit. Bake 1 hour uncovered. It is important to have the fruit well drained. This may be made the day before and reheated when needed. Serve with meat, especially good with ham.

Mrs. R. S. Hummel, Tipton

Baked Pineapple Casserole

(to serve with meat)

Mix:

1 No. 2½ can crushed pineapple (do not drain)
¼ to ½ pound cheddar cheese, grated

Add:

¾ cup sugar   2 rounded tablespoons flour
                    ½ teaspoon salt

Put in buttered flat casserole, cover with buttered crumbs. Bake at 350 degrees for 30 to 40 minutes.

Mrs. Forest Cobb, Jr., Cedar Rapids

150

Pastries

Oh ! So yummy

Calories —— too!

If you have to diet,

Then —— these are taboo!

Butter Crunch Pie Crust

½ cup butter
¼ cup brown sugar, packed
1 cup sifted enriched flour
½ cup chopped pecans, walnuts or coconut

Heat oven to 400 degrees. Mix butter, brown sugar, flour, and nuts with hands. Spread in oblong pan, 13x9½x2-inches. Bake 15 minutes. Take from oven and stir. Press the hot Butter Crunch against bottom and sides of a 9-inch pie pan.

Fill with favorite cream filling. (Chocolate is excellent). Top with meringue. Bake 15 to 20 minutes at 375 degrees. Serves 8.

Mrs. Keiffer Garton, Tipton

Pie Crust

3 cups flour
1 cup lard (home rendered, preferred)
¾ teaspoon salt

1 egg plus
1 teaspoon vinegar
Plus water to make
½ cup

Blend flour, salt and lard. Slightly beat egg, add vinegar and water to make ½ cup. Add to flour mixture and mix. Roll and use as desired.

This can be handled more than most pastry without becoming tough. It can be frozen in pie pans. Makes 5 crusts.

Rose Wagner, Stanwood

To give pies an expert look:
For a shiny top, brush crust with milk before baking.

For a golden brown glazed top, brush top crust with water; sprinkle evenly with granulated sugar before baking.

For a glazed top, brush top crust lightly, before baking, with beaten egg or egg yolk mixed with a little water.

Grasshopper Pie
(Frozen)

14 chocolate sandwich style cookies
2 tablespoons butter
24 large marshmallows
½ cup milk
4 tablespoons green creme de menthe
2 tablespoons white creme de cacao
1 cup whipping cream

Crush cookies into crumbs. (These are the commercial cookies put together with frosting). Melt butter and blend in. Press mixture into an 8 inch pie pan. Chill and use as a crust.

Melt marshmallows in milk over hot water in double boiler. Let cool. Stir in creme de menthe and creme de cacao. Whip cream and fold in. Pour into pie shell and freeze. Serve frozen. Makes 6 servings.

This is a very refreshing dessert to serve after a heavy meal. It is company fare and can be kept frozen for some time.

Mrs. Adolph Elvers, Elkader
Wife of State Senator

Pineapple Chiffon Pie

1 tablespoon (1 envelope) gelatin
4 tablespoons water
4 large eggs, separated
¾ cup sugar
1 tablespoon flour
1 tablespoon lemon juice
¼ teaspoon salt
¾ cup drained crushed pineapple
¼ cup pineapple juice

Soften gelatin in 2 tablespoons of the water and set aside. Beat egg yolks slightly, add other 2 tablespoons water, half the ¾ cup sugar, the lemon juice, salt, pineapple juice and flour. Mix well and cook in double boiler, stirring constantly until mixture thickens (don't cook any longer). Add the pineapple and let cool while you whip the egg whites stiff, then add the rest of the sugar to egg whites. Fold whites in pineapple mixture and pour into baked crust. Put in refrigerator to chill. Makes 2 8-inch pies.

Mrs. Elmer Cruse, Tipton

153

Nesselrode Chiffon Pie

Soften 1 tablespoon unflavored gelatin in ¼ cup cold water.

Scald in top of double boiler 1 cup milk and 1 cup light cream. Combine 3 slightly beaten egg yolks, ¼ cup sugar, and ½ teaspoon salt.

Stir hot milk mixture into egg mixture. Cook over hot water, stirring constantly, until mixture coats spoon. Remove from heat and stir in gelatin. Cool. Add 1½ teaspoons rum flavoring. Chill until slightly thick; beat until smooth.

Beat ⅓ cup sugar into 3 stiffly beaten egg whites. Stir ¼ of egg whites into cooked mixture. Fold in remaining egg whites and ¼ cup chopped maraschino cherries, rinsed and drained. Pour into cooled, baked ten inch pastry shell. Top with whipped cream and shaved sweet chocolate.

Mrs. Albert Conrad, Tipton

Cherry Pie

(Won National Championship for Mrs. Lush's daughter in 1942)

Filling:

Combine 4 tablespoons cornstarch, ¼ cup cherry juice. Add 1 cup honey and beat slowly until thick. Add 3 cups red tart cherries, well drained. Add 1 tablespoon butter. Set aside.

Crust:

Mix ¼ teaspoon salt with 1½ cups flour. Cut in ½ cup cold lard with short, brisk jerks until mixture resembles meal. Add ice water in small portions until you can pick up dough with well floured hands. Divide dough. Roll half out. Spread on 1 tablespoon extra lard, fold edges in. Reroll until ⅛ inch thick or less. Fit into pie tin. Put all cherries in and all juice the pan will hold. Moisten edges, place top dough on, pinch edges, trimming extra dough.

Top crust should have design. Sprinkle with sugar and butter.

Bake 30 to 40 minutes or until done.

This recipe was broadcast over NBC in New York.

Mrs. J. L. Lush, Ames
Iowa Mother of Year, 1963

Best Ever Apple Pie

Cream apple pie is to our family the best apple pie ever made. Use your own favorite pastry recipe. Peel and slice enough apples to fill crust. Sprinkle apples with ½ teaspoon nutmeg, ½ teaspoon cinnamon and a pinch of salt. Mix together 1 cup sugar, 1 tablespoon flour and ¾ cup sweet thick cream. Pour over apples. Place strips of pie dough over the top. Bake pie in a hot oven at 425 degrees for 10 minutes. Reduce heat to 350 dgrees. Bake until done, from ¾ to 1 hour in all.

Mrs. Felix Derynck, Tipton

Glazed Peach Pie

Prepare and bake 1 pie crust. Slice enough fresh peaches to yield 2½ cups. Sprinkle with 1 tablespoon lemon juice. Add ¼ cup sugar and mix. Set aside for 1 hour.

Drain peaches. Add enough water to juice to make 1 cup. Mix together in a pan ½ cup sugar and 3 tablespoons cornstarch. Cook rapidly, with the juice, until thick and clear. Remove from heat, add ⅛ teaspoon salt and ⅛ teaspoon almond flavoring, also 2 tablespoons butter. Add the peaches. Turn into baked crust and cool. Serve with ice cream or whipped cream. Very good.

Mrs. Rex Berry, Tipton

Crumb Topping for Fruit Pie

Mix until crumbly:

> ¼ cup brown sugar (packed)
> ½ cup flour
> ¼ cup soft butter

Use this mixture in place of top pie crust. Bake at 425 degrees 35 to 45 minutes or until nicely browned.

Mrs. Kenneth Oldham, Tipton

155

Rhubarb Cream Pie

3 cups rhubarb, diced
1½ cups sugar
3 tablespoons flour

½ teaspoon nutmeg
1 tablespoon butter or
  margarine

2 well beaten eggs

Blend sugar, flour, nutmeg and butter. Add eggs and beat until smooth. Pour over rhubarb which has been placed in a 9 inch pie pan, lined with favorite pastry. Top with pastry, cut in fancy shapes. Bake in hot oven, 450 degrees for 10 minutes; decrease heat to 350 degrees and continue baking for about 30 minutes.

Mrs. Harry Gerber, Tipton

Rhubarb Cream Pie

2 tablespoons butter
2 cups rhubarb
1¼ cups sugar
2 tablespoons cornstarch

¼ cup milk or cream
2 egg yolks
Salt
Egg whites for meringue

Melt butter, add rhubarb, and 1 cup sugar. Cook slowly until done.

Mix ¼ cup sugar, cornstarch, egg yolks, milk, and salt. Add to rhubarb and cook until thick; pour into baked pie shell and top with meringue.

This is very good in a butter crust:

1 cup flour
½ cup butter or margarine

1 tablespoon sugar

Mix until crumbly and press in pan. Bake in 350 degree oven until lightly brown.

Mrs. Fred Kleppe, Tipton

The old slogan "Let us eat, drink, and be merry for tomorrow we die" should be changed to read "Let us eat, drink, and be merry so that we may live joyfully today, tomorrow, and for many days."

Pecan Pie

3 eggs
¾ cup brown sugar
¼ teaspoon salt

1 cup light corn syrup
1 cup pecan halves
1 teaspoon vanilla

Plain pastry

Beat eggs, add sugar and salt and mix well; add corn syrup, pecans and vanilla. Line a 9 inch pie pan with pastry. Pour in pecan mixture. Bake in hot oven 425 degrees 8 to 10 minutes, then finish baking in a slow oven 325 degrees, 45 to 50 minutes or until set.

Lenore Sullivan, Ames
from "What to Cook for Company"
Iowa State University Press

New Orleans Pecan Pie

2 tablespoons shortening
1 cup brown sugar
2 tablespoons flour
1 cup light corn syrup

¾ teaspoon salt
1 teaspoon vanilla
3 beaten eggs
1 cup broken pecans

Cream together shortening, sugar, and flour. Add syrup and beat very well. Add eggs, vanilla and salt and again beat very well.

Add pecans. Place in unbaked pie shell, 9 inch, and bake 15 minutes at 400 degrees, then 35 minutes at 325 degrees.

Mrs. Alvin Davidson, Mechanicsville

Buttermilk Pie

Cream together 1 stick margarine, 1½ cups sugar and ¼ cup flour. Add 3 eggs, beaten; ⅔ cup buttermilk, 2 teaspoons vanilla.

Mix well. Put in unbaked pie shell and bake at 350 degrees until set.

Lura Hoon, Tipton

157

Marshmallow Custard Pie

2 cups milk
12 large marshmallows
⅓ cup sugar

3 eggs
¼ teaspoon salt
Nutmeg

Dissolve marshmallows, sugar, and salt in milk over low heat. Beat eggs lightly. Add a small amount of hot milk to the eggs and then add them to the scalding milk mixture. Pour into unbaked crust and sprinkle with nutmeg. Bake for five minutes at 400 degrees, then at 325 degrees until silver knife comes out clean.

Mrs. Vernon Kimberling, Tipton

Angel Food Pie

Cook together about 10 minutes:

4½ tablespoons cornstarch
¾ cup sugar
1½ cups boiling water

Add ⅛ teaspoon salt to 3 egg whites and beat until stiff. Add 3 tablespoons sugar and 1½ teaspoons vanilla, beating until egg whites are creamy. Pour hot cornstarch mixture over egg whites, beating constantly. Cool. Fill a baked pastry shell. Beat ½ cup cream and spread over top of pie. Sprinkle ½ square bitter chocolate, grated, on top.

Mrs. Hermann Onken, Tipton

Strawberry Pie

1 package strawberry gelatin dissolved in ¾ cup hot water. Cool and add:

2 10-ounce boxes frozen strawberries or 4 cups fresh strawberries
2 cups cream, whipped
¾ cup sugar

If fresh strawberries are used add an extra ½ cup of sugar. Pour into a baked pie shell and refrigerate for 3 or 4 hours. This recipe makes 2 large pies and can be prepared the day before serving.

Mrs. Leo Loes, Tipton

Lemon Puff Pie

2 egg whites
4 tablespoons sugar
1 package lemon pie filling
   mix
⅓ cup more sugar

2 cups water
2 egg yolks
2 tablespoons lemon juice
1 teaspoon grated
   lemon rind

1 baked 8" pie shell

Beat egg whites until foamy, then add the 4 tablespoons sugar, a little at a time, beating after each addition until sugar is blended. Continue beating until meringue will stand in peaks. In a saucepan combine pie filling mix, the ⅓ cup sugar and ¼ cup water. Add egg yolks and blend well, then add remaining 1¾ cups water. Cook and stir over medium heat until mixture comes to a full boil and is thickened. This will take about 5 minutes. Remove from heat and stir in lemon juice and rind. Pour half of filling into pie shell. Fold remaining half, while hot, into meringue.

Spread evenly over pie filling in shell. Chill and serve.

This is a very colorful dessert.

Mrs. Raymond T. O'Brien, Davenport

Brandied Mince Pie

⅓ cup finely chopped walnuts
2 cups mincemeat
½ cup orange marmalade

1 cup peeled, diced apples
2 tablespoons brandy
2 tablespoons flour

Mix walnuts into your favorite pie crust. Mix together mincemeat, marmalade, apples and brandy. Sprinkle in the flour and mix well. Bake in 425 degree oven for 35 to 40 minutes.

Mrs. B. C. Bunker, Tipton

Good cooks taste; chronic tasters may become overweight.

Raspberry Dream Pie

Crust:

1 cup biscuit mix
¼ cup soft butter or margarine
3 tablespoons boiling water

Heat oven to 450 degrees. Put all ingredients into 9 inch pie pan; stir until mixed. Pat into shape and flute edge. Bake 8 to 10 minutes. Cool.

Filling:

1 package Junket currant-raspberry Danish dessert
⅔ cup water
1 tablespoon lemon juice
1 small package frozen red raspberries

Cook until berries are melted and filling is thick and clear. Cool.

When cool, pour into pie shell and top with 1 package dessert topping. Top with toasted coconut. Chill about 4 hours before serving.

This pie keeps well in the refrigerator.

Mrs. Richard Hambright, Traer

Strawberry Pie

Spread 5 ounces softened cream cheese in bottom of a nine inch baked pie shell. Crush 1 cup strawberries, measure again and add water to make 1 cup.

Mix 1 cup sugar and 3 tablespoons cornstarch. Add to crushed berries and cook until thickened and clear. Add 1 tablespoon butter and a little red food coloring. Put 4 cups fresh berries in pie (whole or halved) and pour sauce over all. Let cool. Serve with whipped cream.

Shirley Nelson, Washington

Lemon Pie

Make pie crust for 9-inch pie.

½ teaspoon ground nutmeg
1½ cups granulated sugar
3 tablespoons flour
¼ teaspoon salt

⅓ cup soft butter
3 eggs, well beaten
2 or 3 peeled lemons, very
thinly sliced

½ cup cold water

In a bowl, stir sugar with flour, nutmeg, salt, butter, eggs, sliced lemons and cold water. Pour carefully into unbaked pie crust.

Bake for 10 minutes in 400 degree oven. Lower temperature of oven to 350 degrees and bake for another 20 to 25 minutes or until firm.

Mrs. R. S. Hummel, Tipton

For a quick lemon pie with the tartness that you might like, Betty Sturdy, Tipton, suggests:

Substitute ½ cup frozen lemonade, undiluted, for ½ cup of the water in recipe when using lemon flavor jello chiffon pie filling. Use this with butter crunch crust, page 152.

Lime Pie

1 crumb or baked pastry 8 inch pie shell
½ cup concentrated lime juice (if fresh limes are used then add
  1 teaspoon grated rind)
1 15-ounce Borden's Eagle Brand condensed milk
Yolks of 2 eggs

Combine lime juice, rind, and condensed milk, gradually stirring the lime juice into the milk. Add unbeaten egg yolks and stir until well blended. Add 1 drop green vegetable coloring for color. Pour into chilled crumb crust or cooled pastry shell. Top with dessert topping or meringue from the two egg whites. If meringue is used, brown as usual.

Ina Barewald, Tipton

Sour Cream Raisin Pie

1 cup raisins, cooked and
   drained
¾ cup sugar

1 cup dairy sour cream
3 egg yolks
¼ teaspoon salt

¼ teaspoon nutmeg

Mix together, pour into unbaked crust. Bake in 375 degree oven for 10 minutes, reduce heat and bake 30 minutes at 350 degrees.

Beat egg whites, sweeten with 6 tablespoons sugar. Add 1 teaspoon cornstarch to meringue and it will never fall or get watery.

May add ½ teaspoon lemon flavoring to meringue if desired.

Spread over pie; return to oven and brown.

Mrs. Ed Mueller, Grand Mound

Raisin Cream Pie

Mix the following:
1 cup seedless raisins
   (soaked overnight)
1 cup cream

¾ cup sugar
1 tablespoon flour
2 egg yolks

Cook until thick (stirring as it cooks), then allow to boil slowly for 5 minutes. Remove from heat and pour into a baked 9 inch pie shell. Top with meringue made of the 2 egg whites, ¼ cup sugar and pinch of baking powder. Bake 12 to 15 minutes at 325 degrees.

Mrs. Merle Dahn, Tipton

Raisin Pie

Prepare an unbaked pie crust

Cream well 2 cups sugar and ¼ pound margarine

Separate 4 eggs. Beat yolks well and add 1 teaspoon vanilla. Add to creamed mixture. Add 1 cup raisins, 1 cup chopped nuts. Beat egg whites and fold in just before you put in oven. Bake 1 hour in slow oven, 325 degrees.

Fern Raney, Tipton

Pumpkin Pie

1 cup pumpkin	1 teaspoon cinnamon
½ cup sugar	½ teaspoon cloves
¼ cup sorghum	½ teaspoon ginger
2 eggs	¼ teaspoon nutmeg
1 cup milk	½ teaspoon salt

Mix pumpkin, sugar, spices and sorghum. Beat egg whites until stiff; add yolks and beat until mixed. Fold into above mixture. Add milk and mix to blend. Pour into unbaked pastry shell; bake 10 minutes at 400 degrees, decrease to 350 degrees and bake 30 minutes more.

Ruth Nebergall, Tipton

Honey Pumpkin Pie

2 eggs	½ teaspoon salt
1½ cups pumpkin	¼ teaspoon ginger
¾ cup evaporated milk	1 teaspoon cinnamon
¾ cup honey	¼ teaspoon nutmeg
¼ cup orange juice	¼ teaspoon cloves
¼ teaspoon grated orange rind	1 tablespoon boiling water

Beat the eggs slightly, add pumpkin, evaporated milk, honey, orange juice and rind, salt, and the spices which have been dissolved in boiling water. Pour into unbaked 9 inch pie shell and bake at 425 degrees for 15 minutes, then lower heat to 350 degrees and bake until barely firm, about 25 minutes.

Mrs. Don Dallas, Stanwood

Crunchy Cover for Pumpkin Pie

Blend 1 tablespoon soft butter with 3 tablespoons brown sugar.

Add 3 tablespoons coconut and ¼ cup chopped pecans. Sprinkle crumb mixture over pumpkin pie 5 minutes before pie has finished baking.

Marie Miller, Iowa City

163

No Bake Pumpkin Pie

2 cups pumpkin
⅓ cup cornstarch
¾ cup sugar
½ teaspoon salt

1 teaspoon cinnamon
¼ teaspoon ginger
¼ teaspoon nutmeg
¾ cup milk

2 eggs, well beaten

Cook all ingredients except eggs for 20 minutes. Add slowly to beaten eggs, stirring constantly. Cook another four minutes. Beat well. Pour into graham cracker pie crust.

Mrs. W. Conrad, Tipton

Paradise Pie

(A cool dessert for a hot day)

10 inch baked pie shell
2 cups milk
2 tablespoons flour
1 tablespoon cornstarch
⅓ cup sugar

⅛ teaspoon salt
2 egg yolks, slightly beaten
1 teaspoon vanilla
2 tablespoons butter
2 ripe bananas

1 package red jello

Scald milk. Combine next four ingredients; add small amount of scalded milk and mix to smooth paste. Gradually add remaining milk and cook, stirring constantly, until thickened, about 3 minutes. Stir small amount of hot mixture into egg yolks, then gradually add remaining mixture, return filling to sauce pan and continue cooking for 3 minutes. Remove from heat; add butter and vanilla. Cool and pour into pie shell. Be very sure your pie is cold before putting jello on top. Dissolve jello as directed on package; chill until partially set. Peel 2 bananas; slice and place on top of filling. Pour jello over bananas; place in refrigerator until firm. Serve plain or with whipped cream or dessert topping.

Mrs. Ray Buckman, West Liberty

Avoid the pan scouring blues; soak egg and milk scalding pans in cold water.

164

Ambrosia Chocolate Pie

Crust:

1¼ cups graham cracker crumbs
2 tablespoons sugar

½ teaspoon cinnamon
½ cup finely chopped pecans or almonds
⅓ cup soft butter

Combine crumbs, sugar, cinnamon and nuts. Add soft butter and mix well. Press firmly on bottom and sides of 8 inch pie tin. Chill 1 hour before filling.

Filling:

1 package chocolate pie filling
¾ cup sweetened condensed milk (not evaporated milk)
1¼ cups half and half cream

Prepare according to directions on package. Cool. Pour into chilled crust. Cover with sweetened whipped cream. Decorate with chocolate curls. Using a vegetable peeler shave off curls from a piece of sweet chocolate.

Mary Anne Nelson, Cedar Rapids

Chocolate Cheese Pie

Crust:

20 graham crackers, crushed
¼ cup soft butter or margarine
¼ cup white sugar

Filling:

1 cup evaporated milk, frozen to crystals
6 ounces semi-sweet chocolate bits, melted

Beat 3 ounces soft cream cheese and ¼ cup sugar until smooth.

Add milk gradually, continuing to beat, until thick and fluffy.

Beat in chocolate. Pour into pie shell; refrigerate covered, overnight. Garnish with whipped cream and chocolate curls. Makes 6 to 8 servings.

Mrs. George Lemkau, Tipton

165

Choco-Cake Pie

1 unbaked pie shell

Make a sauce as follows:

Melt 1½ squares unsweetened chocolate with ½ cup water and ⅔ cup sugar. Bring to a boil, stirring. Remove from fire and add ¼ cup butter and 1½ teaspoons vanilla. Set aside.

Heat oven to 350 degrees. Make batter of 1 cup sifted flour, ¾ cup sugar, 1 teaspoon baking powder, ½ teaspoon salt. Add ¼ cup shortening (vegetable), ½ cup milk, ½ teaspoon vanilla. Beat 2 minutes. Add 1 egg. Beat 2 minutes. Pour batter into unbaked pastry. Stir the sauce and carefully pour over the batter. Sprinkle top with ½ cup finely chopped nuts. Bake 55 minutes. Garnish with whipped cream. Serves 8.

Mrs. Robert Laake, Davenport

Hershey Bar Pie

1 recipe Butter Crunch Crust:*

Cover bottom of 9 inch pan with crust

Filling: Melt 5 small size Hershey bars (with almonds) with 20 large marshmallows and ½ cup milk. Cool. Fold in 1 cup cream, whipped. Put in crust. Refrigerate for 12 hours before serving.

Mrs. Charles Towle, Davenport

Chocolate Velvet Pie

2 4½-ounce almond Hershey bars. Break up in double boiler.

Add 6 tablespoons water; heat and stir until smooth. When cool, fold in ½ pint cream, whipped. Cover bottom of 9 inch cake pan with butter crunch pastry.* Add filling and let stand at least 6 hours. Serve garnished with shavings of chocolate, a few crumbs reserved from crust, or whipped cream and red cherry.

Betty Sturdy, Tipton

*Butter Crunch Crust Page 152

Jewell Hawk's Coffee Pie

Meringue Shell

2 egg whites
¼ teaspoon salt

½ cup sugar
1 cup ground nut meats

Beat egg whites until stiff but not dry. Mix sugar and salt and add gradually, continuing to beat until mixture is stiff and satiny. Fold in finely ground nuts and spread meringue to line a well-greased 9 inch pie pan, taking care not to cover the rim of the pan. Prick well with fork and bake at 275 degrees 1 hour. Cool.

Coffee Filling

1½ tablespoons instant coffee
½ cup water
½ pound marshmallows

2 slightly beaten egg yolks
½ teaspoon almond extract
1 cup whipping cream

Combine coffee powder, water and marshmallows in top of double boiler. Heat over hot water until marshmallows are melted.

Add marshmallow mixture to slightly beaten egg yolks, gradually stirring it in, then return mixture to double boiler and continue cooking for 1 or 2 minutes, stirring.

Chill until mixture begins to set, then beat smooth at medium speed of mixer. Whip cream until stiff, add almond extract and fold into filling. Pour into cooled meringue shell and chill several hours before serving. Garnish, if desired, with whipped cream and/or chocolate shavings. Pie can be frozen. 8 servings.

Mrs. Jewell Hawk, Grinnell

167

A dinner at home need not be set with the formality of an embassy banquet, but it should be an event to be enjoyed. A child may have traveled only to his first grade class that day, but a traveler returns with some experience. It should never be, "Where did you go?' "Out" "What did you do?" "Nothing."

Notes:

Salads
Salad Dressings

Toss it —— Dress it ——

Or set it to Jell ——

If you make a good salad,

As a cook —— you excel!

Double Bean Salad

1 can (1 pound) tiny green lima beans, drained
1 can (15½ ounces) small whole green beans, drained
½ cup sliced pitted ripe olives   ⅓ cup salad oil
¼ cup finely chopped pimentos   ¼ teaspoon Worcestershire
¼ cup finely chopped onions   sauce
⅔ cup vinegar
¾ cup brown sugar

Combine first five ingredients. Make dressing with remaining ingredients. Marinate vegetables in the dressing for sveral hours in the refrigerator. Serve in lettuce lined salad bowl. Makes 6-8 servings or serves 4 very generously.

(This is a marvelous salad with casserole or beef stroganoff.)

Mrs. John Kyl, Bloomfield
Wife of U.S. Representative

Lively Bean Salad

1 No. 303 can green beans   ½ cup chopped green
1 No. 303 can wax beans   pepper (optional)
1 No. 303 can kidney beans   ⅓ cup thinly sliced onion
                                1 cup celery

Drain vegetables and combine.

Make a dressing of:
⅔ cup vinegar   1 teaspoon salt
¾ cup sugar   ⅓ teaspoon pepper
            ⅓ cup salad oil

Mix well and pour over beans. Let stand overnight.

Duetta Schwitzer, Tipton

If your family likes extra seasoning, try adding 1 teaspoon each of dry mustard, paprika, and celery seed to the above dressing.

24-Hour Cabbage Salad

2 tablespoons unflavored
    gelatin
1½ cups sugar
1 teaspoon salt
1 cup salad oil
2 carrots, shredded

¼ cup cold water
1 cup vinegar
1 teaspoon celery seed
¼ teaspoon pepper
6-8 cups shredded cabbage
8 red radishes

1 small onion, grated

Combine gelatin and cold water and let stand to soften. Heat sugar and vinegar together until sugar is dissolved. Add seasonings and stir in gelatin. Let cool to thickness of cream, then beat in oil. Combine vegetables and toss with enough dressing to moisten. Refrigerate 24 hours. Serves 16.

Evelyn Nebergall, Tipton

Salad and Dressing

Soak 1 tablespoon Knox gelatin in ¼ cup cold water. Heat 1½ cups sugar, 1 cup vinegar, 1 teaspoon celery seed, ½ teaspoon pepper and 1 teaspoon salt. Add gelatin. Cool to the thickness of cream, and add one cup salad oil.

Mix with vegetables, any kind, red cabbage, white cabbage; both are very good; celery, peppers, carrots, onion.

This will keep for days in covered bowl in refrigerator. Use as needed.

Mrs. Fred Voigts, Butler County

Hot Slaw

Put 1 tablespoon butter in bottom of heavy pan, then shred medium size head of cabbage. Add salt, pepper, and ⅓ cup water; cover with lid, cook over low heat about 20 minutes.

Beat one egg in bowl and add

¾ cup sour cream
⅓ cup vinegar
½ cup sugar

Stir well and when cabbage is done pour this dressing over it. Let cook up, then serve.

Mrs. Earl M. J. Escher, Tipton

171

Cornhusker Salad

Break crisp lettuce into small pieces. Add sliced radishes, cucumber, a quartered tomato, julienne-cut green pepper, celery, carrots, green onions and 1 cup ham cut in medium size chunks.

Special Olive Oil Dressing

⅛ cup finely cut chives
   or onion tops
2 cups pure olive oil
1 freshly peeled garlic
   clove
¼ teaspoon salt
⅛ teaspoon dry mustard

Dash pepper
⅛ cup wine vinegar
⅛ cup tarragon vinegar
Juice of 2 large lemons
Dash of sugar, Maggi
   seasoning, and
   Worcestershire sauce

Crush garlic with salt. Mix with dry ingredients. Add vinegar, lemon juice, chives, sugar, Maggi seasoning and Worcestershire sauce. Mix well. Add olive oil, stirring constantly. Makes a little over a pint of dressing. Serve with Cornhusker or any vegetable salad.

LaPerche Peasley, Tipton

Tossed Salad

1 head lettuce, torn into bite
   size pieces
1 onion, sliced in rings
Sliced radishes
1 green pepper, diced

Several stalks celery,
   diced
2 or 3 tomatoes, cut in
   eighths
2 hard cooked eggs

Toss with a small amount of true mayonnaise. Before serving add cut up anchovies and French dressing.

Mrs. C. S. Miller, Tipton

For that special tossed salad:
Add bits of crisp bacon or butter slices of bread, sprinkle with Parmesan or other favorite cheese. Dry and brown slightly in oven (250 degrees). Crumble and sprinkle over salad just before serving.

Potato Salad with Mayonnaise

Boil potatoes in their jackets in a covered saucepan until tender.

Chill for several hours; peel and slice. Marinate them well with French dressing. Make the salad very moist as it will absorb a great deal of liquid. It may be made in advance; in fact it seems to be better the second day.

Chop or slice and add: hard cooked eggs, onions, olives, pickles, celery, cucumbers and capers. Season the salad well with salt, pepper and a few grains of cayenne. After one hour or more add mayonnaise.

Dorothy E. Miller, Tipton

Sauerkraut Salad

1 No. 2 can sauerkraut
⅔ cup sugar
½ cup diced celery
½ cup diced red and green pepper
½ cup diced onion

Drain juice from sauerkraut. Toss with other ingredients, chill and serve. Delicious!

Mrs. Wayne Henry, Tipton

Spring Salad

1 cup grated carrots
1 cup drained crushed pineapple
1 tablespoon lemon juice
1 cup cottage cheese
1 cup marshmallows
½ cup mayonnaise
2 tablespoons sugar

Mix all together. Serve on lettuce.

Mrs. B. C. Bunker, Tipton

Physical fitness and good nutrition go hand in hand.

Cinnamon Applesauce Salad

2 packages lemon gelatin
2 cups boiling water
1 tablespoon lemon juice
2 3-ounce packages cream
   cheese

½ cup red cinnamon candies
2 cups unsweetened
   applesauce
½ cup broken walnuts
¼ cup milk or light cream

2 tablespoons salad dressing

Dissolve gelatin and cinnamon candies in boiling water. Stir in applesauce and lemon juice and chill until partially set. Stir in nuts. Pour into 8x8x2-inch pan. Blend remaining ingredients and spoon over gelatin mixture. Swirl through salad to give marble effect.

Elsie O'Neal, Tipton

Seven-Up Applesauce Salad

Dissolve 1 package raspberry gelatin in 1 cup hot applesauce.

Add juice and grated rind of 1 orange and 1 7-ounce bottle Seven-up. Mold as desired. A beautiful color. Tasty!

Margaret Kuhn, Tipton

Cinnamon Waldorf Salad

1 package cherry gelatin
1½ cups boiling water
¼ cup red cinnamon candies

1 cup pared, chopped
   apples
1 cup celery, diced
½ cup chopped nuts (optional)

Place gelatin in bowl and add 1 cup boiling water. Stir until dissolved. Combine candies and remaining ½ cup boiling water. Stir until dissolved. Add enough water to make 1 cup liquid. Add to dissolved gelatin. Cool until consistency of unbeaten egg white.

Fold in apples, celery and nuts.

Mrs. Charles Thomson, Stanwood

174

Apricot Salad

2 packages gelatin, lemon or
  orange
½ cup sugar
Juice of 3 oranges and 1 lemon

1 cup pineapple
1 cup apricot nectar
  or apricots, cut up
½ cup almonds, blanched
  and slivered

Mix sugar with gelatin. Dissolve in 2 cups hot water. Add remainder of juices plus enough cold water to make 2 cups liquid.

When mixture begins to congeal, add other ingredients.

Margaret Worsham, Tipton

California Special Salad

2 packages lemon gelatin
3¾ cups water
Juice of 1 lemon
1 cup celery, chopped fine

1 No. 2½ can Royal Anne
  cherries, drained and
  pitted
½ cup walnuts, chopped

Dissolve gelatin in 2 cups boiling water. Add 1¾ cups cold water.

Add lemon juice and the cherries and stir well so that the cherries will fill with the gelatin and plump up. Set until partially congealed, then add celery and nuts. This is very good for a jello mold.

Mrs. Kenneth Showalter, Franklin County

Ginger Ale Salad

1 package lime or lemon gelatin
½ cup boiling water
1½ cups ginger ale
¼ cup nuts

1 cup white cherries
½ cup pineapple
¼ cup diced celery
Maraschino cherries, as
  desired

Dissolve gelatin in water. Cool slightly and add other ingredients.
Mold.

Verda Wilson, Tipton

175

Cranberry Salad

1 package lemon gelatin
1½ cups hot water
½ cup crushed pineapple
¼ cup chopped nut meats

1 cup thick cranberry sauce
½ cup diced celery
2 tablespoons lemon juice

Pour water over gelatin and stir until dissolved. Let stand until partially set. Sweeten cranberry sauce to taste. Combine all ingredients. Add gelatin mixture and mix thoroughly. Chill until firm.

Elsie O'Neal, Tipton

Cranberry Salad

Grind one pound cranberries and 3 large red apples, pared, through food chopper. Add 1 cup sugar. Let stand for at least 30 minutes.

Mix in ½ cup walnut meats and a 10-ounce package miniature marshmallows.

Add 1 cup whipped cream. Pour into a 9x9-inch dish or pan. Put in refrigerator. Cut in squares on crisp lettuce leaf. (freezes wonderfully).

Mrs. Harry Dodds, Tipton

5-Cup Salad or Dessert

1 cup mandarin orange
  sections, drained
1 cup pineapple chunks

1 cup dairy sour cream
1 cup quartered marsh-
  mallows, (8 or 10)
1 cup coconut

Combine all ingredients and refrigerate 24 hours. This can be made ahead. (A favorite of men who do not like salad dressing).

Mrs. C. W. Norton, Davenport

176

Jewel Salad

3 envelopes unflavored gelatin
   soaked in 1 pint cold water
   for 5 minutes

2 cups sugar
1½ cups liquid (pineapple
   juice and water)
½ cup vinegar

Boil sugar, water, juice, and vinegar 10 minutes. Add gelatin.

When almost set add No. 2 can pineapple cut in pieces, ½ cup slivered almonds, 1 cup chopped sweet pickles. Mold.

Dorothy Randall, Tipton

Tart Salad

Mix:
    1 package lemon or lime gelatin
    1 cup sugar
    1 teaspoon dry mustard
    ½ teaspoon salt

Add:
    1 pint boiling water (scant)
    ½ cup vinegar

Cool.

Add: 1 cup celery
      1 medium onion,
         chopped fine
      2 cups cabbage

½ cup pimentos
Olives, green peppers, if
   desired

Mrs. Ray Schnack, Bennett

Zesty Salad

Dissolve in 1 cup boiling water:

1 package lemon gelatin   1 package lime gelatin

Stir in:

1 cup mayonnaise
2 teaspoons horseradish
1 large can evaporated milk
½ cup nut meats

1 carton small curd
   cottage cheese
1 No. 2 can crushed
   pineapple, drained

Mold as desired.

Mrs. Raymond Fenstermaker, West Liberty

Cranberry Fluff

Combine, cover and chill over night:

> 2 cups raw cranberries, chopped
> 3 cups tiny marshmallows
> ¾ cup sugar

Add:

> 2 cups diced, unpeeled, tart, red apples
> ½ cup seeded grapes
> ½ cup broken nut meats
> ¼ teaspoon salt

Fold in one cup cream, whipped, and ¼ cup mayonnaise. Chill.
Makes 8 to 10 servings.

Mrs. B. C. Bunker, Tipton

Cranberry Tokay Salad

2 cups fresh cranberries
1 cup Tokay grapes
1 cup pineapple tidbits
1 cup sugar
¼ cup broken walnuts
½ cup cream, whipped

Put cranberries through food chopper, using coarse blade. Stir in sugar and let set over night. Stir, pressing lightly to remove excess juice. Cut grapes in half and remove seeds. Drain pineapple, add grapes, nuts and pineapple to cranberry mixture. Just before serving, fold in whipped cream and garnish with grapes.

Elsie O'Neal, Tipton

Pimento Cheese Salad

1 glass pimento cheese spread
½ cup salad dressing
1 cup whipping cream, whipped
20 large marshmallows (cut up)
9 ounce can crushed pineapple, drained

Mix and let set over night.

Margaret Daugherty, Tipton

Tart Beet Salad

1 package lemon gelatin
2 cups hot water
¼ cup vinegar
2 cups diced cooked beets, drained

¼ cup chopped celery
1 tablespoon prepared horseradish
½ teaspoon salt

Dissolve the gelatin in the hot water. Add the vinegar, and chill until slightly thickened. Add the beets, celery, horseradish and salt. Chill until firm. Unmold, garnish with endive. Serve with mayonnaise or salad dressing.

Especially good with ham or seafood. Makes 4 to 6 servings.

Mrs. Keiffer Garton, Tipton

Tomato Aspic

2 envelopes unflavored gelatin
¼ cup cold water
1¾ cups tomato juice
1 8-ounce can tomato sauce
1 tablespoon lemon juice

1 teaspoon sugar
½ teaspoon seasoned salt
1 tablespoon grated onion
2 tablespoons diced green pepper

½ cup diced celery

Soften gelatin in cold water. Dissolve in hot tomato juice. Add tomato sauce, lemon juice and sugar. When it begins to congeal, add remainder of ingredients. Mold as desired.

Frieda Fields, Tipton

V8 Salad (serves 8)

1¾ cups V8 juice
1 package lemon gelatin
1 tablespoon apple cider vinegar
½ cup cottage cheese

½ cup green pepper, chopped
½ cup chopped celery
3 tablespoons mayonnaise

Heat to boiling, one cup V8 juice and dissolve gelatin in it. Add ¾ cup cold V8 juice, vinegar and mayonnaise. When this begins to congeal, add pepper, celery and cottage cheese. Put in large or small molds.

Mrs. A. W. Kemmann, Tipton

179

Hawaiian Salad

(Especially good with ham)

1 package lime gelatin	⅔ cup crushed pineapple
¾ cup pineapple juice	1 cup diced cucumber
½ teaspoon minced onion	4 tablespoons green pepper

¾ cup mayonnaise

Heat juice and add gelatin. Let stand until partially set then add all but mayonnaise which is folded in last. Chill and serve on lettuce or endive.

Jeannette Platt, Davenport

Cucumber and Cottage Cheese Salad

Grate 1 good sized peeled cucumber and 1 small onion or 2 tablespoons grated onion. Soak in salted ice water for 1 hour.

1 package lemon gelatin	1 cup hot water

1 tablespoon very sweet pickle vinegar

When this begins to set, add ⅓ cup mayonnaise, 1 cup drained cottage cheese and the grated cucumber and onion which has been thoroughly rinsed after removing from the salt water and all moisture drained. Mix well and mold.

Mrs. Pearl DeHart, Ames

Tasty Lime Salad

2 packages lime gelatin	1 tablespoon grated onion
2 cups hot water	1 teaspoon paprika
1 cup cold water	1 cup salad dressing
1 teaspoon vinegar	1 cup chopped green pepper
1 teaspoon salt	1 cup diced celery
1 cup small curd cottage cheese	½ cup grated carrot

Dissolve gelatin in hot water. Add cold water, vinegar, salt, paprika, onion, cheese and dressing. Let stand until it begins to congeal; beat until fluffy. Add remainder of ingredients. Mold in 8x12-inch pan or ring. Serves 12.

Mrs. Leonard Hayes, Tipton

180

Frosted Apricot Salad

2 packages orange gelatin
3½ cups boiling water
16 marshmallows, quartered

1 No. 2½ can apricots, diced
and well drained
1 9-ounce can crushed
pineapple, well drained

Frosting:
¼ cup sugar
1½ tablespoons cornstarch
½ cup pineapple juice

½ cup apricot juice
1 egg, well beaten
1 cup cream, whipped
⅛ teaspoon salt

Dissolve gelatin in boiling water. Add marshmallows, stir until dissolved. Chill until partially thickened. Fold in fruit. Turn into 1 large mold, or individual molds, and chill until firm.

To prepare frosting, mix sugar, cornstarch and salt in heavy pan.

Add fruit juice and egg. Cook, stirring constantly until thick. Chill thoroughly. Fold in cream. Frost salad with mixture.

Mrs. Fred E. Wier, Letts
Wife of State Representative

Pineapple Salad

2 packages lemon gelatin
4 cups hot water
2 cups crushed (drained)
pineapple

1 package miniature
marshmallows
3 sliced bananas
⅓ cup pecans

Chill and set.

Topping:
1 egg, beaten
½ cup sugar
Little salt

2 tablespoons flour
1 cup pineapple juice

Cook until thick. Cool. Add:
1 glass pimento cheese to 1 cup whipped cream.
  3 teaspoons sugar   ¼ teaspoon vanilla

Mix together and spread on top of salad and chill.

Mrs. William Schlueter, Durant

181

Bing Cherry Party Salad

1 No. 2 can crushed pineapple
1 No. 2 can bing cherries
⅓ cup lemon juice
3½ cups water, pineapple
    syrup and cherry syrup

2 packages cherry gelatin
3 tablespoons cream
1 3-ounce package cream
    cheese
½ cup chopped pecans

Dissolve gelatin in 3½ cups boiling juices and water. Divide into 2 equal portions. Chill 1 portion until partially set. Add pineapple and pour into 8x8-inch pan. Chill until firm. Soften cream cheese with cream. Spread over gelatin. Chill until firm. Chill remaining gelatin until slightly set. Add pecans and cherries. Pour over cream cheese mixture and chill. Cut in 9 portions. May garnish with whipped cream or dessert topping mix.

Gladys Bartlett, Tipton

Grape-Cherry Salad

2 8-ounce cans
    spiced grapes
2 packages cherry gelatin
1 No. 2 can pitted bing
    cherries

¼ cup lemon juice
1 cup sliced pitted ripe
    olives
¾ cup broken walnuts or
    pecans

Drain juice from grapes, add water to make two cups of liquid and heat to boiling. Dissolve gelatin in it.

Drain cherries, add lemon juice and enough water to juice to make two cups liquid. Stir into gelatin mixture; chill until slightly set, in flat dish. Add drained fruit, olives and nuts to gelatin mixture. Chill until firm.

Topping:

    Dissolve
        1 package lemon gelatin in
        1 cup boiling water; cool.

    Add
        1 package Philadelphia cream cheese
        1 cup crushed pineapple, strained
        1 cup cream, whipped

Pour over the cherry-grape mixture and chill.

Mrs. Roy Glick, Tipton

Fruit Salad Parfait

1 envelope gelatin
½ cup cold water
1 cup salad dressing
1 8-ounce package
  cream cheese
¼ cup maraschino cherry
  juice
1 cup crushed pineapple,
  drained

1 cup drained coarsely
  chopped canned apricots
¼ cup chopped maraschino
  cherries
1 cup heavy cream, whipped
2 tablespoons confectioner's
  sugar

Soften the gelatin in cold water and dissolve over hot water.

Cool. Gradually add salad dressing to cream cheese, mixing until smooth and well blended. Add cherry juice, sugar and gelatin.

Chill until slightly thickened. Add fruit and fold in whipped cream.

Refrigerate.

Mrs. Robert Hambright, Van Buren County

24-Hour Fruit Salad

1 2½ can pineapple
  (sliced or chunks)
1 egg, beaten
½ cup sugar

1½ tablespoons cornstarch
2 cups marshmallows,
  bits or cut
½ pint whipping cream

Maraschino cherries

Mix egg, juice from pineapple, sugar and cornstarch and boil until it coats the spoon (gets a little thick). Cool. Quarter marshmallows and cut up cherries and pineapple. Whip cream. Mix boiled mixture, whipped cream and other ingredients. Leave in refrigerator over night.

Mrs. Joseph P. Deeney, Waukon

For a distinctive flavor in your salads, try substituting minted pineapple for the plain.

183

Orange Sherbet Salad

1 package orange gelatin   1 cup hot water
                    ½ cup orange juice

Cool. When cool and almost set, whip. Add ½ pint orange sherbet, 1 can mandarin oranges (drained). Put in mold or individual molds.

Fern Raney, Tipton

Reception Salad

1 package lemon or lime gelatin   ⅔ cup walnut meats, cut fine
1 No. 2 can crushed pineapple   ⅛ teaspoon salt
2 small packages cream cheese   ½ pint cream, whipped
1 small can red pimentos or   ½ cup celery, cut fine
1 glass pimento cheese spread

Dissolve gelatin in warm water and the pineapple juice, enough to make one pint of liquid. Let stand until it begins to thicken. Put in remaining ingredients (mash pimento with cream cheese), mix well, and let stand in refrigerator until firm.

Bernice K. Briceland, Iowa City

Pineapple Cottage Cheese Salad

1 package lime gelatin   1 cup cottage cheese
½ pound marshmallows   ½ cup mayonnaise
            1 small can crushed pineapple, drained

Dissolve gelatin in pineapple juice and enough hot water to make 2 cups. Add marshmallows and stir until melted, then stir occasionally until partially set.

When gelatin starts to set, fold in cottage cheese and pineapple and mold as desired. Refrigerate.

Mrs. Forest Cobb, Jr., Cedar Rapids

184

Pineapple Salad

1 package lemon gelatin   20 marshmallows
2 cups hot pineapple juice

Stir until marshmallows are dissolved, let cool then add:

1 cup less 2 tablespoons salad dressing
1 small package cream cheese; crumble
1 cup drained pineapple   ¾ cup evaporated milk, whipped

Fold cheese and pineapple into whipped milk, then into gelatin mixture. Put into flat cake pan; let set firmly. Pour over top, one package cherry gelatin dissolved in two cups hot water.

Mrs. Hans Freese, Tipton

Rainbow Salad

Dissolve 1 package lime gelatin in 1 cup hot water. Set aside to cool.

2 packages cream cheese (3 ounces)
1 small can drained crushed pineapple
1 small cup nut meats   1 cup cream, whipped

Cream cheese with 2 tablespoons mayonnaise, add pineapple, nuts and cream. Mix through lime gelatin. Let set well in refrigerator.

1 package cherry gelatin   1 cup hot water

Set aside to cool.

When lime mixture is cool and set, pour cooled cherry mixture over top and refrigerate. This makes a very pretty holiday salad, but good any time.

Mrs. Robert Stafford, Tipton

Frozen Fruit Salad

2 tablespoons lemon juice
2 tablespoons cream
2 tablespoons sugar
½ cup mayonnaise
2 3-ounce packages cream cheese (cut fine)

Mix well. Add:

1 can pineapple chunks (drained)
½ cup maraschino cherries
12 large marshmallows (cut fine)
½ cup nut meats

Add:

1 cup cream (whipped)
1 can fruit cocktail (drained)

Put in ice cube trays and freeze. Take out of freezer and put in refrigerator at least four hours before serving.

Frances Hegarty, Tipton

Frozen Rhubarb-Cheese Salad

2 cups cottage cheese
2 cups cooked rhubarb sauce, sweetened
1 teaspoon unflavored gelatin
2 tablespoons cold water
1 cup heavy cream

Sieve the cottage cheese. Measure 2 cups of hot cooked rhubarb and sweeten to taste. Soften the gelatin in the cold water and mix with hot rhubarb sauce. Combine with cottage cheese and chill. Whip cream and fold into chilled mixture. Freeze two hours.

Mrs. Dwight Dean, Tipton

Frozen Salad

1 cup crushed pineapple
½ pound marshmallows, cut fine
½ pound almonds, blanched, cut in strips

Let mixture stand over night. Mix yolks of four eggs with four tablespoons sugar. Cook in double boiler and cool. Add above mixture and ½ pint cream, whipped. Tint light green and freeze in molds.

Mrs. Eli Stutsman, Washington

186

24-Hour Salad

1 No. 2 can sliced pineapple 15 large marshmallows
1 No. 2 can Royal Anne cherries ½ cup pecans

Cut pineapple in pieces. Mix drained pineapple, cherries, marshmallows (cut in sixths) and pecans. Set aside.

Dressing:

1 cup pineapple juice 3 tablespoons flour
3 tablespoons sugar 1 egg yolk
Juice of 1 lemon

Mix above ingredients and cook until thick. Let cool. Fold dressing into ½ pint whipping cream (whipped). Add fruit carefully and let stand 24 hours.

Mrs. Jim Shontz, Tipton

Strawberry Salad

2 3-ounce packages strawberry gelatin
1½ cups boiling water
1 10-ounce package frozen strawberries
3 bananas, mashed
1 No. 2 can crushed pineapple, (do not drain)
1 cup cultured sour cream
Nuts if desired

Dissolve gelatin in boiling water. When slightly thickened, add strawberries, bananas, and pineapple. Put one-half of mixture in a 12x8-inch pan. Let harden; spread with sour cream and sprinkle with nuts. Top with remainder of mixture. Let stand until hard.

Donna Gault, Tipton

Only a person who likes everything can safely let himself eat only what he likes.

187

Chicken Salad

1 package lemon gelatin   1 cup boiling water
½ teaspoon salt

Let cool, and when starting to congeal, whip. Add:

1 cup salad dressing   ½ pound pimento cheese,
3 cups finely cut celery   cubed
3 hard cooked eggs, diced   2 cups cooked chicken
1 cup English walnuts   (or shrimp)
½ pint cream, whipped

Place in refrigerator until firm. Makes 8 generous servings.

Margaret Daugherty, Tipton

Pea And Ham Salad

2 cups cooked ham cut in ½-inch cubes
1 package (10 ounces) frozen green peas, cooked
2 hard cooked eggs, diced
¼ cup sweet pickles, chopped
1 tablespoon grated onion
¾ cup mayonnaise
¼ cup green pepper, diced

Combine thoroughly chilled ingredients gently. Cover and return to refrigerator for an hour or two so flavors will blend.

Serve in lettuce cups. (4 servings)

Mrs. Henry Mente, Tipton

Shrimp Gelatin Salad

2 5-ounce cans shrimp   1 can tomato soup
2 small or 1 large package   (undiluted)
cream cheese   2 tablespoons unflavored gelatin
1 cup mayonnaise   softened in ½ cup cold water
1 tablespoon grated onion   ½ cup chopped green pepper
½ cup chopped celery

Method: Boil soup, add softened gelatin, add cheese and beat until creamy. (Mixture will have some lumps). Cool and add remaining ingredients. Pour into mold and chill.

Blanche Roland, Tipton

Honey Dressing

⅔ cup sugar
1 teaspoon dry mustard
1 teaspoon paprika
¼ teaspoon salt
1 teaspoon celery seed

⅓ cup honey
5 tablespoons vinegar
1 tablespoon lemon juice
1 teaspoon grated onion
1 cup salad oil

Mix dry ingredients, add honey, vinegar, lemon juice and grated onion. Pour oil into mixture very slowly, beating constantly.

Elsie Glassbeoner, Washington

Sweet Dressing

3 cups sugar

1½ cups vinegar
3 teaspoons salt

Boil to completely dissolve. Chill. Add one cup pineapple juice. (Good on cabbage or fruit salad)

Agnes Daniels, Cedar Rapids

Sweet Oil Dressing
(for fruit)

1 cup sugar
1 teaspoon salt
4 tablespoons vinegar

1 teaspoon celery seed
1 teaspoon paprika
1 teaspoon dry mustard

Mix above well, add 1 small grated onion or juice. Slowly pour in 1 cup salad oil. Store in cool place.

Mrs. L. E. Aker, Tipton

Anchovy Dressing

1 pint true mayonnaise
2 teaspoons Anchovy paste
2 teaspoons garlic powder

1 8-ounce bottle
French dressing
1 small can Parmesan
cheese

Mix well. Makes one quart.

Ina Barewald, Tipton

189

Blue Cheese Dressing

¼ pound blue cheese
½ cup salad oil
½ teaspoon salt
1 clove garlic, minced, or
garlic salt

¼ cup lemon juice
½ cup dairy sour cream
¼ teaspoon coarse black
pepper

Have cheese at room temperature. Place in mixing bowl. Mash well with fork. Gradually beat in lemon juice. Add oil, sour cream, salt, pepper and garlic, blending well. Cover and chill several hours in refrigerator. Makes about 1⅓ cups.

Edna Hamilton, Tipton

Tossed Salad Dressing

(Roquefort or Garlic)

1 pint true mayonnaise
⅓ cup milk or cream

1 teaspoon Worcestershire
sauce

Season with either:

1 teaspoon garlic powder
or
3 tablespoons grated Roquefort cheese

Maurine Forest, Tipton

Super Salad Dressing

⅔ cup sugar
1 teaspoon salt
1 teaspoon paprika
¼ cup vinegar

⅓ cup catsup
⅓ onion, grated
½ cup salad oil
1 teaspoon celery seed

Juice of ½ lemon

Mix in order listed and chill before using.

Ruth Nebergall, Tipton

190

Cooked Salad Dressing

¾ cup vinegar
¾ cup water
2 cups sugar

1 teaspoon dry mustard
4 tablespoons flour
3 eggs (or yolks)

1½ cups milk

Beat eggs and add sugar and flour. Add small amount of milk.

Add vinegar and water and heat. Gradually add rest of milk and cook until thick.

Mrs. Dean H. Weih, Bennett

Celery Seed Dressing

1 teaspoon dry mustard
1 teaspoon salt
¾ cup sugar
½ cup vinegar

1 teaspoon paprika
1 teaspoon celery seed
1 cup salad oil

Mix dry ingredients. Add vinegar. Boil 1 minute; cool. Add oil slowly, beating constantly. Store in refrigerator; if mixture separates, shake before using.

Mrs. L. W. Mathews, Tipton

Sala Dress For Cabbage

1 cup mayonnaise
1 tablespoon vinegar

½ cup sugar
1 heaping tablespoon
prepared yellow mustard

Mix. Whip 1 6-oz. can evaporated milk and add to the above.

Mrs. Carl Frederick, Tipton

Tossed Salad Dressing

1 cup sugar
1 cup vinegar

1 teaspoon salt
1 teaspoon paprika

Mix in pint jar; shake well; let stand until dissolved. Keeps well.

Excellent used over fresh vegetables.

Mrs. George Blair, Tipton

191

Thousand Island Salad Dressing

1 cup mayonnaise
1 teaspoon paprika
¼ cup chili sauce or catsup
2 teaspoons vinegar
½ cup celery

½ cup stuffed olives
¼ cup walnuts
1 small onion
2 teaspoons minced parsley
3 hard cooked eggs

Mix and chill.

Suzie Schafer, Tipton

Want something different in dressings? Try these three quick ones.

For COLE SLAW:

Two parts commercial sour cream to one part frozen lemonade.
Do not dilute lemonade.

For VEGETABLE SALAD:

1 cup vinegar
¼ cup olive oil
1 cup sugar

2 egg yolks
½ can tomato soup
Garlic salt

Shake or beat well.

For FRUIT SALAD:

One package instant vanilla pudding mix and about 1¼ cups orange juice. Mix as for pudding.

Jeanette Platt, Davenport

To frost grapes for a lovely garnish — Dip small clusters in slightly beaten egg white. Drain off excess. Dip in granulated sugar and dry.

For food most people spend a large part of their income. What a pity if they buy sickness instead of health!

A Miscellany of Traditional Foods

From many countries to our state

Our grandmas brought these dishes;

A foreign food gives meals a lift——

You'll find these just delicious!

Dutch Appel Koek

2 cups hot applesauce
3 tablespoons cocoa
½ cup shortening
2 cups sugar
1½ teaspoons soda
1 tablespoon hot water

1 teaspoon cloves
½ teaspoon nutmeg
½ teaspoon baking powder
3½ cups flour
1 cup raisins
1 teaspoon cinnamon

Cream shortening and sugar. Dissolve soda in hot water and add, along with applesauce, to sugar mixture. Stir in sifted dry ingredients and mix well. Stir in raisins.

Pour batter into oiled 9x13-inch pan and bake at 325 degrees for 40 minutes. Don't frost.

The appel koek (apple cake) is one that is always on hand in a Dutch home. A homey sort of every-day cake, it is a little tough, quite chewy and not very sweet. It is delicious.

Mrs. Adrian Schagen, Pella

Kolaches

(Bohemian)

⅔ cup lard or other shortening
⅓ cup sugar
1 teaspoon salt

1 pint milk
2 eggs
2 cakes of yeast

6 cups flour (approximately)

Scald milk, add shortening, sugar and salt. Cool to lukewarm, add beaten eggs. Dissolve yeast in 2 tablespoons of water. Add to liquid. Add flour, 2 cups at a time, and beat well. Put in greased bowl. Let rise until double in bulk. Mix down on floured board and make into small balls. Put on greased baking sheet. Let rise again. Press center down for filling. Let rise just a little, put desired filling in centers.

Bake in 450 degree oven 10 to 12 minutes or until done.

Helen Furhmeister, Iowa City

Never Fail Kolaches

1 cake yeast
1 cup lukewarm water
½ cup sugar
½ cup shortening

1 egg
1 cup milk
1 teaspoon salt
5 to 6 cups flour

Dissolve yeast in lukewarm water. Heat sugar, shortening, egg, milk and salt in a pan to lukewarm and add this mixture to the yeast mixture. Gradually add flour, beating well after each addition. Let dough rise to double in bulk.

Form into small balls and let rise again. Press the center of each ball and fill with any desired filling. Bake in 400 degree oven for about 10 minutes or until golden brown.

Fillings

POPPY SEED

1 cup poppy seed (ground)
½ cup sugar

1 cup water
Pinch of salt

Combine and cook slowly about 20 to 30 minutes. Then crumble 2 butter cookies and add to thicken. Raisins may also be added.

HICKORY NUT

1 cup chopped hickory nuts
½ cup sugar

1 teaspoon butter or cream
Pinch of salt

1 cup milk

Combine and cook slowly over low heat until thickened. Pecans may be substituted for hickory nuts.

Mrs. John Krob, Tipton

Kolaches Sweet Dough

2 cups milk
½ cup sugar
2 tablespoons salt
2 egg yolks

2 packages dry yeast or
1 large package (soft)
½ cup soft shortening
7 to 7½ cups sifted flour

Heat milk, add softened shortening, yeast, sugar, beaten eggs and salt. Add enough flour to make soft dough. Set in greased pan to rise until double in bulk. Make into small balls, let rise. Push down in center and fill with prunes or apricot filling. Bake in 350 degree oven for 20 to 25 minutes.

Ida Wright, Olin

195

Swedish Rye Bread

1½ cups lukewarm water
¼ cup molasses
⅓ cup sugar
1 tablespoon salt

2 tablespoons lard
2 cakes or packages of yeast
2 cups sifted rye flour
3 to 3½ cups sifted all
    purpose flour

Mix yeast, ¼ cup water and 1 tablespoon sugar. Let stand 5 minutes.

Mix remainder of water, sugar, molasses, salt and fat. Add 1 cup rye flour, yeast mixture, then remainder of rye flour and white flour.

Use enough white flour to make a soft dough but possible to handle. Turn dough on lightly floured board, cover and let rest 10 minutes. Knead until smooth and elastic. Place in greased bowl. Cover with damp cloth and set to rise until double in bulk, about 2 hours. Punch down, and let rise again until not quite double in bulk, about 45 minutes.

Punch down and divide in half. Shape into 2 loaves. Brush top wiith melted shortening, cover and let rise until double in bulk, about 1 hour.

Bake about 35 minutes in 375 degree oven. Cool on rack.

For those who prefer a heavier bread, more rye and less white flour may be used. 1 teaspoon caraway seed or grated rind of one orange may be added.

Olivette Werling, Tipton

Finsk Brodt

2¾ cups flour
2½ sticks butter or margarine

½ cup sugar
1 teaspoon vanilla

Mix sugar and butter well. Stir in flour and vanilla. Roll a small piece of dough at a time in strip about size of a pencil or a little larger, flatten with rolling pin, brush with beaten egg and sprinkle with sugar. Cut in any size you desire.

Bake in 325 to 350 degree oven for 10 to 12 minutes. Watch carefully as they burn easily. Delicious with coffee!

Mrs. Robert Stafford, Tipton

Scandinavian Bread

2 packages granular yeast
½ cup lukewarm water
½ teaspoon sugar
1 pint scalded and cooled milk
1 cup butter or margarine
1 cup sugar
1½ teaspoons salt

2 beaten eggs
½ teaspoon ground cardamon
7 or more cups flour
½ package raisins
1 package candied fruit
1 beaten egg yolk
¼ cup milk

Pour yeast into ½ cup water, adding ½ teaspoon sugar. Stir, let stand 5 minutes. Cream butter, cup of sugar, and salt; add beaten eggs and cardamon. Pour milk into mixing bowl. Add yeast mixture to milk and then add 3 cups flour and beat until smooth.

Add the butter mixture and blend well. Stir in remaining flour, or enough to make a dough that forms a soft ball when being mixed. Beat until smooth. Place in a greased bowl. Cover, let rise in a warm place until doubled in bulk. Mix in the raisins and fruit which have been lightly floured. Let rise again until double in bulk. Place dough on floured board and divide into six portions. Roll each into a roll 10 or 12 inches long. Twist rolls together, loosely, in greased bread pans. Let rise until double in bulk. Bake 50 to 60 minutes in a 350 degree oven. Remove from oven and brush with egg yolk and ¼ cup milk.

Mrs. Camille Seys, Tipton

English Tarts
(Obtained from an English lady)

Beat:

3 eggs

⅛ teaspoon salt

1 cup sugar

Add:

½ cup melted Iowa butter
¾ cup nut meats

1 box seeded raisins (large)
2 teaspoons vanilla

Pour into previously made raw pastry shells (small or large muffin tins). Bake in 325 or 350 degree oven until mixture is set and pastry brown. Makes delightful Christmas gift in a small box.

Ruth Liddy
Wife of Iowa Secretary of Agriculture

197

Blitz Kuchen Cake

½ cup sugar
½ cup butter
Salt (pinch)
4 egg yolks (well beaten)

½ lemon rind (grated)
and juice
1 cup sifted flour
1 teaspoon baking powder

Cream butter and sugar. Add sifted dry ingredients with well beaten egg yolks to which lemon juice and rind have been added.

Pour into two greased 9 inch layer pans. The batter will just cover the bottom of the pans.

Beat 4 egg whites stiff, gradually adding 1 cup of sugar. Spread over each layer and cover with ¼ cup chopped walnuts and 3 tablespoons of cinnamon sugar. Bake in slow oven (325 degrees) for approximately 40 minutes.

Cool and spread custard filling between layers and add a few more nutmeats on the top.

Custard Filling

3 tablespoons flour
⅓ cup sugar
⅛ teaspoon salt

1 cup milk
1 egg (beaten)
½ teaspoon vanilla
1 teaspoon butter

Combine dry ingredients. Add milk and egg. Cook over boiling water, stirring constantly, until thickened. Add vanilla and butter.

Cool. Drop by spoonfuls on cake.

Mrs. Don Safley, Tipton

Mexican Wedding Cookies

1 cup plus 2 tablespoons butter
½ cup powdered sugar

2 cups sifted flour
1 teaspoon vanilla
1 cup slivered almonds

Combine ingredients. Form dough into small balls about the size of a walnut. Sprinkle with sugar. Bake at 350 degrees for 12 to 15 minutes.

Mrs. Frank Miller, Decorah

Danish Cookies

1 cup butter
1 cup white sugar
2 cups flour
1 egg

½ teaspoon vanilla
½ teaspoon almond extract
½ teaspoon cream of tartar
½ teaspoon baking soda

Make into balls. Dip balls first into a little water, then in sugar and flatten with bottom of glass. Bake at 350 degrees for about 15 minutes.

Mrs. Julius Petersen, Davenport

Danish Syrup and Molasses Cookies

1 cup sugar
½ cup molasses

½ cup syrup
½ cup vegetable shortening

Boil the above together until all have melted. Cool until lukewarm.

Put into this mixture 1 teaspoon salt, 1 teaspoon cinnamon, 1 teaspoon cloves, 3 teaspoons cream of tartar, and 2 teaspoons soda in ½ cup boiling water. Add flour to make a fairly stiff dough.

Roll out on a well floured board until quite thin and cut with knife into diamond shapes. Bake at 350 degrees for 15 minutes. Place ½ of a blanched almond in the center of each.

Mrs. Walter Peterson, Waterloo

Danish Christmas Wreath Cookies

1 pound almonds (with skins)
5 egg whites

2 pounds powdered sugar
3 tea rusks

Grind almonds and tea rusks together. Beat egg whites until stiff.

Combine almond mixture, egg whites and powdered sugar.

Using the star design of cookie press, press out cookies. Cut into 4 inch pieces, form a wreath and place on a well greased cookie sheet. Be sure the sheet is well greased and covered with tea rusk crumbs. When baked, remove cookies by picking them up by fingers. The buttered and crumbed sheet can be used again without adding more crumbs. Cool and store in a tight container.

Bake in 275 degree oven for 20 minutes.

Mrs. Walter Peterson, Waterloo

The St. Nickolas Koekjes (Dutch)

2 cups shortening
2½ cups sugar
1 cup sour cream
6 cups flour

2 teaspoons soda
4 teaspoons cinnamon
½ teaspoon cloves
1 teaspoon nutmeg

Cream shortening and sugar and add sour cream alternately with sifted dry ingredients. Form into 2 rolls 12 inches long and 3 inches in diameter. Roll in waxed paper and chill. Slice and bake 10 to 12 minutes at 350 degrees.

These are the famed Santa Claus cookies that usually are pressed into molds to make fancy shapes. I do them the easy way, as refrigerator cookies, to make them every-day cookies despite their name.

Mrs. Adrian Schagen, Pella

Swedish Kringler

Cut together ½ cup butter and 1 cup sifted flour. Mix like pie dough with 1 to 2 tablespoons water. Roll out to 12x9-inches. (Cut 3 strips 12x3 inches). Place on cookie sheet.

Melt over medium heat ½ cup butter and 1 cup water. Add 1 cup flour and ¼ teaspoon salt. Cook over medium heat, stirring constantly until mixture leaves side of pan. Remove from heat and add ½ teaspoon almond extract. Beat in 3 large eggs, one at a time, until glossy. Spread mixture on strips. Bake in 350 degree oven 55 to 65 minutes. Frost while warm.

Frosting for Swedish Kringler

1 tablespoon soft butter
¾ cup powdered sugar

½ teaspoon almond extract
1 to 2 tablespoons cream

Add nuts if desired. Cut on angle.

Mrs. Raymond E. Spencer, Tipton

Yule Kaka (Scandinavian)

½ cup butter
2 cups sugar
3 eggs
1 pint sour cream
1 teaspoon soda dissolved
   in warm water

1 level teaspoon cardamon
   (crushed, must be powdered)
2 teaspoons baking powder
1 cup blanched almonds,
   cut fine
5 cups flour

Mix and let stand overnight. (Add about 3 cups of flour when the mixing starts and then the rest of the flour when first part is well blended).

Bake in well greased, medium sized loaf pans in 325 degree oven for 35 to 40 minutes. Remove from oven and cool on wire rack.

Then cut each loaf into slices about ¾ inch thick and cut these slices in a diagonal fashion. Arrange on baking sheets and re-bake at 275 degrees for about 30 minutes. Store cakes in tight container; they will keep—if you keep your hand out of the cookie container.

Mrs. J. G. Westby, Forest City

Spanish Fudge Cake

1½ cups brown sugar
1 cup sweet milk
1 teaspoon vanilla
2 cups sifted flour

½ cup butter
2 egg yolks and 1 whole egg
1 teaspoon cinnamon
2 teaspoons baking powder

Cream shortening and sugar, add egg yolks and 1 whole egg, also vanilla. Sift cinnamon and baking powder with flour and add alternately with milk. Bake about 30 to 35 minutes in a 9x13-inch pan in 350 degree oven. Remove from oven and whip the 2 egg whites, add 1 cup brown sugar. Mix well, put on cake, and return to oven to brown a little. Leave in pan until served.

Mrs. Charles Harmsen, Tipton

201

Irish Imperial Biscuits

1 cup flour
½ cup butter or margarine

¼ cup sugar
1 teaspoon milk

Cream fat and sugar, add milk and flour. Roll out fairly thin and cut with small cutter. Bake in 300-350 degree oven for 10 or 15 minutes, until slightly browned. Ice with colored icing. Can be used as filled cookies.

This recipe came from Ireland.

Aura Bine, Beaman

Swedish Pancakes

4 eggs, beaten until thick
4 tablespoons sugar,
    added gradually to eggs
4 tablespoons melted butter

2 cups milk
1 cup flour
1 teaspoon salt

Add butter and milk alternately with flour and salt to eggs and sugar. Beat until smooth. Bake on a greased, heated skillet. Pour batter and tilt to spread thin. Cook 1 minute until a delicate brown.

Loosen with spatula and flip. Serve with plain or whipped cream and fresh or frozen strawberries, or just any topping for pancakes including syrup made with 1 cup white sugar, 1 cup brown sugar and 1 cup water, brought to a boil.

Mrs. Washburn W. Steele, Cherokee
Wife of State Representative

Czech Raised Dumplings

1 cup lukewarm milk
½ cake yeast
2 eggs, beaten

1 teaspoon salt
2½ cups flour (approximately)
2 slices of toasted, buttered,
    cubed white bread

Stir all ingredients together and at the very last add the toasted bread cubes. Let mixture rise until double in bulk. Form into balls the size of golf balls. Let rise a short time on a floured board.

Cook for 10 to 12 minutes in boiling water. Serve with roast duck.

Mrs. George Blazek, Cedar Rapids

Mother Marie's Buttered Asparagus
(Amana Recipe)

Melt about 3 tablespoons butter in large size frying pan (iron is best). Add bread cubes (dried) to cover bottom of pan and brown evenly. If butter is absorbed, add more to browned bread cubes and add about 2 cups well drained asparagus that has been cooked until tender. Let this mixture brown slowly. Add salt and pepper to taste.

Clabber 2 to 3 eggs briskly, then pour over browned asparagus-bread mixture. Keep flame low and let egg cook until just done.

Quickly remove from pan and serve.

Sometimes this can be rolled from pan. Sometimes it has to be lifted out in large sections with spatula, depending on quantity of eggs and asparagus used.

Very rich—a meal in itself.

Mrs. Fred Heinze, Marengo

Pennsylvania Dutch Hot Slaw Relish

⅓ cup firmly packed light
   brown sugar
2 teaspoons salt
½ teaspoon celery seed

⅓ cup cider vinegar
¼ cup corn oil
2 tablespoons horseradish
   mustard

1 head (2 pounds) cabbage

In a large heavy skillet, stir together the brown sugar, salt, celery seed, vinegar, oil and mustard. Shred the cabbage. There should be about 8 cups, firmly packed. Add the cabbage to the mixed seasonings in the skillet and toss together. Simmer 15 to 20 minutes, or until the cabbage is as tender as you like.

This goes well with any kind of meat. If you want to serve it sandwich-style with frankfurters in buns, there will be enough of the hot slaw for about 12 franks.

Mrs. Francis Lang, Tipton

203

Mexican Luncheon Dish

Brown slightly and pour off excess fat from 1 pound pork sausage.
Add:

1 cup chopped green pepper
1 cup chopped onion
2 tablespoons sugar

2 cups canned tomatoes
1 can evaporated milk soured
with 2 tablespoons vinegar

(2 cups sour cream may replace the evaporated milk, but it curdles easily while cooking).

1 tablespoon chili powder (generous)
2 cups uncooked elbow macaroni

Cook in large skillet at a low temperature until macaroni is tender, but not mushy. If it thickens too much, add more tomato juice or tomato soup. Watch closely, stir often as this sticks easily.

Mrs. Fred Roland, Tipton

German Meat Dumplings

¼ pound pork sausage
¾ pound beef (grind together)
1 egg, beaten

1 cup bread or cracker
crumbs
1 onion

Salt and pepper to taste

Mix above ingredients together. Make into balls the size of a walnut. Drop in broth and cook until done, approximately 30 minutes.

Ella Dinse, Tipton

Bohemian Iced Tea

3 tablespoons black tea   Chopped rind of 1½ lemons
2 cups boiling water

Cover and let stand 15 minutes. Strain this and add:

2 cups sugar   Juice of 3 lemons
Water to make 1 gallon

Chill.

Mrs. Kenneth Showalter, Franklin County

Dutch Hotspot

8 large potatoes
4 carrots

4 medium sized onions
Salt and pepper to taste

½ cup evaporated milk

Peel potatoes, cut in quarters. Peel and dice carrots and onions.

Cook, covered in salted water until tender. Drain, then shake vegetable over low heat to dry. Mash vegetables, add salt, pepper and hot evaporated milk until light and fluffy.

Put mashed vegetables in individual baking dishes, sprinkle with grated cheese. Put under broiler for a few minutes until the cheese melts.

Mrs. Walter Conrad, Tipton

Indonesian Pork Chops

6 loin pork chops, 1 inch thick
2 tablespoons drippings
1 teaspoon salt
¼ teaspoon pepper
1 can peach halves, drained
¼ cup vinegar
2 tablespoons brown sugar

2 tablespoons onion, minced
¼ cup soy sauce
1 tablespoon dry mustard
1 teaspoon garlic powder
2 green peppers
2 tablespoons cornstarch
¼ cup water

Brown chops and season. Combine peach syrup, vinegar, sugar, onion, soy sauce, mustard and garlic powder and blend. Pour over chops. Cook over low heat for 45 minutes. Add green pepper cut in inch squares and peaches. Cook about 5 minutes.

Arrange chops, peaches and peppers on heated platter. Thicken liquid with cornstarch and pour over meat.

Winifred Miller, Tipton

Egg Foo Yung

¾ cup cooked, cut lean pork   1 cup bean sprouts
  (leftover roast)   ¼ teaspoon salt
¼ cup minced onion (optional)   5 eggs, well beaten

Combine pork, onions; add salt and eggs, beating until thick.

Drop from large spoon into frying pan covered with 1 inch layer of hot fat and fry about 10 minutes, turning to brown on both sides. Serve hot with pork gravy or gravy made from bouillon. 6 servings.

Margaret Kuhn, Tipton

Spiced Tongue
(Swedish)

1 baby beef tongue   2 bay leaves
2 teaspoons salt   3 whole cloves
            1 teaspoon peppercorns

Cover with hot water and simmer tongue 1 hour. Add the above spices and cook until done. May take 2 hours, depending on size of tongue. Remove the skin and let tongue cool in the spiced broth.

Slice. (Very good cold on a platter of assorted meats).

Ruth Liddy
Wife of Iowa Secretary of Agriculture

Swedish Meat Balls

½ cup fine bread crumbs   2 eggs
½ cup milk   2 tablespoons minced onion
½ pound ground beef   3 teaspoons salt
¼ pound ground pork   ¼ teaspoon pepper
¼ pound ground veal   ¼ teaspoon poultry seasoning

Soak crumbs in milk until they are mushy and then add ground meats. Mix well, beat eggs slightly and add with seasonings.

Form into balls the size of a quarter and brown in hot fat. When browned, cook in a 350 degree oven for 15 minutes.

Mrs. Tom Riley, Cedar Rapids
Wife of State Representative

Vegetables

Take time to serve the vegetables

In a variety of ways;

Your family will want seconds!

And be lavish with their praise.

Green Bean Casserole

2 cans French style green beans
1 can cream of mushroom soup
1 can French fried onion rings

Combine beans and soup in buttered casserole. Bake approximately 30 minutes at 350 degrees. Sprinkle onion rings over top and return to oven for another 5 minutes, or until browned.

1 can each of water chestnuts and pimento may be added. Toasted slivered almonds may be substituted for the onion rings. Serves 8.

Darlene Donohue, Tipton

Oriental Green Bean Casserole

½ cup butter
½ cup chopped onion
2 4-ounce cans sliced mushrooms, drained
1 5-ounce can water chestnuts, (drained-sliced)
2 packages frozen French cut green beans, thawed
4 tablespoons butter

⅓ cup flour
1 teaspoon salt
½ teaspoon pepper
½ cup mushroom liquor
1 cup milk
2 cups shredded cheese
2 teaspoons soy sauce
½ teaspoon tabasco sauce
1 can French fried onions

In the half cup butter, saute onion, mushrooms and water chestnuts until tender. Mix in thawed green beans and set aside.

Make cream sauce by melting 4 tablespoons butter and stirring in flour, salt and pepper. Gradually add mushroom liquor and milk, stirring until smooth and thickened.

Add shredded cheese, soy sauce and tabasco. Stir until cheese melts.

Put half of green bean mixture in bottom of large baking dish.

Cover with half of cheese sauce, then second layer of vegetables, and top with remaining cheese sauce.

Bake in moderate oven (350 degrees) for 15 minutes. Remove from oven and sprinkle crumbled French fried onions on top. Return to oven and bake 10 minutes. Makes 8 servings.

Mrs. Harold Johnson, Washington

Beets in Orange Sauce

Combine 1 cup orange juice with ⅓ cup seedless raisins and heat to boiling.

Mix ¾ teaspoon salt, ¼ cup sugar, 2 tablespoons cornstarch.

Add 2 tablespoons beet juice and stir to a paste. Add to orange juice and raisins and cook until clear.

Add 1 tablespoon lemon juice and 1 tablespoon butter and 1 No. 2 can drained beets.

Elsie O'Neal, Tipton

Piquant Beets

½ cup crushed pineapple, with syrup
2 tablespoons vinegar
2 tablespoons sugar

2 cups diced, cooked beets
2 tablespoons butter
Salt and pepper
2 teaspoons cornstarch

Combine pineapple and vinegar, heat to boiling.

Mix sugar and cornstarch. Stir all at once into hot liquid. Cook and stir until mixture is smooth and thickened.

Add beets, butter, salt and pepper. Heat thoroughly over low heat.

Laura Geller, Tipton

Escalloped Broccoli

¼ cup diced onion
6 tablespoons butter
2 tablespoons flour
Salt to taste

¼ cup water
1 8-ounce jar cheese
3 whole eggs
3 packages frozen broccoli

Saute onion in butter, add flour and water; add salt and beaten eggs, cheese, and thawed, uncooked broccoli. Put in buttered 11x15-inch pan. Top with buttered crumbs. Bake at 325 degrees for 30 minutes. Serves 10 to 12.

Mrs. Wayne Miller, Tipton

Vegetable Casserole
Asparagus or Broccoli

1 can frozen creamed shrimp soup

1 small package cream cheese

2 tablespoons milk

Heat all the above together until melted. Put 2 packages cooked asparagus or broccoli in casserole and pour creamed mixture over top.

Put French fried onion rings on top and bake 30 to 35 minutes at 350 degrees.

Mrs. Dave Cline, Tipton

Baked Cabbage

1 small head of cabbage
2 eggs
1 tablespoon butter

3 tablespoons cream
½ teaspoon salt
⅛ teaspoon pepper

Boil cabbage until tender. Drain, cool and chop fine. Beat eggs.

Add melted butter and remaining ingredients. Combine with cabbage and bake in buttered dish 20 to 30 minutes at 350 degrees.

Mrs. Everett Cone, Tipton

Cabbage Chop Suey

4 cups chopped cabbage
1 green pepper, shredded

2 cups chopped celery
1 onion, minced

Melt 6 tablespoons butter, pour over vegetables in skillet or heavy pan. (I use electric skillet). Add 1 teaspoon salt and ⅛ teaspoon pepper if desired. Steam at least 10 minutes.

Mrs. Ray Schnack, Bennett

Cabbage En Casserole

Shave 6 cups of cabbage. Pack in casserole. Mix ¼ cup water, ¼ cup brown sugar and ½ teaspoon salt. Pour over cabbage.

Place 3 strips of bacon on top. Cover and bake 350 degrees for 45 minutes. Remove cover and bake 15 more minutes.

Margaret Kuhn, Tipton

Cabbage Au Gratin

Cut one medium sized head of cabbage in quarters. Cook in boiling water, salted, until tender. Chop moderately and season with pepper and salt, if necessary; add one green pepper or pimento finely chopped.

Cover with 1¼ cups thin white sauce. Add ⅓ cup grated cheese.

Mix well and sprinkle thickly with ¾ cup buttered bread crumbs.

Place in casserole and bake until mixture is heated through and crumbs are browned.

White sauce:

2 cups milk   3 tablespoons butter

3 tablespoons flour

Cook until thick, pour over cabbage.

Blanche Lambach, Tipton

Red Cabbage

2 tablespoons lard or vegetable   1 cup water
   shortening   4 tablespoons vinegar
4 cups shredded red cabbage   6 tablespoons sugar
Salt and pepper

Melt lard, add cabbage, water and sugar, and cook until tender. Then add vinegar and cook a few minutes longer. This may be frozen.

Welcome Reed, Tipton

Buttered Carrots (Oven Cooked)

For 8 servings:

4 cups carrots, diced, sliced   ⅛ teaspoon pepper
   or in strips   4 tablespoons butter or
2 teaspoons sugar   margarine
1 teaspoon salt   2 tablespoons water

Put all together in a buttered, covered casserole and cook in 350 degree oven about 1 hour.

Bernice Onken, Tipton

Carrot Casserole

3 cups cooked, sliced carrots,
drained
1 can cream of celery soup

1 cup grated processed cheese
½ cup dry bread crumbs
1 to 2 tablespoons butter

Combine carrots, soup and cheese in 1 quart casserole. Top with crumbs that have been mixed with butter. Bake 20 to 25 minutes in a 350 degree oven.

Elaine Martens, Tipton

Hungarian Sweet-Sour Carrots

2 bunches fresh carrots
1 teaspoon salt
2 tablespoons butter

½ cup vinegar
¾ cup sugar
1 tablespoon chopped parsley

Wash and scrape carrots. Cut into strips 3 by ½ inches. Place in saucepan, add salt and cover with hot water. Cook until tender.

Drain. Add butter, vinegar and sugar. Cook slowly until transparent. Serve hot. Garnish with chopped parsley. Serves 6 to 8.

Frances Crawford, Tipton

Scalloped Carrots

2 tablespoons flour
2 tablespoons butter
1½ cups milk
6 to 8 cooked carrots
1 teaspoon chopped onion

⅓ cup American grated
cheese
½ teaspoon salt
⅛ teaspoon pepper
½ cup bread crumbs

3 strips of bacon

Make white sauce of butter, flour and milk. Add seasonings and grated cheese. Butter a baking dish and put into it alternate layers of sliced cooked carrots and white sauce. Sprinkle with crumbs, lay strips of bacon across the top and bake in a moderate oven until thoroughly heated and bacon is crisp. Serves 6.

Marguerite Geiger, Tipton

Creamed Celery

4 cups sliced celery; cook until tender but not soft; drain well. Make a white sauce of:

2 cups milk   3 tablespoons butter
                 3 tablespoons flour

Cook until thick, add 1 pound processed cheese; cook until cheese melts and then season. Add celery. Just before serving add 1 cup toasted slivered almonds. Use less cheese if you wish.

Dorothy Randall, Tipton

Eggplant Casserole

Cook eggplant whole in water until tender. Cool, peel and mash, then combine with: 1 cup brown bread broken in small pieces, ½ to 1 cup processed cheese, 1 egg, beaten, salt and pepper to taste.

Pour into greased baking dish and bake in moderate oven 30 to 45 minutes.

Mrs. Sam Hegarty, Tipton

Hominy Au Gratin

Uncovered casserole. Preheated oven 375 degrees. Baking time 25 to 30 minutes.

1 No. 2½ can hominy   2 cups milk
2 tablespoons butter or   1 teaspoon salt
   margarine   ¼ teaspoon pepper
2 tablespoons all-purpose flour ¾ cup cheese, grated
                                 ½ cup buttered bread crumbs

Drain hominy, make a sauce by melting butter, blend in the flour, add milk slowly, stirring constantly until sauce thickens slightly. Remove from heat. Add salt, pepper, and cheese, stirring until cheese has melted. Place hominy and sauce in alternate layers in greased casserole. Top with buttered crumbs. Bake until crumbs are lightly browned. Serves 6.

Buttered crumbs: melt 3 tablespoons butter or margarine in saucepan or skillet over low heat. Add 1 cup crumbs, stir until crumbs are coated.

Laura Geller, Tipton

Baked Lima Beans

2 cups lima beans and juice
1 cup sliced carrots, drained
¼ cup onions
1 cup tomatoes, juice and all

2 tablespoons butter
1 teaspoon salt
1 tablespoon brown sugar
⅛ teaspoon pepper

Put together in greased casserole and bake with cover on for ½ hour, then 15 or 20 minutes without cover in 350 degree oven.

Mrs. Fred Kleppe, Tipton

Baked Limas with Sour Cream

Soak 2 cups dried lima beans over night. Cook with ½ teaspoon salt and ¾ teaspoon mustard until tender. Drain.

Place in a baking dish. Add ½ cup brown sugar, ⅛ teaspoon pepper and mix well. Pour over 1 cup sour cream and enough hot water to cover. Cover and bake 1 hour at 300 degrees. Remove cover, lay bacon strips on top and return to oven to crisp the bacon. Very, very good.

Norma Brendes, Tipton

Lima Bean Casserole

3 packages frozen lima beans
4 bacon slices (diced, fried)
1 medium onion
1¾ cups milk

1 package dry Italian salad
   dressing mix
½ cup processed cheese,
   grated

3 tablespoons flour

Saute onion slices in bacon fat, set aside. Cook beans until done and drain. Into bacon fat stir flour. Blend in milk. Combine beans and white sauce, add Italian salad dressing mix. Put in casserole alternating layers of beans, onion, bacon, cheese, etc. Bake in moderate oven.

Mrs. Wilbert Mente, Wheatland

Vegetables are at their best when their greens, reds, and yellows are preserved. Boiling colors away also boils away many of their food values. Nothing enhances the flavor of cooked vegetables more than butter. For variety — Heat butter until a golden brown to season vegetables. Chopped onion, celery, dill seeds, or lemon juice add a piquant flavor. Experiment and see!

214

Spanish Lima Beans

¾ cup diced bacon
1 cup cooked lima beans
1 cup (or less) diced onions
1 cup tomato puree

½ teaspoon salt
½ teaspoon paprika
   (optional)
2 tablespoons flour

Fry bacon, add onions, cook to an even brown, add tomato, salt and paprika and the flour made into a paste with tomato juice; stir and cook slowly 10 minutes. Add hot, cooked lima beans, put into a hot dish and garnish with finely chopped parsley.

Mrs. Norwin Martens, Tipton

Onions in Bread Sauce

Peel 2 pounds small white onions. Pierce through with ice pick or nail. Boil in salted water until tender.

While they are boiling, heat 1 quart milk, 1¼ teaspoons salt, ⅛ teaspoon pepper, 1 onion in which 8 cloves have been stuck and 2 cups fine dry bread crumbs. Cook in double boiler for 30 minutes, stirring occasionally.

Remove onion and cloves. Drain boiled onions thoroughly, and add to sauce with 2 tablespoons butter.

Turn into casserole, top with 1 cup crumbs that have been lightly browned in butter. Sprinkle with paprika, dot with butter, and place under broiler until top is crisp, watching carefully. May be made up ahead and reheated.

Grace Hutchison, Tipton

French Fried Onion Rings

Peel and slice onions ¼ inch thick, soak in milk until rings separate.

Make batter of 1 cup flour, ½ cup milk and 1 egg.

Drain onion rings, dip in the batter and fry in deep fat at 375 degrees until golden brown.

Mrs. Louis Thordsen, Tipton

215

Potato Casserole

Early in the day or day before, cook potatoes with jackets on.

Cool thoroughly. Peel and grate into a well-buttered casserole.

Salt and pepper to taste. Pour whipping cream over to barely cover. Bake 1 to 1½ hours at 350 degrees. Will get brown and crusty on top.

Note: An easy, but festive way to fix an old stand-by. Make lots, people love these.

Joyce Hamiel, Tipton

Crispy Potato Balls

Cook quantity of potatoes, either white or sweet, sufficient to serve desired number. Mash and season. For sweet potatoes, add 2 tablespoons brown sugar for each 3 cups.

Cool; shape into balls of desired size. Roll in crushed corn flakes.

Heat in 350 degree oven about 45 minutes or until heated through.

This is an excellent way to use left over potatoes or to avoid last minute preparation.

Margaret Kuhn, Tipton

Parmesan Potatoes

Grease well a casserole with a good fitting lid. Use new potatoes, or cut larger old potatoes in half. Melt a stick of margarine or butter. Roll about ½ package of Rice Krispies into fine crumbs.

Dip each raw potato into the melted butter, then into the crumbs, then into parmesan cheese; or sprinkle well with the cheese.

Place in one layer in the casserole. Salt to taste. Any left over butter or crumbs may be sprinkled on the top. Cover tightly and bake for one hour. Cover may be removed last 10 minutes for more browning. These are just wonderful—for a new way to fix the lowly potato. 350 degree oven.

Vern Berry, Tipton

Cookery is not an art but a master art.

216

Party Potatoes

8 or 10 potatoes
1 8-ounce package cream
  cheese
1 cup dairy sour cream
Butter

Paprika
Chives (optional)
Garlic salt or 1 small chopped
  garlic bud

Cook potatoes, drain. Beat sour cream and cream cheese at medium speed until blended. Add hot potatoes gradually, beating constantly until light and fluffy. If too stiff add a little milk. Season to taste with garlic salt, or if garlic bud is used season with plain salt. Add garlic and chives. Spoon potatoes into 2 quart casserole, dot with butter, sprinkle with paprika and brown.

Can be refrigerated several days before using, then just put in 350 degree oven and bake about 1 hour. If not refrigerated, 30 minutes is enough.

Mrs. Wilbur Conrad, Tipton

Scalloped Potatoes

2 cups potatoes
1 teaspoon salt
1 can condensed cream of
  chicken, mushroom, or celery
  soup

½ cup milk
1 tablespoon grated onion
2 tablespoons grated cheese

Cook potatoes with jackets. Peel and measure 2 cups. Combine soup, milk and onion in sauce pan. Heat, stirring occasionally.

Place about ⅓ of the potatoes in greased quart casserole. Add half of the soup mixture. Add half of remaining potatoes and soup, then all of the remaining potatoes and soup. Sprinkle with cheese.

Bake at 375 degrees for 30 minutes. About 6 servings.

Mrs. J. Henry Lucken, LeMars
Wife of State Senator

Vegetables used to come and go with the seasons. With the magic of freezing, canning, and speedy transportation, they are enjoyed the year around. Fresh vegetables, however, are most economical when in season.

Orange Glaze Sweet Potatoes

2 tablespoons butter
½ cup dark brown sugar,
   packed

1 orange, peeled and
   sectioned
3 cups hot, seasoned mashed
   sweet potatoes

Melt butter in skillet, add sugar and cook over very low heat until it bubbles, about 5 minutes. Add orange sections, simmer 10-15 minutes longer, until oranges look shiny and syrup thickens.

Stir occasionally.

Spoon potatoes into warm serving dish and dribble orange mixture over top. Makes 6 to 8 servings.

Grace Hutchison, Tipton

Zucchini Squash Casserole

1 pound ground beef, brown slightly. Set aside in a bowl. In the skillet in which the beef was browned add 2 tablespoons fat and slice 2 small unpeeled zucchini squash. (Slice crosswise about ⅛ inch thick.) Add a small diced onion and cook about 10 minutes or until the squash begins to get tender. Add 2 cups of cooked (or raw peeled) tomatoes. Salt and pepper to taste. Simmer 5 or 10 minutes.

Into a 2 quart casserole put a layer of the squash-tomato mixture.

Over this sprinkle a very thin layer (⅓ cup or little less) of uncooked rice. Add the browned ground beef and a little salt and pepper. On top of this put the remaining squash-tomato mixture.

Bake covered in 350 degree oven for 45 minutes. Uncover and place slices of processed cheese on top and bake about 10 minutes longer, or until the cheese has melted and browned slightly.

Serves 6.

Edith Hass, Tipton

Keep acorn or any halved squash moist, when baking, by placing upside down in a shallow baking pan. Bake at 375 degrees for 45 minutes, or until done. It may be served unseasoned; natural flavor is excellent when cooked this way. If you prefer, turn cut side up and add equal amounts of brown sugar and butter in hollow. Return to oven for 15 minutes.

218

Corn

IOWA —— The corn state

Our banners do declare!

A vegetable, so versatile

Such healthy, hearty fare.

Corn Bread

¼ cup shortening
½ cup sugar
2 eggs
1 cup flour

1 tablespoon baking powder
1 teaspoon salt
1 cup corn meal
1 cup milk

Cream shortening and sugar; add eggs; mix. Sift flour, salt and baking powder together. Blend in corn meal.

Combine dry and liquid ingredients with egg mixture. Bake in 8x8x2-inch pan in 375 degree oven about 30 minutes.

Mrs. J. A. Waddell, Tipton

Crunchy Corn Meal Spoon Bread

2⅔ cups milk
1 cup corn meal
1 teaspoon salt

1½ teaspoons baking powder
1 tablespoon sugar
3 eggs

2 tablespoons butter

Scald 2 cups milk in the top of the double boiler. Moisten corn meal in the ⅔ cup milk. Add to the double boiler and stir until thickened. Blend in butter, salt, sugar, egg yolks and baking powder. Fold in beaten egg whites.

Pour into greased shallow pan about 7x10-inches. Bake in a preheated oven (350 degrees) 45 to 50 minutes until set in the center.

Serve immediately. Good with bacon or Canadian bacon slices.

Mrs. L. E. Aker, Tipton

Cheese Cornbread

1 cup corn meal
1½ cups flour
3 eggs
1½ cups milk

4 tablespoons sugar
½ teaspoon salt
2 tablespoons baking powder
¼ pound grated cheese

¼ pound melted butter

Mix and bake at 425 degrees for 25 minutes, or until brown. (Do not over mix).

Agnes Daniels, Cedar Rapids

220

Buttermilk Corn Bread

1½ cups buttermilk
1 cup sifted flour
1 tablespoon sugar
1 teaspoon salt

½ teaspoon soda
1 cup corn meal
3 teaspoons baking powder
¼ cup melted lard

Beat egg, add buttermilk and lard. Sift dry ingredients and combine with liquids.

Bake in greased 8x8-inch pan, in 425 degree oven for 20 to 25 minutes.

Dorothy Holtz, Muscatine

Company Corn Bread

1 cup all-purpose flour
1 cup corn meal
2½ teaspoons baking powder
¼ teaspoon salt

⅔ cup sugar
1 egg
¼ cup melted butter
1 teaspoon vanilla

¾ cup milk

Combine the sugar, egg, butter, vanilla and milk. Sift together the flour, corn meal, baking powder and salt and add to the first mixture. Stir until smooth.

Grease cornstick irons or pan. (9x9x2-inches). Bake at 475 degrees until golden brown.

Mrs. Oscar Glick, Tipton

Corn Meal Pancakes

1½ cups corn meal
3 tablespoons butter

2 tablespoons sugar
Salt

Pour 1½ cups boiling water over these and let cool.

Add 1 well beaten egg and ¾ cup milk. Then add ¾ cup flour, mixed with 2 teaspoons baking powder.

Mix quickly and fry as you do pancakes.

Note: This recipe was given me by my sister Lina Reichert Perkins and it is the best of its kind that I have found.

Bertha Reichert Penningroth, Cedar Rapids

Double Corn Cakes

1 cup packaged pancake mix
1 cup cornmeal
1 teaspoon baking powder
2 slightly beaten eggs

2 cups cream-style corn
1 cup milk
2 tablespoons salad oil or
melted shortening

Mix dry ingredients. Combine eggs, corn, milk and oil. Add to dry ingredients, stirring just until all is moistened. Drop batter from ¼ cup measure onto hot lightly greased griddle or skillet. Turn once.

Makes 16 4-inch pancakes.

Mrs. B. C. Bunker, Tipton

Corn Meal Yeast Bread

1 cup milk
1 cup yellow corn meal
1½ teaspoons salt
4 tablespoons fat

1 package yeast
¼ cup warm water
1 egg
3½ cups sifted flour

3 tablespoons sugar

Scald milk. Pour over corn meal, salt, fat and sugar. Stir until fat melts and is smooth. Cool to lukewarm. Soften yeast in ¼ cup warm water. Add to corn meal mixture with 1 cup flour and beat well. Add beaten egg and mix thoroughly. Add remainder of flour.

Knead.

Place in greased bowl and let rise until doubled. Punch down and let rise about 10 minutes. Shape into two loaves or into buns.

Let rise until about doubled. Bake at 350 degrees 35 minutes for loaves; 20 minutes for buns.

Fern Raney, Tipton

To make homemaking an art we must get joy from it.

Corn Fritters

1 cup finely chopped corn
8 tablespoons flour
½ teaspoon baking powder

2 egg yolks, well beaten
2 egg whites, well beaten
Salt and pepper to taste

Sift dry ingredients, add to corn, then add beaten egg yolks and then fold in stiffly beaten egg whites. Drop a spoonful of batter in hot fat, 370 degrees, and fry until brown. Serves 4.

Mrs. Earl Elijah, Clarence
Wife of State Senator

Country Style Corn Fritters

1 cup prepared pancake flour
1 egg
1 tablespoon sugar

½ cup cooked corn
3 tablespoons melted
shortening

Mix enough to make batter of desired consistency. Bake on hot griddle or electric skillet. Crisp bacon is excellent garnish.

Mrs. George Blair, Tipton

Yummy Corn Fritters with Honey Butter

1 cup fresh or frozen corn
2 beaten eggs
½ cup flour

¼ teaspoon salt
½ teaspoon baking powder
1 tablespoon sugar

I like to whirl the corn in the blender, to give more corn flavor to the fritters.

Sift dry ingredients. Add eggs and corn. Drop from teaspoon into hot fat, 370 degrees. Fry until light brown. Serve hot with smooth delicious Honey Butter.

Honey Butter:

In blender or beater bowl break ¼ cup butter in small pieces.
Add ½ cup liquid honey warmed by setting jar in warm water.
Blend 3 seconds, or beat about 3 minutes. Makes about 1 cup.
Also wonderful with hot biscuits, waffles, pancakes, or on toast.

Margaret Worsham, Tipton

Baked Corn

1 quart canned corn
4 whole beaten eggs
2 tablespoons green peppers, chopped

2 cups milk
1 onion, cut fine
1 tablespoon salt
Dash of pepper

Beat eggs light, add salt and pepper, add milk. Then mix corn, green peppers and onion. Put in long pan. Add the liquid. Bake for 1 hour at 325 degrees.

Addie Eves, Tipton

Easy Scalloped Corn

Combine one No. 2 can cream style corn and ¾ cup milk. Add 1 cup cracker crumbs and ½ small chopped onion, 3 tablespoons chopped pimento, salt and pepper to taste. Put into a buttered casserole, dot with 2 tablespoons butter.

Bake at 350 degrees for 30 to 40 minutes. (Butter the casserole and combine everything in it. Saves dish washing).

Mrs. Austin Ford, Tipton

Scalloped Corn

¾ cup cracker crumbs
2 tablespoons melted butter
1 can cream style corn
1 cup evaporated milk

1 egg, beaten
1 small onion, minced
¾ teaspoon salt
⅛ teaspoon pepper

Mix ¼ cup crumbs with butter. Combine the rest of the crumbs and remaining ingredients. Pour into casserole and top with buttered crumbs. Bake at 350 degrees about ½ hour.

Josephine Sheets, Tipton

Corn Pudding

2 cups corn, canned
(fresh is better)
2 tablespoons flour
1 tablespoon sugar

3 tablespoons butter, melted
1 teaspoon salt
⅛ teaspoon pepper
2 eggs, slightly beaten

2 cups scalded milk

Blend together in order given. Pour into greased casserole. Bake at 350 degrees until set, about 30 minutes.

Mrs. J. A. Waddell, Tipton

Corn Souffle

3 egg yolks, beaten
1 cup corn
1 tablespoon flour

1 cup milk
Salt to season
3 egg whites, beaten

Mix all together, fold in egg whites. Bake 20 minutes at 325 to 350 degrees in buttered casserole.

Mrs. Henry Scheer, Cedar Rapids

Iowa Corn Pudding

2½ cups cream-style corn
3 eggs, beaten slightly
½ cup cream
1½ cups milk
1 teaspoon salt
1 teaspoon sugar

¼ teaspoon pepper
1 tablespoon minced onion
¼ cup chopped pimento
¼ cup green pepper, chopped
2 tablespoons butter, melted
½ cup crushed corn flakes

Greased casserole dish

Mix all ingredients together except the crushed corn flakes and 1 tablespoon of the butter.

Mix the corn flakes and remaining butter and sprinkle over the top. Bake in a 325 degree oven for about an hour.

LaPerche Peasley, Tipton

225

Corn and Sausage Casserole

2 cups fresh cooked or
   whole kernel canned corn
1½ cups medium white sauce

1 pound bulk pork sausage
1 cup coarse cracker crumbs

Brown one half of the sausage, stirring, about 6 minutes. Pour off drippings. Use 3 tablespoons drippings for white sauce.

Mix cracker crumbs with some of the drippings. Arrange corn, browned sausage, cracker crumbs and white sauce in greased casserole. Top with layer of crumbs.

Make other half pound sausage into 4 patties. Brown, drain and place on top of mixture.

Bake 30 minutes at 350 degrees. Serves 4.

Mrs. A. W. Kemmann, Tipton

Escalloped Corn and Tomatoes

2 cups canned tomatoes
2 cups canned corn
2 green peppers, diced
1 small onion, sliced thin
3 tablespoons butter or
   meat drippings

2 teaspoons salt
Pepper to taste
2 cups bread crumbs or
   cracker crumbs
¼ cup grated cheese

Simmer tomatoes in a skillet to reduce the juice. Add corn, green peppers, onions, salt and pepper. Simmer for another 15 minutes.

Arrange in alternate layers with the crumbs in a buttered casserole. Use ⅓ of butter to each layer of cracker crumbs. Sprinkle cheese on top. Bake in a moderately hot oven (375 degrees) for 30 minutes. Serves 8.

Mrs. Frank Walton, Tipton

Farms are the source of abundant raw materials for Iowa factories. Corn is used in 850 commercial products.

226

Main Dish Corn

2 cups fresh corn (or No. 2
  can cream style)
2 2-ounce cans deviled ham
¼ teaspoon dry mustard

¼ teaspoon salt
Dash of pepper
1 tablespoon butter
½ cup milk (scalded)

3 eggs, separated

Add milk slowly to beaten egg yolks, stirring constantly. Add butter and let melt in mixture. Add ham, corn, and seasoning.

Beat egg whites stiff (not dry), fold them into the corn mixture.

Bake in 1½ quart casserole in a 325 degree oven for 1 hour or until firm. This recipe makes 6 servings.

Ella Dinse, Tipton

Pride of Iowa Casserole

1 pound sausage
3 beaten eggs
1¼ cups milk
2 cans cream-style corn

1½ cups cracker crumbs
3 tablespoons grated onion
1 teaspoon salt
½ teaspoon pepper

Beat eggs, add milk, corn, onion, cracker crumbs and sausage.

Season with salt and pepper. Stir until sausage is well distributed throughout mixture. Add catsup over top after putting in greased loaf pan. Bake 1 hour at 350 degrees. Serve in squares.

Mrs. H. L. Witmer, Tipton

Corn Oysters

2 cups grated fresh corn
2 beaten eggs
½ cup cracker crumbs

½ cup enriched flour
½ teaspoon baking powder
1 teaspoon salt

¼ teaspoon pepper

Grate corn on coarse grater or cut tips from kernels with sharp knife and scrape cobs with dull edge of knife. Add eggs, cracker crumbs and flour sifted with baking powder, salt and pepper.

Drop from tablespoon into 1 inch of salad oil, hot enough to brown bread cube in 40 seconds. Turn once. Makes 1½ dozen oysters.

Mrs. D. G. Reeder, Tipton

Scalloped Corn and Oysters

¼ cup finely chopped celery
1 can frozen condensed oyster
 stew, thawed
1 1-pound can (2 cups)
 cream-style corn
1½ cups medium cracker
 crumbs

1 cup milk
1 slightly beaten egg
¼ teaspoon salt
Dash freshly ground pepper
2 tablespoons butter, melted
½ cup medium cracker
 crumbs

Combine first 8 ingredients. Pour into greased 1½ quart casserole. Mix butter with ½ cup cracker crumbs; sprinkle over top.

Bake in moderate oven (350 degrees) 1 hour or until knife inserted halfway to center comes out clean. Makes 6 servings.

Inez Crock, Tipton

King Style Scalloped Corn

1 can (16 ounces) cream-
 style corn
1 cup crushed cracker crumbs
½ cup chopped celery
¼ cup chopped onion
¼ teaspoon paprika

⅔ cup shredded American
 cheese
1 teaspoon salt
2 eggs, beaten
2 tablespoons butter, melted

1½ cups milk

Combine ingredients; pour into casserole. Bake at 350 degrees 50 to 55 minutes. Serves 8.

Fern Raney, Tipton

Corn Saute

2 cups corn, fresh or frozen
½ stick butter or margarine

½ teaspoon sugar
¼ teaspoon salt

Melt butter in heavy skillet, add the rest of the ingredients. Saute corn until thoroughly heated and the milk is set in kernel.

Garnish with sliced tomatoes, green peppers or parsley.

Mrs. George Blair, Tipton

228

Corn Chowder

1 cup diced potatoes
1 cup boiling water
1½ cups canned corn

3 slices bacon (cut small)
1 medium onion, chopped

Cook potatoes in boiling water 10 to 15 minutes. Fry bacon until some of the fat cooks out. Add onion, cook until onion is soft and bacon is browned. Add to potatoes then add corn. Add 1 cup milk, salt and pepper to taste. Cook 10 minutes. Sprinkle on 2 tablespoons parsley before serving. (If you like a thickened chowder, blend 1 tablespoon flour with some of the liquid before adding milk.)

Mrs. Richard Culbertson, Tipton

Javanese Corn

2 boxes frozen corn (not canned)
3 to 4 tablespoons cream

¼ cup butter

Cover with a can of moist coconut. Put in open oven dish and bake about 10 minutes at 350 degrees.

Put under broiler to brown.

Mary Michels, Tipton

Corny Noodles

½ package noodles
1 can corn
1 can tomato soup
1 cup chopped onion

1 soup can water
½ can ripe olives, sliced
1 pound hamburger

Saute meat and onion lightly. Add salt and pepper. Mix all ingredients in baking dish. Bake 1 hour at 350 degrees.

Leanna Thomas, West Branch

Food selection has engaged the attention of men ever since the first pangs of hunger created the demand for food.

Squaw Corn

1 No. 2 can corn
4 slices bacon

3 eggs
Salt to taste

Fry bacon (cut in small pieces) until crisp. While still warm add corn and beaten eggs. Stir until eggs are done. Serve at once.

Mrs. Henry Scheer, Cedar Rapids

Squaw Corn

½ to 1 cup cubed smoked ham
2 tablespoons fat
1 No. 2 can (2½ cups) cream-
    style corn

2 beaten eggs
Salt and pepper to taste

Brown ham in fat; add corn, seasonings and eggs. Mix. Cook over low heat, stirring constantly until eggs are set. Makes 6 servings.

Mrs. D. G. Reeder, Tipton

Succotash

1 cup young lima beans, cooked
2 cups fresh corn or
1 No. 2 can corn
2 tablespoons butter

½ teaspoon salt
⅛ teaspoon pepper
½ cup light cream or
    half and half cream

Combine ingredients. Bring to boiling; turn heat low and simmer for about 4 minutes to cook corn. Serves 6.

Ella Dinse, Tipton

While Iowa is known as the state where the tall corn grows, it is also the state where industry grows taller with each passing year.

Corn Salad

2 cans whole kernel corn,
  drained
¾ cup diced, unpared
  cucumber
¼ cup diced onion
2 small tomatoes, coarsely
  chopped

¼ cup sour cream
2 tablespoons mayonnaise
1 tablespoon vinegar
½ teaspoon salt
¼ teaspoon dry mustard
¼ teaspoon celery seed

Combine corn, cucumber, onion and tomato. Blend sour cream with mayonnaise and remaining ingredients and add to first mixture, tossing gently just to coat vegetables.

Chill thoroughly and spoon into lettuce cups. Makes 6 to 8 servings.

Blanche Roland, Tipton

Corn Relish

18 ears corn
1 quart chopped cabbage
2 cups diced celery
1 cup chopped green pepper
½ cup chopped red pepper
1⅓ cups chopped onion
2 cups cider vinegar

1½ tablespoons tumeric
½ cup lemon juice
1½ cups sugar
3 tablespoons salt
2 tablespoons celery seed
2 tablespoons mustard seed
¼ tablespoon cayenne pepper

Cut corn from ears and combine with other ingredients. Stir well. Cook 35 minutes. Seal in sterilized jars. Makes 7 pints.

Mrs. Richard Culbertson, Tipton

Corn Cob Jelly
(Made from Iowa Sweet Corn Cobs)

Boil 6 or 8 sweet corn cobs (after corn is cut off) for about 10 minutes in water to cover.

Strain the liquid. Measure 3 cups liquid in the same pan. Add 1 box of Sure Jell and bring to rolling boil. Add 4 cups sugar. Again bring to a boil and boil for 1 minute.

You might add a little yellow fruit color. Pour in glasses, same as any jelly.

Fern Raney, Tipton

Old Fashioned Popcorn Balls

1 cup dark syrup	1 teaspoon vinegar
1 cup brown sugar	2 tablespoons butter
¼ cup water	2 quarts unsalted popcorn

Combine syrup, brown sugar, water and vinegar in saucepan.

Cook over medium heat, stirring constantly, until mixture boils.

Cook to hard ball stage, 265 degrees, or until small amount forms a hard ball when tested in cold water.

Remove from heat; quickly add butter and blend. Pour slowly over popcorn in large bowl; mix well.

Butter hands and form into balls using very little pressure. For pastel colored popcorn balls, add vegetable coloring with the butter and tint the syrup to the desired shade.

Mrs. Carroll I. Redfern, Donnellson

Never Fail Popcorn Balls

½ cup molasses	½ cup sugar
	1 tablespoon butter

Combine molasses, sugar and butter in a saucepan. Stir over low heat until sugar is dissolved.

Cook syrup over moderate heat until syrup, when dropped into cold water, separates into thread which is hard but not brittle (270 degrees). Pour syrup over prepared corn. Shape into balls with lightly buttered hands.

Mrs. Lester Gill, Tipton

Caramel Corn

¾ cup white sugar	¾ cup brown sugar
½ cup sorghum	½ cup water

Cook above ingredients to hard ball stage, 260 degrees. Add ¼ cup butter and ¼ teaspoon soda. Pour over 10 quarts popcorn.

Lynette Nebergall, Tipton

This and That

Bits of this —— and bits of that.
And facts and figures too ——
Complete this book from Iowa,
May it be a joy to you!

Wild Game Cookery

Hunting and fishing areas in Iowa provide recreation as well as a fine source for the unusual in food. Families of hunters and fishermen quite regularly enjoy delicacies unknown to those with less active forms of recreation.

Preparing these foods requires a special "know how" and as adventuresome a spirit in the kitchen as in the outdoors. In some cases the men cook their own catch, and in many cases directions or recipes are available only from friends.

Betty and Frank Sturdy think the secret of good fish is to start with very hot shortening, turn the heat down as soon as the fish is popped into the pan, cover, and fry until it is crusty and brown.

They prefer to use Fluffo, but qualify their recommendation with the statement that perhaps this is because it is yellow.

To prepare eel, skin and clean. Cut crosswise into 2 inch lengths, dip in flour, salt and pepper, and fry in about 1 inch shortening.

Many cooks recommend frying pieces of celery (leaves, too) with fish to remove the "wild or gamey" taste that sometimes accompanies fish caught in northern waters. The celery is discarded when the fish is ready to serve.

Turtle is cut into pieces and dipped in flour, salt and pepper, and browned slowly in vegetable shortening, just like one would prepare chicken. Then mix one can cream of mushroom soup and one can water together and pour over turtle. Simmer slowly about an hour and a half, adding extra water, if necessary. Sometimes potatoes and carrots are added to simmer along with the turtle.

It is interesting to note the different types of meat in a turtle.

When cooking raccoon, the important thing to remember is to remove all fat from the animal and the kernels from all four feet and the neck (six in all). Place raccoon in a roaster on its side.

Cover with strips of bacon. Mix one large bottle catsup (1 pound, 4 ounce size), 1 cup brown sugar, 1 teaspoon cinnamon, 1 teaspoon nutmeg, 4 medium sized onions, chopped, and 3 cups water. Pour this over the meat and bake at 350 degrees, basting with sauce frequently until tender (2-2½ hours for a young raccoon).

Cool and pick meat from bones. Place meat and sauce from roaster in a skillet, cover and cook over low heat until sauce has almost cooked away.

Rabbit and pheasant may be cooked the same way as turtle.

However, rabbit may be boiled. Pick the meat off the bones and use in salad or ground up with hard cooked eggs, pickles and mayonnaise for sandwiches. For an elegant dish, cream the meat, using a white sauce, cream of mushroom soup and wine. Served over hot baking powder biscuits, this is really outstanding!

State Senator Charles Van Eaton from Sioux City recommends this way of cooking fish fillets and calls his recipe GOURMET

FISH.

Select a paper bag, the size suitable for the amount of fish you have. Dump a portion of any good pancake flour into the bag along with ground blanched almonds.

Whip up a couple of eggs, or as many as you need, according to amount of fish. Swab each piece of fish in the egg until it is completely coated. Now, with a fork, drop a piece of fish in the bag, close the top and shake well. If you are using an electric skillet, it should be set at 340 degrees. Use a liberal amount of shortening, about ½ inch deep. Do not place the fish in the skillet until it is hot. Then drop the pieces of fish in the skillet and turn once—not over twice. Shake a limited amount of paprika on each fillet just before you turn it. This will make it golden in color. Salt and pepper to taste. Cooking time for average thickness of fillets is about 3 to 4 minutes.

Quantities for Banquet Service

Community and church dinners are traditional both in rural and urban Iowa. Whether their purpose is that of raising money or for good fellowship, they require some planning and knowledge of food amounts needed. The following "Quantities for Banquet Service" has been helpful and correct for our community. We believe it may be for yours too. Make adjustments if your eating habits vary.

MEATS

Roasts—

Allow ½ pound per person if there is bone or any waste

Allow ⅓ pound per person on cuts such as pork tenderloin or beef round where there is no waste

Ham—

Cured, ½ pound for men, ⅓ pound for women

Boneless, 3 ounces per serving

Canned, ⅓ pound per person; must not be overheated or shrinkage will be too great

Cubed or Minute Steaks—

about 5 servings per pound

Breaded Pork Loin—

about 6 servings per pound

Meat Loaf—

Allow ⅓ pound per person for large serving; 2 parts beef to 1 part pork makes good proportion

POULTRY

Chicken—

Broilers: 1½-2 pounds, allow ½ bird per serving; 2-3 pounds, allow ¼ bird per serving

Fryers: 5-6 pound bird (live weight) serves 6 people

Stewers: 3½-4 pound uncooked chicken will give about 1 pound or 3 cups diced meat

6-7 pound chicken will serve from 10 to 15 people in casserole dish, the variation depending on amount of meat wanted in dish

Turkey—

Dressed for roasting, 1 pound meat and bone, yields ½ pound cooked meat. Allow ¾ pound, dressed weight, per serving.

TUNA FISH

6½-ounce can will serve 4-6 people, depending on what is added to it.

VEGETABLES

Potatoes—

Mashed or escalloped, ⅓ pound per person
Chips, 1 pound yields 20-25 servings, 5 to 8 chips each
Baked Potatoes: Allow 1 pound butter for 30 to 35 people
Allow 1 quart sour cream for 40 people
Allow 1 quart cheese sauce for 32 people, 2 tablespoons per serving

Canned Vegetables—

Corn, peas, beets: No. 2 can, 6 servings; No. 303 can, 5 servings
Whole or Frenched green beans and lima beans: No. 2 can, 5 servings; No. 303 can, 4-5 servings
No. 10 can vegetables, 25 to 30 servings
Carrots: 1 pound yields 2½ cups diced raw, 3⅛ cups shredded, 2 cups diced cooked. Allow ½ cup diced cooked per serving

Frozen Vegetables

2½-pound package, 15 servings
1½-pound package, 9 servings

Butter for Vegetables

Allow 1 tablespoon for No. 2 or 303 can
Allow ¼ cup for No. 10 can
Allow ½ pound (1 cup) for 100 servings

Cream Sauce for Vegetables

Allow ¼ cup per person or 16 to 20 servings per quart

GRAVY

Allow ¼ cup per person or 16 to 20 servings per quart as for cream sauce. Thickening for gravy, use at least ½ cup flour for each quart liquid; when making very large amounts that amount may need to be increased.

SALADS

Gelatin: As a general rule 1 package flavored gelatin will make 6 servings; 12x20-inch pan will cut 40 servings

Bulk Salads: 1 quart, 8 to 10 servings, ½ cup each

Cabbage: 4 pounds, 25 servings. For cream dressing on cabbage slaw, allow 1 quart cream for 100 servings.

Tomatoes: 5 pounds, 25 servings — when served as sliced tomatoes or salad

Lettuce: Head, 1 pound, 12 to 15 edible leaves
—Leaf, 1 pound, 25 leaves

Dressings:

Mayonnaise: 1 quart dressing plus 1 pint cream or 1 14½-oz. can evaporated milk whipped will make 150 small servings or 100 generous servings

French Dressings: 1 cup, 20 servings; 1 quart, 75 servings

RELISHES

For an inexpensive relish plate for 100 people
  1 large bunch celery
  4-5 bunches radishes
  1 dozen carrots
  1½ quarts pickles

Cranberry relish: 3 pounds cranberries, 100 servings

Cranberry sauce: 6 pounds cranberries, 100 servings

Sweet pickles: 1 quart halves, 25 servings

Sweet pickles: No. 10 can (halves), 130 servings

Dills: No. 10 can, 100 servings

BREAD

Rolls—
Allow 2 per person for men; mixed groups or women, allow
1½ per person

Vienna Bread—
1 loaf unsliced, 10 people
1 loaf sliced, 10 to 12 people

Butter—
1 pound, 64-72 pats, depending on cutter
Allow 1½ pats per person

Jelly—
8-ounce glass serves 12 to 15 people

DESSERTS

Package Cakes—
1 package, 12 large servings
2½ packages baked in 12x20-inch pan will serve 36 as cake,
shortcake or upside down cake

Ice Cream—
1 quart, 8 average size servings
1 quart, 12 servings for pie ala mode or small sundaes

Whipping Cream—
1 quart, 60 servings

Toppings (fruit or sauce)—
For ice cream: 1 quart will serve 50, using 1 tablespoon per
serving
For cake: 3 quarts needed for 50 servings, using approximately ¼ cup per serving

COFFEE

Boiled Coffee—
1 pound coffee, 3 gallons water will make 60 servings

Drip Coffee—
48 cup dripolator, 2½ to 3 cups coffee, depending on brand
and strength desired

Percolated—

Follow mark on percolator for water. Amount of coffee will vary
according to brand and strength desired.

100 — 4 to 4½ cups coffee
75 — 3¼ to 3½ cups coffee
60 — 2½ to 2¾ cups coffee
40 — 1¾ cups coffee
30 — 1⅓ cups coffee
24 — 1 to 1⅛ cups coffee

Coffee Cream—

For most groups 1 pint cream will be sufficient for 100 people.
If all women, less will be used. If several pitchers need to be
used more may be needed for filling them.

TEA

1 cup tea leaves, 2 ounces
For large quantity make tea essence using ½ cup tea and 2
quarts freshly boiled water. Steep 3-5 minutes. Add 1 cup
essence to 2 quarts water. This amount will make 40 servings.

PUNCH

1 gallon, 35 3-ounce servings. This is the approximate amount
served in each punch cup.

NUTS

1 pound, 50 servings

MINTS or SMALL CANDIES

1 pound, 40-50 servings

FLAT MINTS

Allow 1½ per person

—Frances Crawford
—Olivette Werling

240

It Helps To Know

Measures and Equivalents—

3 teaspoons — 1 tablespoon
16 tablespoons — 1 cup
2 cups — 1 pint
4 cups — 1 quart
1 pound sugar — 2 cups
1 pound brown sugar — 2⅔ cups
1 pound powdered sugar — 2⅔ cups
1 pound confectioner's sugar — 3½ cups
1 pound flour — 5⅓ cups
1 pound cocoa — 4 cups
1 pound coffee — 5⅓ cups
1 pound shortening — 2 cups
1 stick shortening — ½ cup
1 pound cheese —4 cups grated
½ pound marshmallows — 32 large or 4 cups miniature
1 cup uncooked rice — 2½ to 4 cups cooked, variation due to
    type of rice and method of cooking
1 cup macaroni — 2 cups cooked
1 teaspoon double acting baking powder will leaven 1 cup
    flour
1½ teaspoons tartrate or phosphate baking powder will
    leaven 1 cup flour
½ teaspoon soda plus 1 cup sour milk will leaven 1 cup
    flour
3 tablespoons cocoa plus ½ to 1 tablespoon fat may be sub-
    stituted for 1 square chocolate
Add 1 tablespoon vinegar or lemon juice to 1 cup sweet milk
    and use as sour milk

Sizes and contents of common cans and jars—

can size	weight	cups
8-ounce	8 ounces	1 cup
No. 300	14-16 ounces	1-1¾ cups
No. 303	16-17 ounces	2 cups
No. 2	20 ounces	2½ cups
No. 2½	28 ounces	3½ cups
No. 3	32 ounces	4 cups
No. 5	46 ounces	6 cups
No. 10	96-106 ounces	12-13 cups

Fruit Cake
(Large Recipe)

1½ cups shortening
2 cups sifted sugar
4 cups flour (sifted before measuring)
8 or 9 eggs
¼ cup brandy
2 teaspoons cinnamon
1 teaspoon baking soda
1 teaspoon nutmeg

1 teaspoon cloves
½ cup black coffee
½ cup baking molasses
1½ pounds black walnuts
1½ pounds almonds
7½ pounds candied fruit
    (about 3 pounds pineapple
    and 4½ pounds cherries, both
    red and green)

Sift flour three or four times, then use 1 cup to dredge the candied fruits and nuts. In the balance of 3 cups of flour, sift the spices.

Cream shortening, adding sugar gradually, and beat until very light. Gradually add the eggs which have been beaten thoroughly. Save a little of the egg white to glaze the cakes after they are baked; put on while hot. Slowly add the mixture of molasses, brandy, coffee and soda, adding the soda last. Add the flour slowly to the above mixture. Batter will be medium thin. Pour batter over the candied fruit and nuts and stir well. It will be fairly stiff, not too runny.

Pour batter into greased pound loaf pans or coffee cans. Bake at 275 degrees for 30 minutes, increase temperature to 325 degrees for 20 minutes; finish baking at 350 degrees. Bake for 1¼ hours or until done.

This recipe will make around 14 or 15 pounds. It may be decorated with fruit and nuts, and given as Christmas gifts.

Mearle Dodson
Davenport

Choice
Additions

We've added some extras

In this latest edition

For – To grow and improve

Is an Iowa Tradition.

Friendship Tea

1 pound-2 ounce jar Tang
½ cup Instant Tea
1 package Wyler's lemonade
2 cups sugar
2 teaspoons cinnamon
1 teaspoon whole cloves

Mix well and store in closed container. To serve, dissolve 2 heaping teaspoons in 1 cup hot water.

Mrs. Ray Gammell, Emerson

Dip For Raw Vegetables

1 cup mayonnaise
1 tablespoon minced onion
1 teaspoon horseradish
1 teaspoon curry powder
1 teaspoon garlic salt
1 teaspoon tarragon vinegar

Mix with spoon several hours before serving. Refrigerate. Should there, by chance, be any left over, it will keep a long time in the refrigerator.

Mrs. Howard Green, Cedar Rapids

Fruit Slush

1 No. 5 can pineapple juice   5 cups water
4 cups sugar

Combine and heat until sugar dissolves.

Add:

1 6 ounce can frozen
   lemonade
2 6 ounce cans frozen
   orange juice
5 bananas, mashed

Mix, pour into covered container and freeze at least 24 hours. It never freezes hard.

To serve:

1. Spoon into glasses and fill with 7 Up, or
2. Serve over ice cream, or
3. Add fresh or canned fruits, or
4. Serve "as is" in sherbet glasses

This keeps well in freezer, is refreshing in hot weather, and serves quite a few people.

Mrs. Raymond Spencer, Tipton

244

Adaptable Fudge

Chocolate:

2 cups sugar
¼ pound butter or margarine
½ cup milk
¼ cup white corn syrup
2 tablespoons cocoa
¼ teaspoon salt
½ cup chopped nuts

Combine ingredients in 1½ quart saucepan and, stirring constantly, bring to a boil. Cook to 233 degrees Farenheit or for seven minutes after mixture has reached rolling boil. Remove from heat; add 1 teaspoon vanilla and beat until it begins thickening and loses gloss. Add nuts. Drop by teaspoons onto waxed paper or pour into buttered pan.

White Fudge: Omit chocolate. Candied fruit may be added.

Penuchi: Substitute brown sugar for white sugar and omit chocolate. Cook to 234 degrees.

An excellent fudge, very quick to make and one which never seems to sugar.

Olivette suggests this recipe as one superior to hers on page 82.

Oven Baked Caramel Corn

7½ quarts popped corn, unsalted
2 cups brown sugar
½ cup white corn syrup
1 cup margarine
1 teaspoon salt

Boil sugar, syrup, margarine and salt for 5 minutes (about 245 degrees F.). Remove from stove and add 1 teaspoon soda. Stir and pour immediately over corn. Mix well. Add some peanuts if desired. Put into large roaster or on cookie sheet and bake 1 hour at 200 degrees. Stir every 15 minutes while in oven and several times during cooling.

Store in tight containers and this will stay crisp.

Mrs. Helen Krull, George

Peanut Brittle

3 cups sugar · 2 cups dark corn syrup
1 cup water

Mix ingredients and boil rapidly until mixture reaches 240 degrees Farenheit. Add 4 cups raw Spanish peanuts. Continue cooking until it reaches 280 degrees. After peanuts are added, stir continuously to prevent burning.

Remove from fire and add: 1 teaspoon soda and 1 teaspoon salt.

Stir thoroughly and pour at once onto greased cookie sheets. Spread very thin. As soon as it can be handled, pull as thin as possible with hands. Candy hardens very rapidly, so this step needs to be watched carefully.

Break into pieces of desired size.

Elizabeth Dallas, Tipton

Almond Filling For Coffee Cake

1 cup top milk or evaporated
milk
2 beaten egg yolks
3 tablespoons butter or
margarine

½ cup sugar
1½ tablespoons cornstarch
1 teaspoon salt
1 teaspoon almond
flavoring

Mix sugar, cornstarch and salt with milk. Cook until thick, stirring constantly. Add beaten egg yolks to which small amount of milk was added; cook a minute or two longer. Add butter and almond flavoring. Cool.

Use the above filling as an interesting and delicious variation for Versatile Coffee Cake, page 34.

Mix coffee cake as directed in recipe.

Divide dough, which has been chilled according to directions, into 4 parts; roll each into a circle 12 to 14 inches in diameter. It will seem thin, but can be handled. Transfer to greased 9-inch round cake pan. Brush about ½ tablespoon melted butter over center; spread with cold filling and fold in outer edges. Let rise 2 hours; bake 20 to 25 minutes at 325 degrees. Frost when cold.

Mrs. H. N. Struve, Clinton

246

Toasted Almond Bread

1 cup shortening
1¾ cup sugar (less
   1 tablespoon)
2 eggs
1 cup cultured sour cream

3½ cups sifted flour
1 teaspoon soda
1 teaspoon lemon juice
1 cup sliced almonds
¼ teaspoon salt

Cream shortening, add sugar and mix well. Add eggs and mix. Add dry ingredients, which have been sifted together, alternately with sour cream and lemon juice. Add almonds.

Bake in two waxed paper lined 5x9 inch loaf pans at 350 degrees for about an hour or until cake tester comes clean.

Cool completely. Slice. Place slices on cookie sheet and toast in 350 degree oven for ten minutes on each side.

If top is crusty so slicing without crumbling is difficult, wrap loaf in damp cloth or paper towel until crust softens.

Darlene Donohue, Tipton

Convenient Overnight Coffee Cake

Sift together:

2 cups sifted flour
1 cup sugar

½ teaspoon salt
½ teaspoon cinnamon

1 teaspoon soda

Mix with ½ cup brown sugar

Cut in 2/3 cup shortening

Add 1 cup sour milk and 2 beaten eggs which have been mixed together. Mix well.

Pour ½ of batter into 9x12 pan. Sprinkle ½ of topping over batter, pour remaining batter into pan. Sprinkle rest of topping over this. Refrigerate until time to bake — may be kept up to 24 hours. Bake at 350 degrees for 20-30 minutes.

Topping: Mix together:

½ cup brown sugar
½ cup chopped nuts

½ teaspoon cinnamon
½ teaspoon nutmeg

Mrs. Richard Hass, Cedar Rapids

247

Sour Cream Coffee Cake

1½ sticks margarine
1½ cups sugar
2 eggs
1 cup cultured sour cream

2 cups sifted **cake** flour
1 teaspoon baking powder
¼ teaspoon salt
½ teaspoon vanilla

Sift flour, baking powder and salt together. Cream margarine and sugar, add eggs and beat with mixer until fluffy and light. Add sour cream and vanilla and blend well. Fold in dry ingredients mixing until well blended. Pour into a 9x13" greased and floured pan, sprinkle with topping and bake about 45 minutes or until done. (Test with toothpick). This may also be baked in 2 round aluminum foil pans, 7½"x1¼".

Topping:

4 tablespoons brown sugar
2 teaspoons instant cocoa mix
¾ cup chocolate chips

1 teaspoon cinnamon
1 cup chopped nuts

This cake freezes well. Before serving, heat in 200 degree oven for about 30 minutes.

Mrs. Howard Hamilton, Tipton

Steak Bread

Dissolve 1 package dried yeast and ½ teaspoon sugar in ¼ cup lukewarm water. Allow this to stand about 5 minutes before adding to following dough mixture.

Pour 2 cups boiling water over:

2 tablespoons shortening
1 tablespoon salt

2 tablespoons sugar

Cool to lukewarm and add:

2 cups flour — beat well

Add yeast mixture and about 4 cups flour.

Turn onto floured pastry cloth; allow to rest 5 minutes. Knead.

Let rise in greased bowl until double in bulk. Punch down and divide into 2 loaves. Let rest 10 minutes. Shape each into a loaf about 15 inches long. Place on greased baking sheet. Let rise to double. Slash diagonally every 2 inches, ⅛ inch deep. Bake for 15 minutes at 375 degrees. Remove from oven and brush top with egg yolk mixed with 1 tablespoon water. Sprinkle with Sesame Seed. Bake 15 or 20 minutes longer.

A simple bread to make, with an excellent flavor.

Mrs. Darrel Dircks, Clarence

Date Treasure Loaf

Sift into large bowl:

1 cup sifted flour	½ teaspoon baking powder
1 cup white sugar	½ teaspoon salt

Add whole:

1½ pounds (about 3 cups) pitted dates
1   8-ounce jar Marischino cherries, drained
2   cups walnut halves.

Stir into flour mixture until well coated.

Beat 4 eggs well; pour over fruit mixture and blend well.

Line greased loaf pan (5½x7½x2¾″) with greased heavy brown paper. Spoon in batter. Bake at 325 degrees 1¾ to 2 hours. Remove from pan; let mellow 24 hours before slicing. Keeps well in air tight container.

A new fruit cake that you'll enjoy making at holiday time. It's excellent!

Betty Huber, Tipton

Walnut Glory Cake

¾ cup sifted flour
2 teaspoons cinnamon
1 teaspoon salt
    9 eggs, separated (or enough to make 1¼ cups whites)

1½ cups sugar
2 teaspoons vanilla
2 cups chopped walnuts

Sift flour with cinnamon and salt. Set aside. Beat egg whites until soft mounds form and gradually add ¾ cup sugar. Continue beating until very stiff, straight peaks form. **Do not underbeat.**

Combine egg yolks, ¾ cup sugar and vanilla in small bowl. Beat until thick and lemon colored. Fold in dry ingredients. Fold batter gently but thoroughly into egg whites using rubber spatula. Fold in walnuts. Turn into ungreased 10" tube pan.

Bake at 350 degrees for 55-65 minutes. Invert immediately. Cool completely before removing from pan. Frost with vanilla glaze, whipped cream or sprinkle with confectioners sugar.

Beverly Reid, Tipton

Apple Cake

4 cups apples, peeled and
    diced or shredded
2 cups sugar
2 eggs, beaten

2 cups sifted flour
2 teaspoons soda
3 teaspoons cinnamon
1 teaspoon salt

Cover apples with sugar and let stand ½ to 1 hour or until juice has been drawn out. Add beaten eggs and dry ingredients which have been sifted together. Mix well and bake in floured 9x18" deep-sided pan at 350 degrees for 45 minutes. While baking make topping.

Topping:
Combine 1 cup each of brown and white sugar, 6 tablespoons flour and 2 cups water. Boil slowly until thick. Remove from heat and add ½ cup butter or margarine and 1 teaspoon vanilla. Pour over cake as soon as it is baked and cover with foil until time to serve.

Mrs. Dale Vogt, Atkins

One half cup nuts may be added to either cake or topping.

Rhubarb Pizza

1 cup sifted flour   2 tablespoons shortening
1 teaspoon baking powder   ¼ teaspoon salt
1 egg

Cut shortening into dry ingredients. Add slightly beaten egg and pat into 9x13" pan.

Cut rhubarb into pieces to make 3 cups. Scatter onto crust. Over this sprinkle 1 cup sugar and 1 package strawberry gelatin.

Mix together ½ cup flour and ⅓ cup margarine. Sprinkle on top. Bake at 375 degrees for 30 to 40 minutes. Serve **warm** with cream or ice cream.

Pretty — different — delicious.

Mrs. Rex Berry, Tipton

"3 Of A Kind Ice Cream"

3 oranges   7   cups milk
3 bananas   2   cups cream
3 lemons   1½ cups sugar
1 envelope plain gelatin   ¼ cup cold water
½ teaspoon salt

Mash bananas, squeeze juice from lemons and oranges; pour over bananas immediately. Add sugar and mix. Soften gelatin in ¼ cup cold water and dissolve in 1 cup hot milk. Combine with juices. Add remainder of milk, cream, and salt. Mix well and freeze in ice cream freezer. Makes 1 gallon.

Mrs. Charles Driscoll, Mechanicsville

Lime Sherbet

Dissolve 1 package lime gelatin in 1 cup boiling water. Add juice and grated rind of 2 lemons. Add 1 cup sugar. Cool.

Add 1 quart milk gradually.

Pour into 2 ice cube trays and freeze at low temperature for 1 hour. Remove from trays, beat and complete freezing.

Other flavors of gelatin may be used and fruits added.

Mrs. H. L. Witmer, Tipton

Vanilla Ice Cream

(To be frozen in ice cream freezer)

1 cup sugar	1 quart milk
⅓ cup flour	2 eggs
	1/8 teaspoon salt

Mix sugar, flour and salt; add to milk (reserve small amount to add to beaten eggs) and cook slowly until slightly thick. Stir to avoid lumping. Add beaten eggs to which small amount of milk was added. Cook 2 or 3 minutes longer.

Cool well.   Add:

1 quart cream	2 teaspoons vanilla - or more
1 cup sugar	

Pour into freezer can (1 gallon size); add milk to about 2 inches from top of can.

Freeze slowly according to directions with freezer.

Mrs. Harold Hass, Tipton

Red Oak Grove Presbyterian Church served this ice cream for many years at its social each summer. People came from many miles to enjoy it.

Lorren Voss was persuaded to enter Cedar county's cook-out contest only after his family and sponsor agreed that should he win locally, he would have their permission to enter the state contest. And should he win there, he could enter the national contest.

His wife and two small boys were his testers, tasters and inspiration. The boys reminded him again and again of the story where the little engine kept repeating, "I think I can. I think I can."

When he was crowned 1969 National Pork Cook-Out King, they were the first to say, "We knew you could. We knew you could."

Following is the recipe with which Lorren won the national title.

Lorren's Hobo Ribs

Select meaty, country-style spareribs* (2½ lbs. serves 4). Remove chine bone or have your meat man do this for you. Cut between bones 3 times to give you four servings. Simmer strips, covered, in salted water one hour or until tender. Lace par-boiled ribs on skewers and baste with barbecue sauce. Place on grill, basting several times, for 20 minutes or more. (Loin back ribs may be used if preferred. However, country-style ribs have the most meat.)

* Country-style spareribs are made from a loin roast.

Lorren's Barbecue Sauce

1 cup Heinz catsup
⅓ cup Worcestershire Sauce
1 teaspoon chili powder
1 teaspoon salt

1 cup water
1 teaspoon celery seed
1 dash Liquid Smoke
1 dash Tobasco Sauce

Yield — approximately 2 cups

Combine all ingredients. Heat to boiling. Simmer 30 minutes. If sauce gets too thick, add a small amount of water. This sauce is **great** on chicken and hamburger and can be kept in the refrigerator for weeks.

Company Chicken Casserole

An interesting variation of Yorkshire Pudding.

Coat meaty parts of frying chicken with flour. Brown in ½ cup butter. Save drippings for gravy.

Sift together:

1½ cups sifted flour 1½ teaspoons baking powder
1 teaspoon salt

Beat 4 eggs until very light.

Add: 1½ cups milk

3 tablespoons melted butter

Add dry ingredients, mixing until smooth. Pour into a greased 10 inch baking dish, 3 inches deep. Arrange browned chicken on top. Bake at 350 degrees for 1 hour or until puffy and brown. Serve immediately with gravy made from drippings. Serves 4.

Jean Furnish, Tipton

Vegetable Casserole

Olive Gaul, Tipton, gives the following suggestion for a vegetable casserole that is sure to satisfy the preferences of all guests or family members and can be prepared in advance.

Select two or three vegetables with interesting color and flavor combinations. Cook separately until tender. Drain, but save liquid for gravies or soups. Arrange vegetables in buttered casserole, keeping each in its own area. Cover with your favorite cheese sauce; sprinkle with buttered crumbs or bread cubes. Bake about 40 minutes in slow oven, 325 degrees

Interesting combinations:

Sliced carrots, cauliflower, french-style beans
Corn, lima beans, carrots
Peas, carrot sticks, cauliflower

Sue Larson, Tipton, suggests cauliflower, brussel sprouts and broccoli spears as another excellent combination. She uses cream of mushroom soup with cheese added for the sauce. One nine-ounce frozen package of each is the correct amount of vegetables for one can soup.

Lamb D'Oeuvres

1 pound ground beef and	¼ teaspoon nutmeg
1½ pound ground lamb or	¼ teaspoon allspice
2½ pounds lamb	¼ teaspoon pepper
4 slices bread, crumbled	½ teaspoon salt (plain
¾ cup milk	or seasoned)
2 eggs	

1-2 inch onion, finely minced

Beat eggs in large bowl. Add other ingredients and mix **well.** When thoroughly mixed, shape into 1" balls. Let dry briefly on oiled paper. Brown in oiled (lightly) fry pan. When browned on all sides, drain off excess fat that has accumulated. Add ½ cup beef or chicken bouillon and let simmer. Serve directly from fry pan on colored tooth-picks, or freeze and reheat. Large quantities may be reheated in an electric roaster. Makes 80.

Mrs. Carl Hoover, New Sharon

Formed into larger balls, this may be used as your meat dish for 12 servings.

Lamb Riblets In Orange Sauce

1 pound lamb riblets; lamb breast cut into 1 inch strips may also be used. Salt and pepper.

Flour	½ cup water or orange juice
1 tablespoon shortening	1 teaspoon sugar
½ cup orange juice	1 teaspoon flour
1 teaspoon shredded orange	Cooked lima beans
peel	

Season riblets. Roll in flour. Brown in hot shortening in skillet. Pour off excess fat. Add orange juice. Cover. Simmer one hour. Blend peel, sugar and flour with water. Stir into drippings in skillet. Cook five minutes. Serve hot with seasoned, cooked lima beans.

Yield 3 to 4 servings.

Mrs. Max Crawford, Tipton

Sunrise Lamb Chops

4 lamb blade chops cut
¾ inch thick
2 tablespoons lard or
drippings
1 teaspoon salt
¼ teaspoon pepper

4 orange slices, cut ⅛ inch
thick, peeled
¼ cup brown sugar
¼ cup orange juice
¼ cup lemon juice
¼ cup water

Brown lamb chops in lard or drippings. Pour off drippings. Season with salt and pepper. Place an orange slice on each chop. Combine brown sugar, orange juice, lemon juice and water. Pour mixture around chops. Cover tightly and simmer 50 to 60 minutes or until meat is tender. Makes 4 servings. For a less tart product use half as much lemon juice.

Mrs. H. L. Witmer, Tipton

Roast Leg Of Lamb

Wipe leg of lamb with damp cloth. Cut lemon in half and rub over entire surface until all lemon juice is absorbed. Cut small pockets in lamb and insert slivers of garlic. Sprinkle with seasoned salt. Place lamb in roasting pan, fat side up. Insert meat thermometer in the fleshy part away from the bone and fat. Bake at 300 degrees until the thermometer registers 180 degrees. A 6 pound roast takes 4 hours.

Baste roast with the following sauce applied with a pastry brush:

¼ cup fresh lemon juice
½ cup mint jelly

¼ cup salad oil
Sprinkle of salt

Heat altogether. Any remaining sauce may be used as table sauce for lamb.

Mrs. Eleanor West, Iowa City

Esther suggests the following Spiced Apricot Glaze as an interesting variation from the above sauce:

1 cup apricot preserves
⅓ cup lemon juice

¼ cup finely chopped parsley
1 teaspoon rosemary

Combine ingredients, blend. Spread one-half of preserve mixture over lamb. Continue basting during roasting time. Serve lamb with remaining apricot sauce.

Golden Salad

Dissolve 1 package orange gelatin in 1 cup boiling water. When slightly thickened add:

1 cup salad dressing	1 teaspoon grated onion
1 cup grated carrots	1 tablespoon lemon juice
1 cup diced celery	1 cup cottage cheese
1 tablespoon chopped green pepper	¼ teaspoon salt

Mold. A practical salad yet very pretty for a party and uses ingredients usually on hand.

Mrs. Robert Laake, Davenport

Green and Yellow Layered Salad

Dissolve 1 package lime gelatin in 2 cups hot water. When partially set add 1 cup small curd cottage cheese. Pour into 8x12 oblong pan, ring mold or glass bowl. Allow to set.

Dissolve 1 package lemon gelatin in 2 cups hot water; add 1 cup miniature marshmallows. Stir these to dissolve also. When partially set, add 1 cup crushed pineapple. Pour over lime layer which has set.

A refreshing summer salad but equally good for other seasons.

Mrs. Frank Malone, Cedar Rapids

Sea Food Salad

Dissolve 1 package lemon gelatin in 1 cup hot water. Add 1 teaspoon salt and 1 tablespoon grated onion. Cool until slightly thickened.

Add:

3 hard cooked eggs, diced	1 5-ounce can tuna or shrimp
½ pound pimento cheese, cubed	½ cup salad dressing
1 tablespoon green pepper, minced	½ cup cream, whipped
3 cups diced celery	1 cup chopped nuts

Mold as desired. Serves 10 to 12. Very good for a main luncheon dish. It can be prepared at least a day ahead of the time of using.

Mrs. A. C. Leopp, Cedar Rapids

Cheese Or Ham Souffle Sandwiches

12 slices bread*
½ pound cheddar cheese slices
    or 6 slices ham

2 cups milk
4 eggs
1 teaspoon salt

1 teaspoon paprika

Cut crusts from bread slices and spread one side of each with butter. Place six slices in a greased, flat pan, buttered side down. Put a slice of cheese or ham on each and cover with the other bread slices, buttered side up.

Make a custard mixture of the remaining four ingredients by beating eggs slightly and adding paprika, salt and milk. Blend well. Pour over sandwiches and refrigerate several hours or overnight. Bake at 350 degrees for 45 minutes.

Serve hot with asparagus or mushroom sauce made as follows: Melt 2 tablespoons butter and add 2 tablespoons flour. Gradually stir in 1½ cups milk. Cook, stirring constantly, until smooth and thick. Season with 1 teaspoon salt and ¼ teaspoon pepper.

Add 1-9 ounce package frozen asparagus pieces, cooked and drained, or add ½ pound mushrooms, sliced and sauteed in 3 tablespoons butter. Serves 6.

*We use home baked bread.

Whipple House Salad

1-10½ ounce can condensed
    tomato soup
1½ tablespoons unflavored
    gelatin
½ cup cold water
2-3 ounce packages cream
    cheese

1 cup mayonnaise
1 cup diced celery
2 tablespoons finely diced
    green pepper
1 teaspoon chopped onion
½ cup sliced stuffed olives

Heat soup. Add gelatin which has been softened in cold water. Cool. Add other ingredients. Chill until firm. Serves 8 to 10.

Heavenly Chocolate Pie

Have ready one baked pie shell.

2 egg whites	¼ teaspoon cinnamon
½ teaspoon vinegar	¼ teaspoon salt
	½ cup sugar

Beat together egg whites, vinegar, cinnamon and salt until stiff but not dry. Gradually add the sugar and beat until very stiff. Spread over bottom and sides of pie shell. Bake at 325 degrees for 15 to 18 minutes. Cool.

1-6 ounce package semi-sweet chocolate bits
2 egg yolks   ¼ cup water

Melt chocolate chips over hot, not boiling water. Blend in egg yolks which have been beaten with the water. Stir until smooth. Spread three tablespoons of the mixture over the cooled meringue. Chill remainder of chocolate mixture.

1 cup whipping cream   ¼ cup sugar
¼ teaspoon cinnamon

Whip cream until stiff. Add sugar and cinnamon. Spread half of this over the chocolate layer in the pie shell.

Fold chilled chocolate mixture into remaining whipped cream. Spread over center of pie. Chill 4 hours before serving.

Mrs. Oren Jones, Atalissa

259

INDEX

262

265